Ludopolitics

Videogames against Control

Ludopolitics

Videogames against Control

Liam Mitchell

Winchester, UK
Washington, USA

First published by Zero Books, 2018
Zero Books is an imprint of John Hunt Publishing Ltd., No. 3 East St., Alresford,
Hampshire SO24 9EE, UK
office1@jhpbooks.net
www.johnhuntpublishing.com
www.zero-books.net

For distributor details and how to order please visit the 'Ordering' section on our website.

Text copyright: Liam Mitchell 2017

ISBN: 978 1 78535 488 5
978 1 78535 489 2 (ebook)
Library of Congress Control Number: 2018932660

A CIP catalogue record for this book is available from the British Library.

Design: Stuart Davies

Printed and bound by CPI Group (UK) Ltd, Croydon, CRO 4YY, UK

We operate a distinctive and ethical publishing philosophy in
all areas of our business, from our global network of authors to
production and worldwide distribution.

Contents

Preface

What can videogames tell us about the politics of contemporary technoculture, and how are designers and players responding to its impositions? To what extent do the technical and aesthetic features of videogames index our assumptions about the world, or about what exists and what is denied the status of existence? And how can we use games to identify and shift those assumptions?

This book responds to these questions. Through close readings of both the design and play of videogames, *Ludopolitics* offers a critique of one of the defining features of modern technology: the fantasy of control. Videogames promise players the opportunity to map and master worlds; they offer closed systems that are perfect and perfectible, in principle if not in practice; and although they provide players with a means of escape from a world that can be unpredictable and unjust, they aren't only escapism. The numerical, rule-bound, and goal-oriented form of the videogame corresponds, albeit imperfectly, to the form of other digital media, expressing assumptions about both the technological world and the world as such.

As an index of our assumptions about what the world *is*, videogames also suggest what we feel the world *should be*. They express the desire to see it changed. We can therefore look to the dominant ways that videogames are designed and played in order to identify the ways in which contemporary cultural and political phenomena coalesce around the pursuit and valorization of technological control.

At the same time, we can look to different forms of design and play for a different sort of politics. It wouldn't be fair to call these other modes of gaming marginal, subversive, or even alternative, both because many of them are so commonplace and because the opposition between dominant and alternative im-

plies the possibility of an escape. The technological and ontological form of power that this book examines – a form in which
"politics" doesn't mean the violent coercion that we normally
associate with the term, but rather entails the definition, delimitation, and disclosure of existence – calls for an aesthetic response that doesn't resort to an outside. This is a response, conveniently enough, that can already be found in contemporary,
critical practices of videogame design and play. Designers craft
power fantasies to satisfy players' desires for control, but they
also make games that leave players feeling impotent, guilty, or
confused – in a good way. Likewise, players enjoy the sensation
of power that the seamless integration into a digital system can
deliver, but they derive just as much pleasure from exploring
and repurposing those very systems – even if that pleasure is
of a different sort. Fun and critique come in varied but similar
shades, and they can be used to color within the lines just as
compellingly as without.

Because there are more than enough popular and academic
commentaries dissecting the problematic politics of many videogames and much of game culture, and because critical forms
of design and play are as beautiful, complicated, and delightful
as they are underappreciated, *Ludopolitics* turns to them instead.
Moreover, rather than focusing on design and play practices that
pose explicit criticisms of the unconscious pursuit of control, *Ludopolitics* highlights examples that work indirectly, addressing
mainstream audiences in the process. Games like *Spec Ops: The
Line*, *Braid*, *Undertale*, and *Bastion* are at once critical and a whole
lot of fun, and play practices like speedrunning, theorycrafting,
and myth-making are no longer strictly peripheral hobbies, if
they ever were.

As a theoretically-minded exploration of the politics of a
technocultural form, *Ludopolitics* makes reference to political
theory, media theory, and game studies. It is not, however, a
purely academic text. The first chapter is a dense and sometimes

philosophical articulation of the problem of control that the following chapters critique through cultural objects and practices: the second and third chapters focus on game design, and the fourth and fifth on play. While the book is therefore intended to be read from start to finish, readers who find themselves more interested in games than theory should feel free to skip Chapter One.

Any book, like any cultural object, is an expression of the author's understanding of the world and a working-out and solidifying of what that understanding is. As the product of several years of thinking about videogames and of many more years of playing them, *Ludopolitics* is no exception. I am indebted to many colleagues, friends, and gamers for their help in the composition of this book and the framing of the problematic that guides it: to the editors at Zero Books, for the opportunity to write between the popular and the academic; to *Loading...The Journal of the Canadian Game Studies Association*, where I initially published a shorter version of Chapter Three; to the Department of Cultural Studies at Trent University, the Department of Political Science at the University of Victoria, and the Canadian Game Studies Association, for years of institutional support; to Keith Barron, Michael Epp, Hugh Hodges, Jeremy Leipert, Brad Pejril, Daniel Perry, and all of the other friends with whom I've gathered around a table over the years; to Cole Armitage, Marta Bashovski, Bradley Bryan, Suzanne de Castell, David Cecchetto, Allan Cecil, Dwayne Collins, Kelly Egan, Jennifer Jenson, James Kerr, Arthur Kroker, Gary Larsen, Matthew Lilko, Paul Manning, Michael Morse, Karleen Pendleton-Jiménez, Danielle Taschereau-Mamers, Joshua Noiseux, and Liam Cole Young, for conversation, editorial labor, and inspiration. Above all, I wish to express my gratitude for Jeanette Parker, without whom this book would not exist, and for Maeve, who plays.

Introduction: Gaming Time

In the fall of 2014, game developer Almost Human released *Legend of Grimrock 2*. As a grid-based, fantasy-themed action-role-playing game in the vein of classic dungeon crawlers like *Eye of the Beholder*, *Grimrock 2* appealed to me for a number of reasons: it presented satisfying puzzles, fun exploration, and challenging combat, and it scratched a nostalgic itch that I, as a child of the 1980s growing up with a personal computer, knew that I had. I was in my third year of university teaching at the time, and I couldn't wait for the semester to end so that I could devote a week to the game.

Christmas came and went, and, with my partner away for two weeks visiting family, I devoted the week before New Year to the game. I beat it within four or five days of fairly continuous play, but I knew, by the end, that my first playthrough had left something to be desired. My characters could have been stronger if I'd balanced their attributes differently; I could have outfitted them with better and more interesting equipment; my party could have been improved by choosing different characters entirely. I went online to read other players' strategies and created a second, improved party. Armed with my knowledge of the now-demystified Island of Nex, I ran through hard mode with a satisfying efficiency, defeating the Island Master and completing the game's optional ending.

"So you're done with it now, right?" My partner was on the phone. "I mean, classes are starting soon, and I'll be back in just a few days..." Of course I was done with it. I wasn't going to rush back into teaching, but I was going to turn my attention to another new game, Supergiant's *Transistor* – something that I would be "reading," something that would be "serious" and "important" and contribute to my "work."

"Good," she said. "Hey, how's that turkey soup you made?"

"Oh, right – yeah, it's pretty good. I mean, I haven't made the actual *soup* yet, but I totally made the stock yesterday. Yeah. It's going to be a good, healthy dinner. I'm going to start making it right after I get off the phone."

It was New Year's Eve, and I was ushering in 2015 with lies. I hadn't made any stock and had vague intentions but no real plans to make soup: the week-old turkey carcass was graying in the fridge, and I was making dinners out of odds and ends. I didn't plan on going out to celebrate, and I wasn't even ready to start playing *Transistor*. Serious gaming could wait.

One of the interesting features of *Grimrock 2*, particularly from the perspective of someone looking for interesting things to do with the game, is its alchemy system. Although limited compared to the crafting systems of similar games, *Grimrock 2's* alchemy system lets the player expand the skillsets of their party members: player characters with the Alchemy skill can brew potions and make bombs made from herbs scattered around the Island of Nex. While these generally provide only temporary benefits, the rarest herb in the game, the Crystal Flower, provides permanent ones: each Crystal Flower can be used to increase a single attribute by a single point, affecting the character's ability to hit harder, carry more, cast stronger spells, take bigger hits, and so on. There are only a few Crystal Flowers in the game, so these permanent improvements are limited. One character class, however, can generate more: for every 4500 steps that an Alchemist takes with a Crystal Flower in their inventory, a new Crystal Flower is generated.

By the time of that phone call with my partner, I had beaten the game twice and knew exactly how the Alchemist worked: two of the four characters in my second party had been Alchemists, and they had generated some 14 attribute-increasing potions between them by walking more than 31,500 steps. (The game tracks player statistics in detail.) I was still reading the game's forums, though, looking for ideas – not yet wanting to be finished with this particular gaming experience. I suspected that something more could be done with the Alchemist – that there was some exploit I hadn't considered. That was when I came across this suggestion on the game's official forum:

> One tip, if you want to walk forever and go to sleep. Close the pressure pad gate in Keelbreach Bog (top left so bugs can't get through) then swim around to Forgotten River and back to Keelbreach Bog to the other side of the teleporters. Then just put a weight on you[r] keyboard "w" key and walk into the teleporters.
> This way you can walk forever.[1]

When my partner arrived home three days later, she noticed something odd about my computer: "Why is there a screwdriver propped up on your keyboard?"

The Politics of Play

Videogames are digital systems governed by rules. They fit the classical definition of games in that they enable players to "voluntarily attempt to overcome unnecessary obstacles," as Bernard Suits puts it, but they complicate that definition because of the ways that they are encoded and because of the ways that they mediate players' experience of time.[2] As such, they provide substantial insight into both the *digital* and the *ludic*, or gamelike, aspects of the contemporary world, or into a world increasingly *modeled on* videogames. They are an indirect means by which algorithmic phenomena as disparate as ubiquitous surveillance, big data, drones, nanocomputers, traffic signals, high-frequency trading, and actuarial science can be understood. If the world is quantifiable, then digital games offer a way to understand something unique about contemporary cultural conditions. And if the world is *not* quantifiable, then our infatuation with these games tells us something else.

Videogames can help us think about apparently non-digital, non-algorithmic phenomena as well as about their technological counterparts. They can offer us a way of understanding the modern condition as such, where "modern" is understood with sufficient breadth: much of what is true for us today was true 500 years ago as well, if not before; the logic of computation preceded and enabled the advent of the computer.[3] That logic is not neutral in terms of its values or benign in its societal implications, though it is not straightforwardly malign either. Computation, digitization, rule – whatever you want to call it: this mode of societal organization normalizes particular modes of behavior while rendering others abnormal.[4] This is an exercise of power that only seems non-coercive. As the sets of instructions that computers follow in order to carry out their work, algorithms help to condition the conditions of possibility of human action; they conduct the conduct of the individuals who make use of them, or the individuals who are digitized and fed into them, by encoding certain possibilities while excluding others.[5] In this context, games in general, and videogames in particular, thematize a set of more-or-less perennial concerns (the sculpting of human behavior) with more-or-less important consequences (the outcomes of that behavior). Thinking through how this thematization works, and thinking about the implications of the political and ethical preoccupations and pitfalls of modernity that videogames illustrate, is the goal of this book.

In this line of questioning, one of the central issues at stake is the relationship of people to systems in the light of the politics of fear. Digitization is, in part, a response to an uncertainty about the future and a desire to shape it in a particular way, or to *control* it. This uncertainty, or this preoccupation with contingency and finitude, happens to be central to political thought. In fact, the attitude of political thinkers and agents to uncertainty might be said to characterize the passage from pre-modern to modern political thought.[6] Niccolò Machiavelli's *The Prince* illustrates the pre-modern attitude: the city cannot ultimately be controlled – there are too many contingencies to take into account, too many unpredictable citizens, too many unruly outsiders and unpredictable foreign economies – so the prince can only hope to *influence* city politics. Accepting this limitation, this prince needs to accept another, too: "since our free will must not be eliminated, I think it may be true that fortune determines one half of our actions, but that, even so, she leaves us to control the other half, or thereabouts." This is to say that the individual is constrained by the world but free to choose "his" reactions to it, free not to control others, that is to say, but to control himself. From this almost Stoic understanding of things, Machiavelli derives one of his central lessons for political actors in general: follow policies that "correspond to the needs of the times," and when even these fail, respond with resolute equanimity. Dance with Fortuna, but when she spurns your advances, try not to be too upset.[7]

Contrast Machiavelli's attitude to the modern one so forcefully described in Thomas Hobbes' *Leviathan*. Written a little over a hundred years later, it is radically different in tone and prescription: for Hobbes, it is the role of the sovereign to preclude the violence of unpredictability by encoding acceptable behavior in law, speech, and thought, and by enforcing it through the unilateral exercise of legitimate violence. It is precisely *because* there is so much unpredictability in the world that a *predictable* world must be created: the violence of the state of nature must give way to the peace of the social contract. The failure to create that predictable world results in the admission of violence into the state. The modern sovereign therefore encodes acceptable behavior by systematically describing it, offering what "he" insists are self-evident definitions that found a linguistic system from which political conclusions necessarily follow. For instance: life "is but a motion of limbs, the beginning whereof is in some principal part within,"[8] and these principal parts can be understood in terms of movements toward certain objects "which he for his part calleth *good*" and away from others, "object[s] of his hate, and aversion, *evil*."[9] For Hobbes, good and evil are not moral absolutes but terms retroactively applied by a subject moving toward the objects of his affections and away from those of his fear. If this mechanical description of human agency follows, then there is no reason why a sovereign, properly equipped, cannot shape the actions of his mechanically comprehensible subjects: they will move away from that which threatens them and toward that which promises safety. Modern governance, then, involves the creation of adequately convincing definitions and their application to the movements, internal and (then) external, of human subjects.[10]

One of the problems or challenges of this form of political nominalism, and one with serious consequences for the code that underlies videogames, concerns definition. Hobbes despises imprecise phrasing, but he all but acknowledges the impossibility of ever doing away with imprecision.[11] If political systems could in fact function on the basis of perfect definitions, the sovereign would be nothing *but* this definitional function. Unfortunately, exceptional situations that don't fit the established definitions and the systems that flow from them always arise, and the sovereign needs to decide how to respond to them.[12] But what if these decisions on the exception didn't have to be made? What if uncertainty could be written out from the beginning – encoded? There seems to be no better nominalism than that enforced by the certainty of zero and one. Code is law: it enables some actions while strictly proscribing others, often without any obvious violence or compulsion. And code governs more and more of our everyday interactions with the world.[13] Just as the slotted park bench makes it impossible to sleep elevated above the cold, wet ground, Internet Protocol makes it impossible for datagrams to be sent without being broken down into packets. Neither "encourages" behaviors that their designers desire – they *ensure* these behaviors. The homeless person *will* move away, and the user's data *will* pass through TCP/IP. The ambiguity of the spoken word is eliminated by code just as surely as the movements of urban populations are guided by concrete and steel.

But of course these are fictions. They are powerful fictions that do political work, and they should be taken seriously, but coercive technologies like concrete and steel can't ultimately proscribe anti-statist action: the city's architectural coherence is challenged formally by municipal politicians and activists, but also informally by protesters taking to the streets, graffiti artists tagging buildings, and people erecting tents in city parks right next to those slotted benches. These informal challenges don't destroy the buildings that are the physical instantiations of the law, but they do call attention to them, subvert them, *play with* them. Similar contests can be waged against the apparent inviolability of code, which, as it turns out, is not nearly so absolute.[14]

Here, in this context of soft challenges to hard rules, I want to return to the way that Suits defines games in terms of rules: the constitutive elements of a game, it is the players' acceptance of the game's rules that makes gameplay possible.[15] The strength of this definition is redoubled when the game goes digital: the rules that could be undermined in a traditional game cannot be so easily undermined when they are enforced by the computer. If a player steps away from Chess, the other player can shift a piece on the game board. No such cheating is possible in *Battle Chess*.[16] To use Suits' language, it is all but impossible to voluntarily adopt an inefficient means of achieving a goal in a video-game since all of the legitimate means are already encoded. The videogame fosters a different relationship to rules and goals.

In *The Grasshopper: Games, Life, and Utopia*, Suits follows his definition of gameplay with a four-part division of approaches to games. Conventional players play games according to the (voluntarily adopted) rules and with the game's goal in mind, but triflers, cheats, and spoilsports do otherwise. The cheat and the spoilsport resemble one another in their disregard for rules, but are differentiated by their attitude toward goals: the cheat cares about the goal without caring about rules, while the spoilsport cares for neither. The player and the trifler both observe the rules of the game, but the normal player actively tries to achieve the game's goal. The trifler, interested in something else, doesn't bother. When play loses the voluntary element that Suits attributes to it thanks to the digital foundation of the videogame, players sometimes incline toward trifling: they become interested less by the goal than by the rules according to which the game is played, repurposing them, and achieving something resembling mastery over the means of mastery themselves.

The Eternal Return of the Game

This is what I was doing when I loaded up a new game of *Grimrock 2* for the third time. I built a party of four Lizardman Alchemists (choosing the Lizardman for its optimal "racial traits"), played through the first several hours of the game so that I could acquire the first two Crystal Flowers, walked my party to the first Windgate in Keelbreach Bog, and stood a flathead screwdriver up on the "W" key. The Windgate – a bright, shimmering teleporter – set my party back to where they started, but the screwdriver impelled them forwards, again and again, accumulating four new Crystal Flowers with every 4500 steps.

This was clever, I thought, and admittedly absurd, but it was risky: What if the hunger mechanic killed my Alchemists? What if their bags filled up? What if the less important herbs, like Blooddrops and Etherweed, squeezed out the exceedingly rare Crystal Flowers? I went to bed with the computer still running – with the screen still on, in fact, since I worried that shutting off a peripheral might somehow interfere with the game – anxious but excited about what I would find when I looked in the next morning. I needn't have worried: the Alchemists were still there, undeterred by hunger (which, even at its peak, didn't stop them from moving), inventory space (which, though entirely used up, didn't prevent the herbs from stacking), or operating system updates (which seemed to cede priority to the game).

And they were *rich*. The night's sojourn had yielded dozens of Crystal Flowers, which I immediately transformed into Potions of Strength, Willpower, Dexterity, and Vitality. Their key attributes nearly doubled. At the same time, they were neither rich nor powerful *enough*. I took my newly enhanced party for a walk to some of the upper level portions of the island, and although the Alchemists were able to hold their own, they were hardly decimating the wargs, elementals, and undead. I returned to the Bog, picked up the screwdriver, and returned them to work. I wanted to see what a few more days might do.

Technology and Time

Because videogames offer players control over clearly comprehensible worlds, they help inculcate a desire for mastery over them. The pleasure to be derived from control and mastery can seem like their very purpose.[17] Players achieve this mastery through their intimate relationships with the games' rules. Cheats and spoilsports care about rules only insofar as they are concerned with breaking them, admittedly, but triflers and gamers want to learn them in detail. The desire to master these rules, learning them so well that the player can do things the designer did not anticipate, is one of the key characteristics of gameplay as such. The political consequences implied by this desire include a particular relationship to time.

Time is not an objective fact – or, rather, the objective fact of clock time is far from the most important thing about temporality. The ways in which time has been historically organized are culturally influenced, and they themselves influence culture. Clock time, for instance, arose in the West in large part because of monasteries' need to routinize work and devotion, but it then produced routine as such. Lewis Mumford describes it this way:

The instrument presently spread outside the monastery; and the regular striking of the bells brought a new regularity into the life of the workman and the merchant. The bells of the clock tower almost defined urban existence. Time-keeping passed into time-service and time-accounting and time-rationing. As this took place, Eternity ceased gradually to serve as the measure and focus of human actions.[18]

With the clock, we see a technology that has been influenced by a mode of life then influence that mode of life. To put it in terms of the apparently non-coercive form of politics that I articulated above, the clock at the center of the monastery conducted the conduct of the people who lived within earshot; it created a framework that enabled certain behaviors (properly observing the canonical hours, arriving at work on time, paying a debt, and so on) while proscribing others.[19] The effects of this enabling and proscribing were as profound and long lasting as they were unpredictable: Pope Sabinian probably didn't suspect that his papal bull would result in Eternity "ceasing to serve as the measure and focus of human actions."

But to say only that technology, whether clock or computer, influences and is influenced by a "mode of life" is too vague to tell us much, let alone to help think about videogames. Technology doesn't straightforwardly determine our relationship to grand categories like temporality, culture, action, or thought, but it does relate to these modes of expression of our mode of life in a non-arbitrary fashion. There is *some* relationship here.[20]

If securitization is the sovereign's aim, then time itself is the sovereign's enemy.[21] Time, bound by the clock or not, means the inescapable ends of people and things. Finitude, change, and entropy are the enemies of stasis, which a certain conception of securitization requires and promotes. That which can be secured is what exists *now*, but the now is continually passing out of existence; threatened by the fact of every individual's eventual demise, security can only ever be approximated in the fantasy of presence and stability that the boundaries of the state enclose and enable. The fact that Hobbes' personal fear of death would be redoubled in his characterization of the state is no coincidence.[22]

Time's forward march threatens the fantasy of stability and security that characterizes the deathbound individual and the shifting state alike, and we see evidence of this threatened feeling in technologies both exotic and everyday.[23] Consider the work of the SENS Research Foundation, for instance, which funds research and development into "strategies for engineered negligible senescence" – that is, strategies to halt and reverse aging that range from 3D printed organs to stem cell therapy to genome editing and beyond. Its co-founder and Chief Science Officer, Aubrey de Grey, insists that we live our lives in a "pro-aging trance," impulsively leaping "to embarrassingly unjustified conclusions in order to put the horror of aging out of one's mind" and engaging in "arbitrarily irrational rationalizations to get on with one's miserably short life in a state of minimal preoccupation with that fate."[24] For de Grey, and for the futurists who share his convictions concerning the "rationality" of scientific progress, death is not something to which we must acquiesce. The trance can and should be "combated" with the weaponry of modern technology.

If this example of death-defying technology seems a little too on-the-nose, consider a more apparently neutral medium, the online archive: increasingly widespread, automated, and algorithmic, our digital detritus is shaped by social media aggregators and data collections agencies into personal records that vastly exceed the scope of any offline record keeper. Why has Facebook invested so heavily into facial recognition technologies? Why is it so intent on streamlining the process of sharing and storing photos? The digital archive obviously enables the capture of particular moments in time in defiance of the eventual deaths of its subjects, but it also enables a fantasy of return to a non-existent origin. The archive promises the freedom of pure beginning and ultimate command: beginning without end, or beginning removed from the necessity of the end. "Freedom" from finitude.[25] And the fact of the archive's digitization, with its corollary aspirations of automaticity, contributes to these dreams of immortality, truth, purity, and freedom.[26]

Modern technology tends toward the defiance of death through the exercise of control.[27] Even technologies that apparently have nothing to do with this defiant exercise exhibit this tendency. In organizing and combatting the disorder and entropy of the world, they index what Lorenzo C. Simpson calls "our uneasiness with our finitude, our uneasiness with time. Technology's success in granting our wish to *domesticate* time has encouraged an attitude towards time that is increasingly pervasive in our culture."[28] We see here a complicated relationship between those modes of expression of our mode of life that I identified earlier, and although the relationship is neither necessary nor necessarily causal, certain beliefs take hold and certain practices are conducted far more often and easily than others thanks, in part, to the "domesticating" tendency of the technology. The particular technology *in question* is not the agent directly responsible for these beliefs and practices – for, for instance, the conviction that human lives can and should be extended indefinitely, or for the adoption of technologies that automatically track and archive peoples' movements, conversations, and actions – but technology *as such* is a tremendously productive lens through which to think about how and why they work the way that they do. Technology provides a lens for thinking about the relationship of contemporary cultural beliefs and practices to categories like time, epistemology, ontology, politics, and ethics.[29]

What, then, can we make of the way that modern technology in general, or technology "as such," shapes our understanding and experience of the world? How does it affect our relationship to time? How loosely or strictly does it constrain the political and ethical possibilities open to us? Twentieth-century philosophers provided good answers to these questions. Martin Heidegger, the most insightful of them, argued that modern technology is a way of revealing the world as a standing reserve, or as something always available to be used and discarded. It refigures the world in its own terms, and confines human actions within them.[30] This is not to ascribe subjectivity to "Technology," as though there were some impersonal but agential force directing human affairs, but to identify the ways that the world exists for modern subjects and to gesture toward what has been denied the status of existence.[31]

This line of criticism is a useful starting place, but it remains a twentieth-century commentary on technology in general when what I'm after is a reading of twenty-first century games. What happens when we ask the same questions about time, technology, politics, and ontology, but give pride of place to the video-game rather than the philosophy?

Structurally defined by rules, videogames are often *thematically* defined by the idiosyncratic relationship between player, time, and system. No other medium claims to offer such comprehensive control over temporality. Saving and reloading, dying and respawning, speedrunning or cheating; slowing it down, speeding it up, replaying it, pausing it entirely: videogames involve *the manipulation of time in the service of mapping and mastering digital worlds*, and this act of manipulation indexes an attitude that extends to the mapping and mastering of the world in general.

As such indices, videogames differ from and resemble traditional games in a few important ways. Videogames, for instance, differ from traditional games in that they offer a technological means of manipulation that is easier and more convincing than other ways of learning systems and turning back time: pressing the quick load button in order to redo a combat encounter is much more straightforward and acceptable than pleading with a dungeon master to reroll dice. But they resemble traditional games, too, in that both involve the willing entry into a magic circle defined by the suspension of the laws of reality and their replacement by arbitrarily chosen but deadly serious alternative laws, including alternative laws for handling time.[32] As just another set of coded rules that are, in principle, disconnected from the laws of reality and their implications for finitude and fate, the algorithms governing videogame time are something to be sussed out and manipulated in the service of some game-defined goal. Time – whether the time of the videogame or time in general – is something to be gamed.

Now, there's nothing necessarily *wrong* with that, of course, just as there's nothing necessarily wrong with the way that film compresses or elongates time in order to convey compelling narrative experiences, but it does illustrate something about our relationship to time outside of the game – if that remains a meaningful distinction. Increasingly, we see time itself as something manipulable, something within our control rather than that which emblematizes its loss, and something that can and should be put to work in the ordering and exhaustion of things. This change in comportment is apparent in videogames even more than in those technologies that extend life or archive its events because of their systematic character: videogames are digital systems that are, in principle if not in fact, complete and perfect. The predominant approach taken to videogame design and play, then, demonstrates a disavowal of time's inevitable progression, or a refiguring of finitude in the context of a winnable system; it indexes the impossible desire to know and control everything, including time. The failure to realize that impossible desire engenders a corresponding frustration and resentment,[33] as well as the related desire to create and explore worlds in which perfect knowledge and control are possible.

The Idle Ideal

It doesn't take extraordinary means to break most videogames: a little bit of ingenuity, a screwdriver, and a small amount of free time will often do the trick. That small amount might only apply to the initial setup, though; after that, it can take your system quite a while to carry out its work. In the case of *Grimrock 2*, I needed several weeks of gameplay to get my characters to where I wanted them to be. Or to where I thought I wanted them to be, anyway. At some point, I finished converting Crystal Flowers into stat potions, walked around and killed enemies with single attacks, and then just...*stopped*. Achieving omnipotence was nice, but I didn't know what to do with it. Or I suppose I knew what to do – I knew exactly the possibilities that were open to me – but I had no interest in doing it.

What explains that loss of interest? The journey had turned out to be more satisfying than the destination, but there was something else going on as well. There was, for instance, something pleasant about waking up each morning to an incremental increase in my characters' abilities, stacking and discarding the useless reagents, converting the Flowers to potions, and then applying them. And there was the pleasure of simply knowing that I had put together one of the strongest *Grimrock 2* parties in existence, and without technically cheating. And then there was the pleasure that came from the automatic nature of my characters' numerical progression itself. This, I think, was the ultimate source of the satisfaction that I derived from gaming *Grimrock 2*, and it touched on the relation that automaticity and number have to any videogame's formal properties. Any progress within a videogame can be quantified, and given a sufficiently clever manipulation of the rules, that progress can be made automatic. In many cases, this makes the accomplishment of the formal objective trivial, subordinating the game's stated goal to a secondary, more *interesting* goal – the gaming of the game.

Grimrock 2 is, of course, not the only game that can be abused in this way, and I certainly have a history of finding ways to break games, or at least of locating and reaching their limits. When I was a child, I spent hours improving my character in the 1989 classic *Quest for Glory: So You Want to Be a Hero*, an adventure/role-playing game, by typing commands ("cast flame," "throw rock") and slowly watching my skills reach their capacity. When I was older, I found ways of automating tasks like these. In *A Tale in the Desert*, a massively multiplayer online game set in ancient Egypt, I created macros to automate the production of charcoal and to walk my character across the vast, empty desert, leaving me free to do other things around the house. In *The Elder Scrolls V: Skyrim*, a popular open world roleplaying game, I crafted and equipped armor that reduced the cost of Alteration magic by 100% and then used another screwdriver to cast Telekinesis for hours at a time, repeatedly maxing out Alteration and thereby bypassing the soft cap on perks and leveling. And in *Clicker Heroes*, a strangely compelling incremental game featuring absurdly simple gameplay, I ran a script that simply played the game for me. In each instance, I was moving toward the optimization and control that the game promised, but I inevitably found myself more engaged by the process of optimization itself than the power that this optimization provided.

The tension inherent to all of this is instructive. If the videogame has ideals, then one might be idleness: the automatic progression from weakness to strength; the hands-free optimization of a knowable system; the freedom to do something else. At the same time, the achievement of this ideal requires work. Discovering the conditions under which progress can be automated usually doesn't require extraordinary knowledge or unusual techniques, but that doesn't make it easy. Moreover, this process often results in the player knowing so much about the game's system and its limitations that the exercise of mastery, once achieved, is no longer desirable.

There is, in other words, a constitutive ambivalence to the

videogame. There is in fact no platonic form of "the videogame," and if there were, it would have no ideal. While videogames are in one important sense "about" power, mastery, and control, as well as the exploration of the systems that make them up, they aren't "about" the slavish adherence to any of these things, despite the apparent rigidity and perfectibility of code. Rather, they clearly demonstrate players' tendency to explore and exploit their rules, bending them, questioning them, and turning them to new ends.

Earlier, I said that videogames incentivize the drive to "achieve something resembling mastery over the means of mastery themselves." This "something resembling mastery" is not mastery or control. The trifler, unlike the fictional, totalitarian sovereign or the equally fictional, naïve programmer, knows from the start that no rule is perfect, no system impregnable, no code unbreakable; the trifler doesn't strive for mastery because they know that this mastery is unattainable. They recognize videogames as ambivalent cultural artifacts despite their tendency toward digitization and systematicity, and they know, consciously or not, that videogames have a lot to say about the ambivalence of technology, sovereignty, and modernity.

Ludopolitics

When games and gaming take place within the framework of modern technology, they take on the impositional logic according to which the world is and should be available for use. The conjunction of the *frame* of modern technology and the *form* of the digital game renders everything a means to the mapping and mastering of worlds. Given the central role that rules play in structuring games, and given the ease with which those rules can be translated to the computer, it is no surprise that actual game design and play practices often find themselves bound by this framework. But this is no necessity: games and gaming can and routinely do play with the logic of modern technology.

They reject its impositions not on the basis of political theory or first philosophy but on the basis of lived, played, and designed experience. A *ludopolitics*, then, documents and accounts for the significance of this experience, or for the means by which designers and players are mounting an immanent critique of the contemporary technocultural moment, playing with and against the impulse to control. This play rarely takes a consciously or deliberately political form, and it never fully escapes the logic that binds it or the world in which it is embedded, but it can nonetheless trace the fault lines of modern technology and perhaps elide its totalizing demands.

In the first chapter, I extend the claims made above, arguing that games exemplify the impulse to control better than any other popular medium because they model this phenomenon: the pleasure of learning and controlling systems in order to achieve particular pre-defined ends is at the heart of gaming, and the valorization of game control symptomatizes the broader *loss* of control and systematicity that characterizes modernity. When our interest in videogames becomes a compulsion – not an addiction, but a preference for treating the world in their terms – we hear an echo of the same loss of comprehension, disappearance of purpose, and trembling of ground that characterizes late modernity, and we witness the melancholia and resentment that rise in response. This reactionary securitization gives rise to the kind of self-destructive politics on display in videogame-specific phenomena like Gamergate, but also to the politics of the "real world": the building of walls, the ejection of migrants, the pre-emption of terror, the harvesting of metadata, and so on can and should be contextualized in specific historical contexts, but they can also be understood in these more general, structural terms.[34] At the same time, however, videogames, like all other technology, fail to deliver what they promise. They provide a fantasy of control, not a return to a stable ground that never was. While it is possible to respond to this failure with denial and a redoubling of efforts, it is also possible to admit to the constitutive incompleteness of things. This does not amount to a stepping outside of the promise of technology, since there is no "outside"; instead, it means a playful working through.

This working through takes place in both play and design. Because game design tends toward controllability, all video-game genres function to a certain extent as power fantasies: they all offer players the ability to learn and master the game's algorithms. But there are many counter-examples that frustrate this medial capacity. There are obvious selections from the indie gameworld that might be made here, but they are not the only avenue for the ludopolitical contravention of control. The mainstream/indie divide is increasingly untenable, anyway.[35] In the second chapter, I therefore highlight several recent, popular, narrative-driven videogames, paying particular attention to *Spec Ops: The Line*, *Braid*, and *Undertale*. The aesthetic force and political significance of these games derives in part from their mobilization of the games' various rhetorical resources: games affect players through familiar artistic features like audiovisual design, storytelling, character development, and so on, but also through mechanics and gameplay.[36] The particular force of *Spec Ops: The Line*, *Braid*, and *Undertale* stems from a masterful combination of all of these, and from these games' thematic focus on issues germane to control, especially control exercised over and through time.

I use the third chapter to conduct an extended analysis of the aesthetic potential of game design for political and ethical argumentation around the theme of control. *Bastion* is deeply concerned with this theme in nearly every facet of its design, though it doesn't seem that way at first: for the majority of the game, the player learns the game's systems and masters its controls, traveling Caelondia and collecting items that are supposed to set the post-apocalyptic world aright. At the end of the game, too, the player seems to have the power of choice: through a feat of magical engineering, they are given the option to "Restore" or "Evacuate," returning the world to a pre-apocalyptic moment or accepting the end and moving on. Through a gentle but ineluctable feature of the game's design, however, *Bastion* imposes Evacuation on the player. In doing so, it suggests an interpretation of the nature of life in control-obsessed society and a claim about the ethical and political disposition that might be equal to this technological epoch. Moreover, it does so experientially and philosophically, or allegorithmically: *Bastion* invites the player to experience a choice on Nietzsche's eternal return. The game's design suggests that the save/reload mechanic at the heart of videogames exemplifies the failure to meet the challenge of the eternal return. Restoring – repeating the same – means avoiding the movement of time. Evacuation, on the other hand, embraces an uncertain and finite future.

Games, like any rule-bound systems, produce behavioral tendencies through their design, but these tendencies can always be countered, elided, redirected, ignored. I begin the fourth chapter by outlining the various different ways in which gamers "play" and the seriousness with which we treat the relationship between the sacred space of play and the outside world: the willful or accidental disruption of the magic circle can upset us so seriously because it forcefully reintroduces the "Law" of "Reality," temporarily suspended by the "Rule" of the game.[37] The importance placed on the boundary of play demonstrates the implicit threat continually leveled against it. At the same time, players, or the triflers who ignore games' objectives to explore their rules, often treat that boundary playfully, calling attention to the various ways that it is constructed and maintained. While alternative player practices like trifling have always been significant modalities of gameplay, they have become increasingly important in recent years thanks to the nature of the videogame and the development of the hobby: the apparent inviolability of hard-coded rules appeals to players' desire to discover them and see if they can't be bent or if some interesting new forms of play can't be found within them, and the internet gives these players the means to commune. These attempts to discover, bend, and repurpose the rules may themselves take the form of games, or may give rise to new games.[38] Since player practices are extraordinarily diverse and wonderfully complex, I highlight only a few: speedrunning *Super Mario Bros.*, fan theorizing and datamining *Undertale*, and myth-making in the social experiment Twitch Plays Pokémon. Each of these player practices attends, in one way or another, to forms of temporality and questions of control, calling attention to the fact of the medium out of which it arises: to its limitations, its construction, and its alternative deployments.

In the final chapter, I study one player practice that pays particularly close attention to time, the tool-assisted speedrun. In it, triflers use game emulators to perform frame-perfect key-presses, discovering and exploiting glitches beyond the reach of even the best players, and then make their play available for viewing and discussion. Many gamers are familiar with the traditional "real-time attack" variety of speedrunning, but fewer know about, let alone understand, its tool-assisted cousin. The Awesome Games Done Quick marathon is changing that. Since 2014, a team from tasvideos.org has presented speedrunners and viewers with TASBot, a combination of a Nintendo "Robotic Operating Buddy" and a specially-built replay board connected to the controller port of a console. While most tool-assisted speedrunning movie files are created once, emulated and recorded, and then archived online for later consumption, TASBot "plays" games "live": runners create scripts that are fed through TASBot in real time, just as though a player were sitting there and pressing the buttons (at 60 frames per second, and often executed on two or more controllers at once). A mildly interesting feat of do-it-yourself engineering, TASBot has proved to be a thrilling performer, since the scripts it executes can do unbelievable things with the games it plays: TASBot has used unmodified consoles and cartridges as the raw materials for creating new games and platforms through a process that the runners refer to as "total control." At the same time, each TASBot performance has also exhibited bizarre glitches and failures. The TASBot team members execute total controls while demonstrating a routine awareness of their inability to give a perfect performance; they know that they cannot account for every element of the code, of the hardware, or even of the electricity itself, all of which is prone to unexpected behavior. During these performances, TASBot offers an implicit, code-minded, playful critique of a collective fantasy that many of us share – namely, that our devices, and the digital architecture that undergirds them, are predictable, fungible, and perfect. TASBot, and other instances of trifling like it, open critical paths to political critique.

Early in *Gamer Theory*, McKenzie Wark offers the following observation on the relationship between videogames and violence: "[t]hat games present the digital in its most pure form is reason enough to embrace them, for here violence is at its most extreme – and its most harmless."[39] Games are juvenile distractions, but they are also serious models of a world no longer defined in terms of Reality or Being or Law.[40] If Wark is right, they are less models of the world than the world itself, and their force lies in how they help to reproduce a singular world in which all of "us" must live. Here, space has become gamespace and life a series of post-Platonic, procedurally generated caves. In the context of this new, ludic hyperreality, the trivial features of videogames can tell us a great deal about how we act, what we value, and who we must be – and they can help us change all of these things, too.[41]

Chapter One

Controlling the Political

Videogames and politics have a lot to say about one another, but not in the way you might think. It's sometimes said, for instance, that games model and promote problematic personal and institutional politics. Just think about 90s games like *Duke Nukem 3D* or *Colonization*, which put the player in the respective positions of a one-liner dropping, jet pack sporting, alien killing ladies' man on the one hand and a European monarch looking to conquer the new world on the other. If these games are unapologetic representations of violence, misogyny, commodification, and imperialism, then you might say that they're encouraging these values, ideals, or ways of thinking. Or you might dispute this line of thinking, arguing that violent games don't make people violent; in fact, you might argue, *Duke Nukem 3D* and *Colonization* are examples of games that encourage critical reflection on the politics that they represent, since their mechanical implementation of various dehumanizations puts the player in a position to experience inhuman actions as they play the game. *Colonization*, in this reading, is in fact only problematic in that it fails to fully represent the horrors of the colonial past, notably omitting the slave trade from its mechanical implementation of history; that, in other words, it's not offensive *enough*.[42]

Whether you think that specific games promote problematic political values or harbor the potential to model, reflect on, and critique them, you might be inclined to limit your argument to those specific games. *Duke Nukem 3D* valorizes sexism and violence, for instance, but other first-person shooters – say, the kid-friendly *Splatoon*, where bullets are replaced by ink and the objective is painting territory rather than killing enemies – do not. Videogames, that is, should be analyzed individually, or at most grouped together according to genre and then thought through. In this understanding of the relationship between videogames and politics, individual videogames can always break the generic political mold, and they should be encouraged to do so.

The most problematic mold is arguably the power fantasy. When a videogame takes the form of a power fantasy, it encourages players to live out their impossible desires in extreme fashion, treating the people of the world as things, the things of the world with dispatch, and the world itself as a playground. Power fantasies crop up in all kinds of media, of course, and they're not necessarily problematic; the feeling that I get from efficiently blasting away sprites isn't "bad." That said, videogames seem especially prone to the sort of escapism that power fantasies offer, since the simple act of playing and mastering the game is the source of that satisfying feeling. Stylish representations of violence can help, of course, but they're not the principal source of that feeling. The sensation of power particular to videogames derives from the mastery of a system.

This sense of power dovetails with the sense of immersion that stems from the "fit" between the player character and the game.[43] Players feel powerful to the extent that they can seamlessly immerse themselves in systems. For Christopher Franklin, the videogame power fantasy tends toward overt representations of violence because videogames excel at simulating space, the setting for bodies and the objects that impact them. They mostly fail to simulate relationships. Consider the difficulty of "systemizing interactions" between two people in a conversation: branching dialogue trees, which are the dominant forms used for modeling conversation, haven't advanced much since the 1980s, and attempts at employing them often leave the player less immersed in the game than they were before. Consequently, "games tend to be more about spatial and physical conflicts, and as a result of that, violence pops up thematically more often than

27

it does in other media."[44] This problem is amplified when the pleasure of systemic immersion and spatial simulation dovetails with big budgets and the traditional thematic fare of masculine power fantasies: superhuman abilities, advanced weaponry, moral decisionism, docile female bodies, and so on.

This is even the case for games that make a pretense of tackling the kinds of "real world issues" that stem from the unequal distribution of power. Big budget videogames might insert seemingly thoughtful fare about this sort of inequality into their dialogue, exposition, or *mise-en-scène*, but the fundamentally empowering nature of their gameplay cannot help but take priority over the politically minded exploration of a theme. *Deus Ex: Mankind Divided*, for instance, is a well-reviewed major studio release set in a dystopian future in which prosthetically-augmented humans find themselves divided from the unaugmented, a political situation the developers described as "mechanical apartheid." The game makes continual reference to this violent inequality, all but hitting the player over the head with the theme: "A wrench is a tool, not a human being!" reads the graffiti; "Augs Lives Matter," say the banners. Even if this mode of exposition didn't trivialize or appropriate the Black Lives Matter movement and apartheid, among others, producing an arguably racist product in the process, it would nevertheless fail to deliver on such serious fare because of the conflicting character of the gameplay: neatly divided off from the thematic material, delivered in non-player characters' barks and assorted visual reminders of the bifurcated character of posthuman society, the gameplay presents the player with the opportunity to master a small variety of action, exploration, and stealth systems while controlling an ever-more-powerful player character who can do nearly anything without narrative repercussion. As Franklin puts it: "It is hard to speak truth to power or discuss the nature of power when your game is itself a celebration of unrestrained and unexamined power."[45]

Not all power fantasies attempt to incorporate political material, of course, and there might be no more straightforward example of violent escapism than *Bulletstorm*, a first-person shooter that puts the player in the position of Grayson Hunt. Angry, sarcastic, and frequently drunk, Hunt is prototypically masculine, a near-parody of the space marine archetype in everything from his personality to his physique to his dialogue. He is armed with the usual battery of weapons, each one more ridiculous than the last: the energy leash lets Hunt pull enemies toward him (slowing time in the process and allowing him to reposition them to be kicked into things), the "flailgun" shoots bolas made of grenades, and the "penetrator" features skillshots with names like "MILE HIGH CLUB" and "DRILLDO." Those skillshots are what helped the game stand out back in 2011: when the player kills an enemy or group of enemies in a creative way, the game offers points and praise as a reward for the demonstration of skill.

While *Bulletstorm* is obviously a violent, escapist power fantasy, it also seems self-aware. In addition to the volume and absurdity of ways to "kill with skill," the game's over-the-top visual style, the fact that developer Epic Games also authored the utterly unironic space marine shooter *Gears of War*, and the fact that the game's 2017 re-release gave players the option to replace Grayson Hunt with a very confused Duke Nukem, consider *Bulletstorm*'s obsession with penises.

The developers and promoters know exactly what guns so often represent (designer director Cliff Bleszinski has said that "[t]he minigun is basically an extension of Grayson's penis"),[46] there are more than a dozen skillshots that make reference to male genitals (including "EJACULATED," "MONEY SHOT," and "BONED"), and the dialogue features no word more frequently than "dick" – often misused with a nudge and a wink. Take the following exchange from the game's second act, knowingly titled "Damsel in Distress," by way of example:

Trishka Novak: "If you shitpiles give chase I'll kill your dicks!"

Grayson Hunt: "What? What does that even mean? You're gonna kill my dick? I'll kill your dick! How 'bout that, huh?"

This might be interpreted ironically, but there are reasons to think that *Bulletstorm* shouldn't be read as a parody. The main character is a muscular white man who speaks in a gruff cadence, the game tries to provide him and the other caricatured characters with human motivations, and the game delivers a straightforward thrill when Hunt successfully executes a chain of skillshots. As G. Christopher Williams puts it: "can a game really be kitsch if it's so close to the truth?"[47]

In any case, *Bulletstorm* is an emblematic power fantasy, and whether you think that it straightforwardly models violence, racism, misogyny, and so on, or that it offers a self-aware critique of these things, your analysis could remain restricted to *Bulletstorm* alone, or to first-person shooters more broadly. But this would be an unfortunately limited approach. Not only are first-person shooters not the only videogame genre to offer players the opportunity to live out power fantasies, they are in some ways the most innocuous genre to do so: they are *transparently* power fantasies. They wear their values on their sleeve. Most other videogames – regardless of genre – work in the exact same way, giving the player the chance to learn and master their algorithms, exerting more and more perfect control as they become more and more familiar with the game. For Wark and many others, this process is less about winning than it is about learning the game's rules.[48] While games in general certainly require a basic understanding of their rules, the videogame requires that the player learn its algorithms, those "finite set[s] of instructions for accomplishing some task [that] transforms an initial starting condition into a recognizable end condition."[49] If a videogame is constituted by a set of more or less opaque algorithms that govern player action, then the power that the player feels derives from learning and mastering them. Given this understanding of videogames, the power fantasy that players are living out has less to do with guns, violence, conquest, or women than with achieving an intuitive relation to a set of rules. First-person shooter games like *Bulletstorm* and *The Division* are obviously power fantasies, but so are real-time strategy games like *Starcraft* and casual games like *Candy Crush*.[50] All of them demand a relationship to the game that moves beyond understanding its basic rules and possibilities, and all of them reward the player for developing that deeper relationship. This might seem innocuous in comparison to the stereotypical power fantasy in which the player is given the opportunity to violate vulnerable bodies, but, as I will argue throughout this chapter, its violence – a violence ultimately enacted at an ontological level – has the potential to be much worse.

An extended example might help make the case for this reading. I focused on *Colonization* before, but the more popular choice would have been *Civilization*, also designed by Sid Meier. The original *Civilization* helped to define the 4X genre ("eXplore, eXpand, eXploit, and eXterminate")[51] and paved the way for five successful sequels, each of which puts the player in the position of an eternal sovereign dictating the course of an empire over thousands of years. And this is a complicated position: the player oversees major developments and turning points, but he or she is also responsible for micromanaging military units, trade deals, urban development projects, and so on. At the same time, the game manages to lull the player into a trance, always taking "just one more turn." The game generates this "smooth flow" out of a "tangle of roles" by requiring the player to enter "an unfamiliar, alien mental state," Ted Friedman argues: it requires them "to think like a computer."[52] And not just to think. *Civilization* is a strategy game, not a roleplaying game, but the player nonetheless *inhabits* the role of the computer; they learn "how to engage and optimize systems," as Brian Schrank puts it, but they also learn "how to manage their desire."[53] A formal critique of *Civilization*, then, has little to do with its progressivist historical narrative, its orientalist presentation of non-Western cultures, its technological determinism, or any other ideological mistake. Instead, this focus on the game's form suggests that *Civilization* should be critiqued on the basis of the way that it teaches its players to think, intuit, and even desire algorithmically.

Thinking in terms and on the basis of discrete, bounded, computerized information-processing systems is an incredibly significant form of contemporary political power: we are building systems that operate in algorithmic terms and we are being entrained to them. Whether miniature consumer electronics or massive infrastructural constellations, these computational systems constitute an opaque machine ecology of their own. Contemporary finance capital is unsurprisingly exemplary here: high-frequency trading, in which proprietary algorithms conduct high volume, short term trades at speeds thousands of times faster than human traders, accounts for half of all US equity trading volume. Because it takes place with incredible speed, and because it takes place between competing and exceedingly complicated algorithms, it can generate unpredictable consequences – black swan events like the 2010 flash crash. High-frequency trading is exemplary, not exceptional; our technological systems tend toward complexity, autonomy, and opacity. As Samuel Arbesman puts it: "many of these systems are actually no longer completely understandable. We now live in a world filled with incomprehensible glitches and bugs. When we find a bug in a video game, it's intriguing, but when we are surprised by the very infrastructure of our society, that should give us pause."[54]

Arbesman's reference to videogames is not coincidental. The algorithm is a form of power that is just as difficult to represent in traditional media as it is easy to depict in videogames. Alexander Galloway extends Friedman's analysis in his own reading of *Civilization*, which he takes as a stand-in for videogames in general:

> In the work of Meier, the gamer is not simply playing this or that historical simulation. The gamer is instead learning, internalizing, and becoming intimate with a massive, multipart, global algorithm. To play the game means to play the code of the game. To win means to know the system. And thus to *interpret* a game means to interpret its algorithm (to discover its parallel "allegorithm").[55]

Videogames, for Galloway and many others, illustrate the technologized condition of contemporary politics; they are, "at their structural core, in direct synchronization with the political realities of the informatics age. If Meier's work is about anything, it is about information society itself. It is about knowing systems and knowing code, or I should say, knowing *the* system and knowing *the* code."[56]

Not only, then, do videogames like *Civilization* operate as allegories for the variety of different algorithmic systems that touch on or even make up so much of the world, they also give us the impression that the world as such, despite its incredible and growing complexity, can be understood algorithmically: everything can be systematized, everything reduced down to a single code. Everything, to add a fifth "X" to the list, can be *exhausted* – understood, played with, and disposed of. Videogames, more clearly than any other medium, present us with an allegorithm for the purported comprehensibility, controllability, and monolithic character of the world. What greater power fantasy is there than that?

Gamer Theory as Media Theory

So videogames operate allegorithmically, which is to say symptomatically – at least in part: they tell us, indirectly, about what we take for granted. Before saying more about these hidden and taken for granted assumptions about what the world is and should be, I want to focus on the character of this allegorithmic or symptomatic function. What *kinds* of things do videogames tell us, exactly, and what *else* do they do?

Videogames are digital media. As media, they perform the same political work that all other media perform, including the political work of inclusion and exclusion; as digital media, they do something new. For Mark Hansen, the novelty of "new media," videogames included, lies in the way that the computer generalizes the machinic symbolization of the world: "the computer marks a certain dissociation of media from technics. Arguably for the first time in history, the technical infrastructure of media is no longer homologous with its surface appearance."[57] What we see on the screen bears no discernible, comprehensible relation to the technical infrastructure that undergirds it. Media have always been a sort of black box, but there is something distinct in the extent to which the computer intensifies the box's opacity. This is particularly significant because of the temporal disjuncture between person and machine: the end user's experience takes place "on the basis of a technical logic that operates at a temporal scale far finer than that of human sense perception... and with a level of complexity that defies capture in the form of (traditional) media."[58]

In the dissociation of media from technics, or in this intensification of mystification, digital media introduce a new function. Media have always exteriorized human experience, allowing them to be transmitted and archived, but they have not always performed such an extraordinary work of epistemological translation – of making human sense of the things taking place at a level that human beings can't directly access.[59] New media "mediate for human experience the non- (or proto-) phenomenological, fine-scale temporal computational processes that increasingly make up the infrastructure conditioning all experience in our world today." New media mediate the "transcendental technicity" or the "technological unconscious" of experience. New media "mediates the conditions of mediation."[60]

Hansen's phrasing is awkward but useful. The verb "mediates" in particular works better than "translates"; to say that new media mediates, affecting thought and action, is to leave the exact outcomes of those effects indeterminate.[61] It is also, however, to tie those outcomes to the technical structure of the medium in question. Different techniques condition thought and action differently. If that's the case, then it's clearly important to think through the features that distinguish videogames from non-digital games and from other narrative media, digital or not.

What are the "structuring," "conditioning," or "determining" functions that all media perform? If media determine our situation, they do so obliquely rather than directly, operating at a level that precedes human thought; they operate both epistemologically and *ontologically*, conditioning not only what and how we think but *what there is in the world* for us to think *about*.[62] This means that media are "deterministic" in the sense not that they force us to think or act in a particular way – they mostly don't work like propaganda; violent videogames don't make kids violent – but in the sense that they delimit the field, both the field of perception and the field of existence. They are causal in this particular sense. But they are more than *just* causal; they are, as I said earlier, symptoms, in that their structure can tell us something about our general understanding of what we take the world to be – a *pre*-understanding of what exists, partial and exclusionary while also definitive and totalizing, limited in that it is a *particular* worldview but expansive in that it is a view of *the world*.[63]

The widest political significance of cultural and technological artifacts like videogames becomes apparent in this conjunction of media and ontology.[64] This is an old conjunction. Things in the world always show themselves in a certain light, whether this is the light of modern technology, the light of ancient Greek *poiesis*, or the light of something else entirely. This is to say more than that the world is perspectival, though; it's to say that things *appear and are* in terms of something else: *x* is as *y*. We all have different ways of looking at things, but those things can only even appear in those different ways because of the way that they are lit up in advance.

If I were speaking Heideggerian, I would phrase things differently: "[a]lways the unconcealment of that which is goes upon a way of revealing," he writes; things can only appear because being discloses itself in a particular fashion, which is to say in terms of something else.[65] Today, that "something else" is what he calls the essence of modern technology – enframing, as it's usually translated, or *Ge-stell*: an all-encompassing imposition according to which things reveal themselves as comprehensible, orderable, and disposable.[66] Being discloses itself as a *number* of beings that can be so recognized and numbered because they are revealed in quantitative and instrumental terms. The owners of a timber company will see the forest from a very different perspective than the scientists working for a conservation group, but both will see it in the same basic light: the forest is a resource to be deployed in one way or another. It shows itself as a standing reserve of timber, as a means of processing carbon dioxide, as a habitat for animals, and so on, but in each case as a thing in the service of something else. It is comprehensible in these instrumental terms. This may not be the *only* way that capitalists and scientists will understand the forest, but it is the predominant one. It adopts an ontological status. The fact that things show themselves in a certain light, or that they reveal themselves in terms of the essence of modern technology, also means that they refuse to show themselves in another. Revealing has an opportunity cost. In the case of the forest showing itself as a means to an end and a storehouse of assorted resources, this means refusing to show itself in any other way – as the locus of spiritual practice, as an incomprehensible and inhuman wild, or as something that cannot be characterized as some *thing*.

We can discern these ontological limitations in a range of different ways, looking to different sites that might make the danger of our ontological limitations clear. Any object of analysis might be susceptible to this kind of ontological critique, but I want to suggest that it's especially productive to think about ontology in the context of media. Media map the world, indicating the borders, boundaries, and limits that distinguish the known and knowable from the unknown and unknowable.[67] Those things that lie beyond the contours of the media – beyond its linguistic and technical definitions, its social norms, its terms of service, its dominant areas of focus, and so on – can find themselves excluded not just from discourse, but from worldhood as such. There is a reflective role of the media, then, that is both epidemiological and causal: media, videogames included, symptomatize *and* engender particular ways of understanding the world. They drive change, perhaps, and they also describe it.[68]

If this claim about the ontological function of the media is true, then we can learn a lot by thinking carefully about the formal elements of videogames. The algorithms that help constitute them and the distinctive patterns of use that they encourage in players can tell us something about the wider context in which an array of techno-social norms are changing: data and privacy, demographics and subjectivity, automated trading and economics, and so on. They can tell us not only about the "social world,"[69] but about the world as such: about what sort of world we must live in so that these things have been able to come to pass.

The smallest of these features and patterns are also, of course, among the most infrequently noted by most critics, but not because they're too small to see. They are right there on the surface. As Galloway argues: "[v]ideo games don't attempt to hide informatic control; they flaunt it."[70] Whether described in terms of cause or symptom, these algorithmic features and patterns should be understood in big terms: they are ubiquitous in that they extend beyond the game, invisible in that they escape notice, and totalizing in that they structure our thoughts and actions while also indicating how our thoughts and actions are already structured. And they do all of this in a complicatedly recursive fashion: our habitual reliance on small things, repeated over and over until naturalized, comes to form the ground for the generation of further small things.

Clockwork Worlds

So what are these small, ubiquitous, structuring things of the videogame world, and what do they tell us about the world more generally? It's probably coincidental that Marshall McLuhan was reflecting on this question during the period when the first true videogames were being developed and played – *Spacewar!* and *The Gutenberg Galaxy* both appeared in 1962, while *Understanding Media* was published in 1964 – but it's a fortunate coincidence. McLuhan spent most of the latter book addressing electronic media, of course, but he also suggested that traditional games could be understood through a similar lens:

> Games are popular art, collective, social *reactions* to the main drive or action of any culture. Games, like institutions, are extensions of social man and of the body politic, as technologies are extensions of the animal organism. Both games and technologies are counter-irritants or ways of adjusting to the stress of the specialized actions that occur in any social group. As extensions of the popular response to the workaday stress, games become faithful models of a culture. They incorporate both the action and the reaction of whole populations in a single dynamic image.[71]

If games in general are "counter-irritants" to the "main drive" of culture, then what is this main drive? In McLuhan's reading, games are so appealing as escapist diversions because they give back that which we do not have but which we are told we require – our "individualism" or our "freedom." We are trapped by a number of different systems or apparatuses – economic, political, educational, communicational, sexual, racial, and so on – that regulate and curtail our freedom, but we are also continually told that we can and should do whatever we like. Games, that is, provide the perfect venue for exercising control in a world where it seems like we never have enough, and digital games render that control numerical and certain. They are, as Paolo Pedercini claims, "built upon technologies of control and quantification, and they are still by and large informed by them." This technological substrate bends games toward a "compulsion for efficiency and control," which means that players "inevitably carry over a cybernetic bias that could reinforce certain assumptions and mindsets."[72] Computers are particularly good at modeling control because they are built that way, and games are the privileged form of this modeling because they make their systematicity explicit. They valorize it. They are, in other words, so appealing not just because of the control that they offer, but because of its clear, uncomplicated perfection. Single-player games become "clockwork worlds."[73]

The often oppressive systems in which we are embedded are not the only factors contributing to these twin impressions – the need for control on the one hand and the absence of it on the other. And they are not only impressions. It is fundamentally, existentially the case that we lack control. The world is finite; events are overdetermined; we will all die. This isn't to say that every feature of our lives is determined in advance, or that the ways that we comport ourselves in the world are unimportant. Rather, it's to say that there are existential conditions that characterize every human life, culturally and historically inflected though they certainly are. Additionally, and importantly, modernity as such – the ideology of rationalism, scientism, and historical progress that characterized the Enlightenment and that continues to inflect our experience of the world – can be defined in part by the knowledge that we moderns know about these conditions, but that we don't know what to do about them. There have, of course, been recent political attempts to forcefully compensate for the absence of God or ground: twentieth-century totalitarianism can be understood as the product of a lack of "bannisters" and the resulting appeal to a system that would do its own thinking.[74] Technological attempts at such compensation have been no less political.[75]

None of these comments about political and technological modernity are intended to suggest that things haven't changed in significant ways since the fifteenth century or that our political solutions to the problem of imperfect control remain the same. The unprecedented character of the totalitarianisms of the twentieth century certainly demonstrates this shift, and I obviously need to push the historical lens further than that if I want to focus on video-games. In fact, my comments on totalitarianism and control, drawing as they do on mid-twentieth century theorists and focusing on mid-twentieth century concerns, could seem a little out of touch. Is it really the case that we can continue to characterize our political and technological problems in terms of the desire to exercise control over the uncertain and worrisome possibilities posed by the future? Isn't it the case that modern management techniques can't be applied to the risk society, and modern perspectives can't comprehend a postmodern world? The complexity of the contemporary context, so this argument goes, means that we have lost the future to the present, the unexpected to the known, hope to fear. We have become more focused on the anticipation of tomorrow than the less predictable possibilities out on the temporal horizon.[76]

If there seems to be a radical break between a modern politics bent on "disciplining," "investigating," and "codifying" the future and a risk society that hopes only to cope, perhaps generating some profit at the same time, then both the full scope of political control and the full sweep of contemporary technology are not yet clear.[77] To be sure, there have been major evolutions in the general style of government from the fifteenth century on – not in the formal terms of "the Government" as, say, monarchic or democratic or socialist, but in terms of the ways in which the actions of people are governed. The sword has always been an effective means of compelling compliance, but it has been joined in the modern period, as Michel Foucault argues, by the disciplining of the individual and the management of the population. Disciplinary institutions and practices – the timetable, the school, the barracks, the prison – train individuals to internalize the will of the sovereign body and soul, willing it themselves rather than complying with an external will out of fear.[78] Biopolitical tools, for their part – demography, eugenics, terraforming, datamining – provide the contours within which populations flourish or perish. Biopower is particularly significant in the contemporary technological context in which value is generated through the incessant and ubiquitous datafication of whole populations. Points rewards cards, RFID chips, global positioning systems, checkpoints, facial recognition software, and smart phones are subtle instruments of biopower.[79]

None of these shifts in modes of governance suggest a wholesale break with the politics of control or a sharp division between one and another. Contemporary sovereignty works biopolitically, but it continues to discipline and to punish. These shifts also do not suggest a complete change of scale. The evolution of biopower does not constitute an abandonment of the shaping of individuals but a widening of scope.[80] Most importantly, these characterizations of sovereign power (as taking life or fostering it) and of society (from discipline to control to risk) all fit within the framework articulated here. They are all different modalities through which the world is enframed. The standing reserve is constituted by individuals, by bodies, and by populations; it is deployed through tools of demographics and risk management; it is, to an increasing extent, technologized. It is not the case that we have become incapable of accounting for, let alone controlling, the future, but rather that sovereignty has shifted to supranational registers and that the modalities through which it exercises control are becoming increasingly effective on macro and micro levels alike. Here, in a biopolitical context in which technology enables the datafication of both individuals and populations and the corresponding ability to speculate on and take hold of the future,[81] the rubric of control is, if anything, more important than ever.[82]

In addition to the widening deployment of technologies of biopolitical control, there remains a discourse according to which technology can succeed where politics has failed. Daniel Innerarity is certainly correct when he says that "concerns about certainty" and "a longing for control... have lost the standing they had when they were assumed without question" in the arena of politics proper, and he is also correct to suggest that contemporary politics "cannot help but disappoint those who expect it to offer assured knowledge, a path to social consensus, and a means to achieving hierarchical control over society."[83] The fact that there are many people who are disappointed by the inability of politics to offer "hierarchical control," however, certainly does not mean that no one is looking for it. Why, in principle, *couldn't* technology accomplish what political processes have failed to achieve? Given the failures of traditional politics to face the "challenges" of the twenty-first century, the most horrifying of which is surely a globe warming its way toward complete and irreparable uninhabitability, don't we *need* these kinds of technocratic interventions?

Influential people certainly hold to this position today. Stephen Hawking is calling for the colonization of the stars. Elon

Musk, the co-founder of PayPal and the CEO of SpaceX, is building rockets that will take us there. Peter Thiel, another of PayPal's co-founders and Facebook's first outside investor, is using his financial and political relationship with Donald Trump to push the US government to support the endeavor. Thiel, in fact, articulates his beliefs in very general terms: true societal change cannot come from society itself, he argues, since society is mired down by petty politics; *technology* is the means for "escap[ing] from politics in all its forms."

We are "in a deadly race between politics and technology," he writes, and "[t]he fate of our world may depend on the effort of a single person who builds or propagates the machinery of freedom that makes the world safe for capitalism."[84] This is only the free market, libertarian, Silicon Valley twist on a very real, very contemporary faith in Science and Reason that is blind to its own theologico-political assumptions. It is shared by people on the progressive end of the political spectrum as well.

Ontotheology

It should go without saying that there is nothing inherently wrong with using technology to render the world available and then to control it. We are never not engaged with, through, and by technology, and there was never a time "before" technology, so protesting technology as such would be hypocritical at best and resentfully nostalgic at worst.[85] There is, however, something "wrong" with certain deployments of technology, or with the ways that they can frame the world. This is particularly evident in the use of network media – social media in particular, of course, provide frames through which we access the world – but it is also evident in those technologies that mediate our sociality more generally. These and other technologies are particularly worrisome for the ways that they conflate freedom with control on the basis of vulnerability. They are the result of "the reduction of political problems into technological ones," as Wendy Chun puts it; they are responses to fears both natural and "paranoid," and they "blind us to the ways in which those very technologies operate and fail to operate."[86] The myth, for instance, that computers are or will be capable of "storing, accessing, and analyzing everything" covers over the fact that "[computers crash on a regular basis, portable storage devices become unreadable, and e-mail messages disappear into the netherworld of the global network, and yet many people honestly believe in a worldwide surveillance network in which no piece of data is ever lost."[87] Like other mythologies, this is a paranoia that works in the service of those who see through it, or those who understand that technologies are not the answer to political problems but the consummate form of politics today. These myths function so effectively because they speak to us about the things that we most fear and desire.[88]

Generalizing, then: the problems that we confront cannot be answered by technological proxy because they require not the safeguarding of vulnerability but an opening up to it. Freedom is not the freedom from human vulnerability, or the freedom to act from a position of safety. Freedom *stems from* vulnerability; it *risks* safety; it *exceeds* control.[89] It begins from the vulnerability inherent to any relationship between one human and another – a relationality that, in a certain sense, precedes the individuals in question – and it is on the basis of this vulnerability and relationality that politics takes place. Technology, exercised from fear, wants nothing more than to control the unexpected coming to pass of natality.[90]

Not only do technologies of control fail on their promise to deliver freedom or safeguard vulnerability: they also fail to deliver control. The disjuncture between the mediated presentation of perfection and the technical complexities taking place inside the black box gives the user a false sense of security, but often the technology fails to work perfectly and transparently in the first place: "[y]our screen," Chun points out, "suggests that your computer only sends and receives data at your request," but any packet sniffer will demonstrate "that your computer constantly wanders without you."[91] Or our values change in response to its implementation, denying us some freedom we had before: the proliferation of tools for controlling your social media presence covers over changing norms around privacy, for instance. Or it leads to blowback, as technologies are repurposed and turned back against their creators: after the US deployed the Stuxnet computer worm to damage uranium centrifuges in Iran, security experts grew terrified about the possibility of that virus being used as a blueprint for future attacks. Or the implementation of the technology leads to an arms race, with one group's attempts at securitization generating better tools used by other groups for undermining that security. Or we witness the rise of whole new modes of exercising power: corporate and government surveillance shifted into a frightening new register with big data.

While there are usually very good and very specific reasons for the different ways that technologies "bite back,"[92] there is also a general explanation: technologies fail to bestow perfect control because the world is not ultimately controllable. Despite the obviousness of this observation, our newest technologies promise ever greater control over ever more phenomena. Digital technologies promise the world literally and metaphorically. Here, I want to highlight two examples in particular, the first for its theological tenor and the second for its foundational promise.

Twenty-first century rhetoric around digital media and new technology often feels spiritual.[93] Think of Apple's Steve Jobs announcing the iPad in 2010, the computer held aloft like one of Moses's tablets, or *Wired* magazine's Kevin Kelly describing technology in the monotheistic terms of "The One,"[94] or the repeated suggestions by Google's Larry Page that the search engine will one day "understand everything in the world," or the insistence of singulatarians like Ray Kurzweil that we are approaching the technological rapture.[95] In describing the promise of digital media, the prophets of technology convey its ostensible characteristics in spiritual terms: it is *permanent*, extending backwards in the form of a global archive and forwards in the data-derived promise of prediction; *ubiquitous*, stretching over spaces and into (the internet of) things; *totalizing*, pushing for the informatic or quantitative capture of all qualities; *invisible*, or "made of sunshine";[96] *autonomous*, increasingly capable of operation without human intervention; in this growing autonomy, *perfectible*; and finally, and perhaps most importantly, unified, coherent, or *monolithic*. As Kelly puts it in his predictions for 2020 and beyond:

> There is only One machine.
> The web is its OS.
> All screens look into the One.
> No bits will live outside the web.
> To share is to gain.
> Let the One read it.
> The One is us.[97]

Omnipresent, omniscient, and soon omnipotent: that's the promise, anyway.[98] This promise takes an extreme form in the beatific reflections of the likes of Kelly, albeit an extreme form that is perfectly understandable given the loss of God and ground that characterize modernity, but it is also apprehensible today in the form and rhetoric of the Cloud. Data processing and storage is moving from independent and stationary personal computers to centralized megaservers accessed by dependent but mobile computing devices, and we seem to be benefitting from this transition every day. I no longer need to manually sync my files between devices, remember passwords, buy and install software, or update my hardware – all of this can be done more easily, from the individual user's perspective, by the Cloud. More importantly, each individual user's contribution to the Cloud adds to the wealth of data stored in these megaservers, and hence to the wealth of the corporations that run them. The Cloud functions on the basis of the immaterial labor carried out voluntarily and involuntarily every time that a user contributes to the network – a contribution which can be as explicit as the downloading or uploading of a file or as minimal as the quiet registration of the user's presence or absence. Cloud computing obfuscates the ways that networks function by giving users the vague sense that something mystical is taking place, enabling a new intensification of capital.

All of this is, as Rob Coley and Dean Lockwood argue, "a monstrous new form of power and control" that "should be understood as central to the newly *intensive* nature of an already established paradigm of socio-cultural connection and integration, entwined with, but not determined by, emergent technical systems." Their reading of the Cloud as singular and divine foregrounds the cultural fantasy of the phenomenon (cloud culture is "defined by the global informatic archive to which we are constantly tethered," and it "fosters a dream-like state in which we can both *possess* and *be* everything we wish *simultaneously*"), since it is this fantasy that is enabled and required by networked capital.[99] At the same time, the "soft tyranny" of cloud culture relies upon the technical form of network protocols. Notably, they argue that this culture and these protocols can be best understood "in terms of the logic of video games": "play," they write, "proceeds in terms of internalizing the code, the protocological and algorithmic architecture of the game."[100] In willingly playing the game according to the rules that the Cloud sets up, users find themselves running along biopolitical channels, conforming in advance to the rules of the network. This requires the user – "the mark" – "to maintain a state of relative autonomy and self-invention":

It is a form of control that foregoes the hegemonic mode of

"power over" and shifts into a mode in which power is exerted from "within," in fact "owned" by the mark as his very capacity to act in the world and discover his own truth. The mark is enlisted in the process of his own control...[This is] the becoming ontological of power.[101]

If the lofty discourse of the Cloud centers on the spirit, its politics both emanates from and works to establish the ground.

A second, foundational ontologization of control is taking place alongside the first. The most adventurous claims for digital technology's world-changing properties come from those research scientists and futurists working in and thinking about nanotechnology, the manipulation of matter at atomic or molecular scales. Formerly speculative, nanotech is now really here: it is currently used in over 1800 consumer products, deployed in commercial industries ranging from computer transistors to solar energy to stain-resistant textiles, and – or so we are told – nearly ready to revolutionize everything from computing to the biomolecular manipulation of the body.[102] In this futuristic discourse, we are moving from science fiction to science fact. But this discursive claim, as Colin Milburn argues, covers over the extent to which science fiction continues to inform the research programs of scientists working in the nanotech field.[103] Pointing to the playful ways in which nanomaterials have been manipulated – shaped into smiley faces, carved into dice, turned into actually functioning but totally useless "nanocars"[104] – Milburn makes it clear that the field of nanotechnology is driven forward not so much by the need for new nanomaterials or processes as by the desire to tinker with reality on a fundamental, atomic level, and by the dream of turning matter into software.[105] These desires and dreams are influencing the actual shape taken by research science, as well as the popular discourse about the potentials of this ever-new field.[106] And again, it is not coincidental that this second ontologization of control also takes a ludic form.

To the carving of nano-dice can be added the playing of nano-tic-tac-toe, nano-chess, and nano-soccer, as well as the gamification of research through crowdsourcing and the use of consumer game consoles and controllers for the hyperreal navigation of nano-simulacra – to say nothing of the appearance of nanotechnology in so very many games.

Cloud computing and nanotechnology take ludic form because games, better than any other medium, model our assumptions about the world. If cloud computing and nanotechnology promise the world, they do so not as outliers distinct from the normal functioning of technology. The claims of these digital technologies are the claims of technology itself. We engage with *mondo nano* through "mediated prehension," Milburn argues, "participating in a cultural logic of experimentation where *to dissect* is *to know* and *to break* is *to see*," but this is also the way that we engage with the world as such. Modern technology reveals the world as digitizable in precisely the way that Milburn, following Galloway and Wark, suggests that videogames perform:

> [H]ack-and-slash game violence...functions as an *allegory* for digitization as such: the chopping of the analog into measurable units, the slicing of continuous differentials into manipulable parts. After all, the dream of digital matter is about the transformation of analog matter into *bits*: bits as binary digits, and bits as matter broken apart. Through the *nano breaking* of matter, we enact our prehension of the molecular world.[107]

In rendering our ontological assumptions visual, tactile, and actionable, games exemplify the political work done by modern technology, which is to say the wide range of consequences that issues from people believing that technology will in fact render the world comprehensible and controllable. These are the political consequences of what Katherine Hayles refers to as the regime of computation: when the world is understood as fundamentally computable – as founded on code, and hence on the ability to render all things discrete and manipulable (to render them *as things*) – ambiguity becomes abject.[108] That which cannot be rendered digital – say, the body, with all of its failings and its grim promise of inevitable death and decay, as well as the radical unpredictability of birth and life – is relegated to the temporal or epistemic outskirts.

I said earlier that there's nothing inherently wrong with technology, and hence nothing necessarily wrong with digital technology or with the videogame. But with these fanciful forms of future media, we see the potential problem take shape. The twinned rhetorics of the Cloud and *mondo nano* provide a theological apex and an ontological foundation, or a framework within which things can be ordered: the ideal form of the digital world (its whatness or its essence) is data, and it operates on the basis of its purportedly programmable ground (its thatness or its existence). These are mutually justifying: the nigh-divine power of data justifies the view according to which the world is programmable, and the understanding of the world as programmable justifies the desire to render it so. If we have a technology that can improve the world, shouldn't we use it? Shouldn't we identify and combat injustices? Shouldn't we prevent suffering – avert the apocalypse? We see here a mutation in our basic apprehension of the world driven by perfectly understandable desires and fears, a historical or epochal shift in our thinking and being in the world according to which the world is understood as *fundamentally* comprehensible, *fundamentally* controllable. As a mutation within the broadest parameters of metaphysics, there is a sense here in which cybernetics, the datafication of things, and the regime of computation are only intensifications of an onto-theo-logic extending back thousands of years.[109] This is the same ontotheology that accounts for the shift from disciplinary power to biopower that I described earlier: it takes place within this fundamental set of assumptions about the world. Nevertheless, it is a change that is accompanied not only by the assumption that the world is controllable, but – because, in part, of our fears of vulnerability and finitude – that it *should be* controlled.

When this impulse shifts from the implicitly political register of technology to politics as it is usually understood, the stakes of digitization become clear. Thinking that the world can and should be controlled, both because it *is* controllable and because the lack of control poses a *threat*, explains the melancholic form taken by phenomena as disparate as border securitization, pre-emptive war, racial profiling, and finance capital.[110] Take the building of perimeter walls as an example: the Berlin Wall, the Israeli West Bank barrier, the Mexico-United States barrier, and the Line of Control on the India-Pakistan border are just a few contemporary examples of the renewal of an impulse that dates back to 8,000 BCE in Jericho.[111] For Wendy Brown, the resurgence of this psycho-political impulse can be explained by the number and quality of threats facing the sovereignty of the nation-state: "globalization," in this context, connotes the instability caused by the free movement of people and capital and all of the things that go with them – plagues, terrors, jobs.[112] Although these are threats to the nation-state itself, they are felt, economically and metonymically, by the citizens of those formerly, ostensibly sovereign states, and so the governments that propose and carry out the erection of border walls find themselves well supported by angry, fearful citizens.[113] The fact that these walls ultimately fail to work and that even their designers and advocates know in advance that they *will* fail is important for demonstrating both the constitutive uncontrollability of state borders and the futility of the political will to close down politics. That, ultimately, is what border walls are: the indices of failed attempts to excise contingency and the markers of a modern, Hobbesian conception of sovereignty that needs to disavow what it knows to be true about the world – its uncontrollability – in order to exist in the first place. In this, border walls are conceptually homologous with code.

Play

The modern conception of sovereignty that gives rise to border walls is problematic in the same way as the ontotheological conception of code that makes data into the basic unit of existence and the ideal form of all things: both framings construe the world and its political possibilities on the basis and in terms of fears about finitude and desires for salvation. We are not, however, bound to abide by these presumptions and prescriptions, totalizing though they can be, both because ontology does not prescribe a single politics and because ontology shifts. Though determinative, it is also historical and cultural; though totalizing, it does not totalize. We can do other than attempt to exert perfect control over a world conceived as standing reserve.

Our systematic, digital, totalizable assumptions about the world are a precondition for treating things and people so violently, but they are far from inevitable. They are also homologous with the assumptions of videogames: the same assumptions that inform the power fantasy also inform ontology, politics, and ethics. The videogame, as the medium that enables the construction and navigation of complete worlds, best instantiates data politics and the ontotheology that grounds and legitimates it. At the same time, the videogame does not totalize; an avenue for the totalizing scope of digitality, it nevertheless also offers the means for its immanent critique. Where Guy Debord saw the potential for establishing distance and weakening apparently objective truths in *détournement*, or in the tactical reversals of signs that prompt critical reflection in a place where before there was none,[114] Wark sees a similar potential in the ability of the gamer to step outside of the confines of one particular game and into another.[115] In moving from one game to another – one *world* to another – the gamer can alter their stance toward "reality" itself. This is less a matter of ideological demystification, revealing how things "really are," than of refusing to become caught in a fight or flight response wherein one either rejects the dictates of modern technology or escapes to somewhere that it has yet to touch. These are not the only options available.

If reality has already become gamespace, then the ways that we engage with games influence our conception of the world as such. When we play to win, we leave the legitimacy of the game unquestioned, but when we *trifle* with it, we play "with style to understand the game as form. [We] trifle with the game to understand the nature of gamespace as a world – as *the* world."[116] Trifling – ignoring the game's objective in order to explore its possibility space – demonstrates that the rules of the game appear to be objective, that they are designed and maintained by particular political actors exercising sovereign authority, that they can therefore be contested, *and* that there is no world outside of these formal constraints. Trifling, in other words, reveals gamespace to be simultaneously absolute and contingent, monolithic and finite, open to contestation and inescapable. In this, gamespace allegor(ithmat)izes our existential condition: we are bound to a finite world that is not ultimately under our control, but we are nonetheless able to act within it in a meaningful way.

In the same way that the trifler can relativize and repurpose the rules of the gameworld without breaking them, Wark's gamer theorist can relativize and repurpose the Law of Reality without escaping it. For although Wark relativizes reality by allegorizing it as gamespace, he acknowledges that games themselves nonetheless differ fundamentally from gamespace in terms of the gamer's position with regard to that most important existential constant, time:

The game is a knowable algorithm from which you know you can escape; gamespace is an unknown algorithm from which there is no escape. The game is just like the gamespace of everyday life, except that the game can be saved. The game can overcome the violence of time. The game ties up that one loose end with which gamespace struggles – the mortal flaw of an irreversible time.[117]

The gamer's ability to reverse time means that "[t]he world outside [of the game] appears as an imperfect form of the computer game," imperfect in the deepest, most originary sense – for the passage of time is the most immediate index of our fundamental lack of control.[118] But the trifler understands that even the most perfect videogame has its limits and that even the strictest rules can be manipulated to achieve unforeseen ends. The trifler understands the imperfection of even the purest digital systems, and they achieve this "understanding" less through the directly political modality of *détournement* than through the experiential and indirect modality of play.

Trifling, hacking, and other similar practices that contravene control resemble *paidia*, or free, spontaneous forms of play, but this does not mean that they are the only means of instituting a playful attitude. Even the strictest form of controlled, rulebound *game*play, or *ludus*, can contravene control.[119] Game design, which is the focus of the following two chapters, can inculcate a critical or ethical attitude, working against the controlling, systematizing tendencies inherent in the form.[120] Both the play and design of games are capable of mounting immanent critiques of the systems in which they are embedded because they index the non-systemic, non-totalizable nature of all structures.[121]

Chapter Two

Design against Control

Videogames are often complicit with the denial of finitude and the desire for control because of their rulebound, digital form, and the consequences of this complicity are widespread: political, ethical, aesthetic, and ontological. Players play videogames in the terms set by the games; play proceeds along predictable lines, within existing structures. It is never completely free. Moreover, this kind of gameplay can produce a desire to understand and exhaust game systems. At the same time, videogames only *tend* to produce this attitude: there are any number of different ways in which it can be contravened, from the perspectives of both the designer and the player. In fact, the rulebound nature of digital games inclines a certain kind of player to find ways to play *with* the game, bending or breaking its rules in creative ways – a subject taken up in the fourth and fifth chapters. This chapter and the next, however, consider the potential for game design rather than game play to issue an immanent critique of control.

Games can work against their own tendencies. They make arguments through stories, mechanics, and the play between these dimensions. When their arguments touch on subjects germane to that modern, controlling attitude, they can put the player in a critical, reflexive position that constitutes an aesthetic space of political and ethical potential. This is particularly the case for single player, story-driven games that thematize time, including those examined below: *Spec Ops: The Line, Braid, Undertale,* and *Bastion*.

A book on games and politics might very reasonably look to games that contain political themes, or games that have been designed with a political takeaway in mind, but I am deliberately avoiding such "serious" games in favor of those that prioritize fun. The simple reason for this is that the players of serious games almost always know in advance that they are playing a game designed to convince them of something, and this knowledge necessarily changes the play experience.[122] Molleindustria, which produces "homeopathic remedies to the idiocy of mainstream entertainment in the form of free, short-form, online games," is exemplary here. Their website is fairly restrained, save for that description from their circumspect About page, but small cues alert the player to the didactic nature of their work. Thumbnails for their games show their names and a brief description: "*Phone Story*: The dark side of smartphone manufacturing"; "*McDonald's Videogame*: An anti-advergame for the fast food industry." The gameplay tends toward unambiguity too.[123] But Molleindustria's better games display more subtlety. *To Build a Better Mousetrap*, for instance, begins when the player uses the cursor to lift up a mouse and deposit it on a platform. A cat mask descends on its head. The newly minted cat takes control of an assembly line manufacturing colored cubes by managing researchers, workers, and an ever-increasing line-up of unemployed malcontents – "human" resources. The game works for the reasons that those other Molleindustria offerings do not: its ambiguous title prompts reflection on the purpose of endless innovation, its lack of instructions invites the player to explore and think through the meaning of its mechanics, and its difficulty encourages the player to replay the game to discover its different endings, many of which, like "Insurrection," are good for the workers but bad for the player. Players who do replay the game can find themselves in a position of comparative mastery, but this itself ends up being a critique of the violence of pointless, limitless production: in an optimized factory, the mice are either incarcerated or underpaid, while the cat achieves mere "retirement." The cubes win.

Framing affects the reception of artistic games as well. When games are only shown in galleries, archived on their designers' websites, or described in books about the artistic potential of videogames, players come to them expecting to have an "artistic" experience. Take *Adam Killer*: Brody Condon modified the *Half-Life* engine to display an infinite number of copies of a 3D model of his friend on a featureless white plane and invited the player to shoot that model over and over, painting the screen with corpses and blood. *Adam Killer* can be read as a critique of the reinforcement and reward patterns of first-person shooter games: in affording perfect and perfectly pointless control, the game undermines the valorization of control that videogames in general encourage.[124] The basic message works – it was copied ten years later and delivered to a much larger audience via *The Onion*'s own satire, *Close Range*, in which the player delivers an endless series of point blank gunshots to unarmed faces – but it might have been more effectively communicated if "the player" here were anyone other than Condon himself: *Adam Killer* was made available in video form, but never as interactive software. It was created by a self-described visual artist as a performance piece – "game art" rather than "game" – and it was received in a similar light.[125]

Players of explicitly political games and audiences appreciating game art know that their experiences are supposed to mean more than the usual play session. They may come to these games intrigued or open, but they also come to them alert. This is not at all to say that the sort of radical games designed by Molleindustria or the game art created by the likes of Brody Condon are uninteresting, ineffective, or unimportant; rather, it's to say that there is interestingly political and ethical material in "the games that we play for fun" as well.[126] There's a real potential to games that take the player by surprise.

Popular games like *Civilization* are, as I noted earlier, "political" not only because they directly thematize politics, but because they institute a way of thinking and acting in their design, and because they interpellate the player through pleasure. Game design concerns the political not in its occasional reference to the "Politics" of parties and office, but in the ways that it addresses or shapes the space of uncertainty between people. Referring to this space, or this mode of existence, as "the political" is a shorthand intended to evoke the interpersonal potential of what we hold in common: that uncertain agonistic space where we share common concerns and decide common affairs.[127] In this context, "Politics" is only the rationalizing negation of political potential that can take place when the collective voices of thousands are channeled through institutions and representatives. It should also be understood in any number of less direct but equally thoughtless ways: through definitions and "common sense"; through conventions of design and sensibility; through pre-understandings of what exists, and how it does so; through algorithms, protocols, and lock-in. By dividing the normal from the abnormal, what may be spoken from what cannot be uttered, and what exists from what does not, the political can be reduced to politics – usually in service of the status quo.[128]

At the same time, since "the political" evokes the commons, or the public, referencing it alone risks missing the similar state of uncertainty and potential that exists between any two people, even in private. More importantly, it risks missing the *responsibility* that arises most clearly in this private state. The face-to-face encounter of one person with another is uncertain in the same way that the political agonism of the commons is uncertain – the outcome is inherently unknown and unknowable – but it is also a call to act and account. The face of the other presents itself in its vulnerability, as well as in its simultaneous similarity and alterity, and it elicits a response that precedes rational reflection.[129] This means that the face-to-face encounter is the space of responsibility, duty, or ethics – but not of morality. Moreover, the requirement to take responsibility in the face of the other extends to the political realm: all political action is ultimately action taken in a space of uncertainty, but this uncertainty does not relieve the actor of their responsibility.[130] The ethics that attends the vulnerability of interpersonal encounter differs from the morality of prescription in the same way that the political differs from politics: ethics and politics both share and give rise to uncertainty and potential, and ethics and politics can both be reduced through their systematization, no matter the means by which that systematization takes place.

So, when I refer to the political and ethical capacity of games, or to ludopolitics, this is the kind of thing I have in mind: the provocative potential of games to challenge their players by opening onto a space of uncertainty and responsibility, or a space where their capacity to control the things of the world is called into question even while their imbrication in the world is reasserted. In this context, all games – even those that seem to be completely devoid of political or ethical themes – have some sort of political and ethical potential, and even those games that appear to be progressive in their narrative themes can belie that potential in their mechanical form.

Open Worlds: *Fallout 3*

With those preliminary comments about the political and ethical potential of game design in mind, consider *Fallout 3*, a game loved by critics, players, and a few moral philosophers alike. A post-apocalyptic open world action roleplaying game, *Fallout 3* gives the player control of the former resident of a nuclear bunker tasked with finding their father and restoring hope to the Capital Wasteland. Early in the game, the player is likely to come across Tenpenny Tower, a walled community relatively safe from the dangers of the wastes. One of those dangers comes in the form of ghouls: mutated, zombie-like humans, some of which retain their humanity and some of which have gone "feral." The player encounters one of the "civil" ghouls, Roy Phillips, during their first approach. Roy is trying to convince the head of security, Chief Gustavo, to admit him and his followers in exchange for caps, the game's currency, but Gustavo flatly refuses. The player can resolve the quest in four ways:

1. Kill Phillips and his followers, eliminating the ghoul threat.
2. Let the ghouls into the Tower, knowing that they will then kill its residents.
3. Broker a deal in which the ghouls will become residents of the Tower, living harmoniously with the humans already there.
4. Leave things as they are.

I, like many other players, negotiated a peaceful deal, helping Phillips and his followers gain entry. Leaving the Tower, things seemed tense but fine, but when I returned later, the human residents were missing. The ghouls had murdered them all.

The Tenpenny Tower quest is one of the best parts of *Fallout 3* because of the way that it breaks roleplaying game conventions: players are used to seeking out and achieving a peaceful "third way," but here, their attempts fail. Miguel Sicart argues that the quest engenders a state of "ethical cognitive friction" in the player since the gameworld itself offers no clear guidelines as to the "correct" outcome, since the outcome is uncertain, and since seemingly "ethical" actions on behalf of the player lead to "unethical" results. This friction "can lead players to be suspicious of their own moral standpoint," which is, for Sicart, the key marker of "ethical gameplay": "an experience in and of play that disrupts the progression toward goals and achievements and forces players to address their actions from a moral ,perspective."[131] It is one of only a few quests in *Fallout 3* that leaves the player uncertain about how to act.

Despite the quest's unusual ambiguity, its thematization of intolerance, and its capacity to generate "ethical cognitive friction," Tenpenny Tower shares a number of problems with the rest of *Fallout 3* that rest on the game's design. Uncertain though the initial outcome is, the game does not in fact call into question the quest's moral status: that morality is coded and enforced through the game's "karma" system, which assesses the player's actions as neutral, good, or evil. Completing quests that help out the Capital Wasteland's common folk gives positive karma; killing drug-addicted raiders gives positive karma; giving purified water to beggars gives positive karma. Completing quests that hurt people, stealing their belongings, or devouring their corpses gives negative karma. In the Tenpenny Tower quest, the player earns negative karma by murdering the humans or the ghouls, either before they gain entrance to the Tower or after they have murdered its residents, and positive karma by convincing the residents to accept them or by murdering Alistair Tenpenny or Chief Gustavo. Accruing karma over the course of the game bestows "karma titles" on the player ranging from the mundane to the divine: from "Vault Guardian" to "Shepherd" and "Messiah," and from "Vault Delinquent" to "Deceiver" and "Devil." By systematizing choice, *Fallout 3* encodes a morality that is recognizably Christian and Kantian. There might be an "ethical dilemma" here, in precisely the *moral* sense in which Sicart uses the term, but there is not what I am referring to as an *ethics*: there is no real confusion about what is made possible by the game's systems or about the ethical valence of these possibilities. They are knowable, if not entirely known, in advance, and they are encoded in an existing moral system that prescribes what the correct action is.

This first problem rests on a second: *Fallout 3* is able to encode its moral system because all of the events that take place in its world take place *in* code *for* the player. The world is enacted at the player's behest, even while it is designed to feel as though it were a living and breathing thing. If I walked away from Tenpenny Tower after seeing Phillips' initial confrontation with Gustavo, nothing would have happened: the ghouls would have remained outside, frustrated and waiting, while the residents stayed in. The passage of time would have changed nothing. The same is true of the other quests and events in *Fallout 3*. Nothing happens without the player's intervention. This is obviously no different than the vast majority of commercial roleplaying games, or games in general, but it's nonetheless a design decision that doubles down on the narrative decision to make the player the center of the universe: Messiah, Devil.

So *Fallout 3* is a power fantasy: it gives the player an array of interesting weapons and the ability to stop time to use them; it offers quick saves that make it possible to immediately reverse the outcomes of any undesirable encounters; it presents the player with a rich set of mechanical systems (attributes, skills, perks, weapons, armor, karma) that can be learned and optimized; it makes the player into a powerful and moral demigod; and it renders the gameworld a standing reserve that takes place only in the player's presence. The challenge it presents the player has little to do with the need to take responsibility for acting into an uncertain world. The Tenpenny Tower quest might constitute a moral dilemma, but it is not political or ethical in the sense that I outlined above.

None of this makes *Fallout 3* a "bad game." The fact that it counts as a power fantasy, or that it works to entrench a protocological understanding of its gameworld, doesn't mean that we "shouldn't" play it, or that we should feel bad for roaming the Waste. *Fallout 3* can be a deeply satisfying, immersive experience – and there's nothing inherently wrong with power fantasies, anyway. *Fallout 3* is not so much *bad* as it is *uninteresting*. The Tenpenny Tower quest could have offered the player more compelling options. What if the game eliminated or at least hid its karma system? The player would be forced to assess their character's actions without the aid of on-screen heuristics. Or what if the game restricted the ability to save and reload? The

Tenpenny Tower quest is actually a good example of how to frustrate a player interested in saving and reloading, since it defers the consequences of the player's decision until a later point by which the player has likely saved several times more, but many other quests and all combat encounters can be bypassed through saving and reloading.[132] More permanent options might result in a greater sense of player investment because of better "exposition" – what designer Greg Kasavin defines as "the deliberate arrangement of its content, including its structure, its systems, and its narrative, in support of the game's experiential goals." Good exposition immerses and invests the player in the experience that the designers are trying to achieve by presenting an "internally consistent" and narratively compelling game-world.[133] And immersion and investment are preconditions for political and ethical experience.

More extensive expository options than those pursued by *Fallout 3* exist too, of course. Take the issue of waiting for the player's actions as an example: nothing happens in *Fallout 3* without the player initiating it. Something might be described by a non-player character as urgent, but in the absence of a ticking clock, the experienced player knows that they are free to explore the world and resolve the action at their own pace. Commercial games occasionally break this convention. *Deus Ex: Human Revolution* begins by asking the player to resolve a tense hostage situation at a manufacturing plant, but it also gives them the opportunity to explore the headquarters first. Worried about missing content in a rush to free the hostages, and knowing that game events usually take place when the player wants them to, the seasoned player might reasonably take their time in Sarif HQ – something that results in the hostages being killed. The player is punished for assuming that the game's narrative is disconnected from its mechanics, and this punishment encourages them to look more seriously on the gameworld. It results in a sense of immersion and investment in a world that seems to have its own pace.

Design decisions like these are interesting in the ways that they encourage players to look differently on gameworlds and in the fact that they affect mainstream gamers. I am, as I noted earlier, less interested in "games for change" or in "artgames" than I am in the political and ethical function of commercially successful games to either entrench existing modes of understanding the world or to undermine them. Because games operate procedurally, and because they cannot help but issue commentary on the world, all games exercise a degree of what Ian Bogost refers to as "procedural rhetoric," or "the art of persuasion through rule-based representations and interactions rather than the spoken word, writing, images, or moving pictures."[134] The "cultural meaning" of the videogame is inextricably tied to its computational character, meaning that there is no such thing as an apolitical game, or a game that does not raise ethical questions. It's just that most games make procedural arguments about the desirability of control and the concomitant disregard for alterity.[135] As Schrank puts it, "[m]ainstream games are designed for players to overcome the 'other,' alterity, and difference...Games are usually about eliminating enemies, dominating spaces, or ordering systems, which is to say that games usually afford a conservative or even fascistic kind of violence"[136] – just the sort of violence that Wark has in mind when he talks about digitality. In this context, then, the question is about the different political and ethical possibilities that computation also affords. What *within* the game can resist the conservatism and violence *of* the game?

Immersion: *BioShock* **and** *Spec Ops: The Line*

One means of mounting this sort of critique would be to directly target what power fantasies promise, particularly the ability to make a limitless number of choices free from the responsibility of their consequences. Choices are foundational for videogames, after all, or at least for what we normally understand videogames to be. When players are made to feel responsible for their choices, games can cause us to feel a range of emotions that might be unique to the medium. In our complicity with the actions of the characters that we play, we can feel empathy, culpability, or discomfort; we can experience some modicum of heroism or villainy, or immerse ourselves in the worlds we explore. Ian Danskin, focusing on four story beats from four indie games, argues for the medium's capacity to arouse these feelings:

> In most media, a storyteller has access to an audience's sympathetic emotions – things that you feel in response to other people's feelings. But here, [in the videogame,] you're not proud of someone else's accomplishments. You're the one acting like a hero, and the other characters become your audience. By having the player *be* the protagonist, suddenly *you* can be clever, or get your *own* heart broken, or act like a hero...There are emotions that we can get our audiences to feel when we tell stories in games that we don't have access to in other media.[137]

Other media, Danskin points out, have their own unique affective affordances. He goes on:

> At the intersection of narrative and computation, there are these things we can do – like invite people to linger and revisit [as in the experimental first-person commentary on memory provided by *Dear Esther*], or unsettle people with game feel [as in the dark platformer *Limbo*], or tell a joke with a system [as in the ironic adventure game *Ben There, Dan That*], or compel someone not to *sympathize* with a character, but to feel what they would feel [as in the action roleplaying game *Bastion*].[138]

For Danskin, it is the interactivity of the medium that affords these "things [designers] can do," enabling them to tell him stories "in ways I've never been told them before."[139] The feelings that result from the choices that players make are, then, a function of this interactivity.

Some of the most interesting moments in videogames, the times when they arouse these unique feelings, happen when the systems that establish choices are laid bare, or when the player's ability to choose among options is frustrated. Designer and critic Raph Koster noted this trend in 2013, when he observed that artgames often restrict player agency in order to deliver their messages. *Freedom Bridge*, for instance, gives the player control of a black square moving from left to right; when the square is forced to cross a tangle of lines, it begins to trail blood. It reaches a bridge after painfully crossing three of these stylized barbed wire barriers, a gunshot rings out, and it dies. The minimalism of the representation doesn't prevent it from arousing sympathy; however, as Koster points out, the game's affective punch relies just as much on its narrative structure as on its aesthetics: "You can't beat it. You can't even make progress. There is only one pattern to perceive: futility."[140] Games like *Freedom Bridge* "are games about people who lack power and lack control. The message gets across because games have always been about agency; gamers are used to having power and control, and to have the game itself deny it is a wake up slap across the face."

Zoe Quinn's interactive fiction game *Depression Quest* works in a similar way, foregrounding the way that it deprives players of control. The game describes the player character as a twenty-something "dealing with motivation issues," and it reinforces this description by actively depriving the player of choices. The first reads like this:

By the time you arrive home and change out of your uncomfortable work clothes the stress is weighing down on you like a heavy, wet wool blanket. Your computer seems to be staring you down from your desk. You want to sit down and work but the mere thought of trying to work sends your stress levels flying; more than anything you feel suddenly and absolutely exhausted, and feel a strong desire to simply hide in bed.

Do you...

1. ~~Order some food, grab a drink, and hunker down for a night of work.~~
2. Reluctantly sit down at your desk and try and make yourself do something.
3. Turn on the TV, telling yourself you just need a quick half hour to unwind from work.
4. Crawl into bed. You're so stressed and overwhelmed you couldn't possibly accomplish anything anyways.

The most "productive," "healthy" option is struck through; the player knows that this would be the best course of action, and so does the player character, but both are unable to choose it. The same pattern recurs throughout the game: "~~Shake off your funk and go have a good time with your girlfriend~~"; "~~Enthusiastically socialize!~~"; "~~Let her know that you've been feeling down lately, and that you appreciate her concern~~." As the player character sinks deeper into depression, the player is deprived of more and more choices. It's a simple mechanical trick, but it effectively communicates something of what it's like to live with depression. At the same time, its framing and its reception as an educational game means that its player knows roughly what to expect.[141] This isn't a strike against *Depression Quest* or games that work in the same way, but it does mean that it *explicitly* thematizes the loss of control.

Indie and art games like *Lose/Lose* and *Mountain* are, in one sense, even more direct assaults on the subject of control, although they can be interpreted more freely. *Lose/Lose*, a shoot 'em up designed by Zach Gage in the vein of *Galaga*, threatens to randomly delete files on the player's computer any time that they destroy enemy ships. Players are welcome to download the game "at [their] own risk," but very few actually do; the score list on the game's webpage suggests that the game has been played fewer than 1500 times, mostly by repeat players. This is understandable, since the loss of control in which the game would result extends beyond the game itself. *Mountain* works in the opposite fashion. An "ambient procedural mountain game," according to its self-description, it was released to critical acclaim and popular disgust in the summer of 2014. Little more than a screensaver, *Mountain* puts the player in the position of the eponymous lump of rock, earth, grass, and trees, which, given the fact that this lump is all that this particular game contains, means that the player is also far more: "WELCOME TO MOUNTAIN. YOU ARE MOUNTAIN. YOU ARE GOD." At the same time, the game offers the player nothing to *do*. Here is the game's complete list of features:

- no controls
- automatic save
- audio on/off switch
- time moves forward
- things grow and things die
- nature expresses itself
- ~ 50 hours of gameplay
- once generated, you cannot be regenerated

The player can rotate the mountain or zoom in, and occasionally they are treated to the sight of an object falling onto the mountain's slope. They hear the mountain itself reflecting on something: "WHY AM I ALL ALONE?" But there really are "no controls." David O'Reilly, the designer, claims that "*Mountain* is a kind of visual silence. You can control parts of it, but it's more about letting go of control."[142] It succeeds in being "about" this letting go precisely to the extent that it upsets players who expect games to deliver them experiences of control – even games that sell themselves on their absence of controls. By this metric, *Mountain* was a runaway success: many users complained that the game was only a "screensaver" that inexcusably hogged system resources, while others offered ironic praise.[143] If O'Reilly had treated *Mountain* as an artgame, players like these might not have found it, and if he had refused to charge money for it, they would not have felt cheated by it. The brilliance of the game lies almost as much in the experience of witnessing the negative reactions to it as it does in "playing" it.

Where *Freedom Bridge* and *Depression Quest* have obviously didactic objectives, *Lose/Lose* and *Mountain* are, despite their controversial design, subtler. Nevertheless, all of these games are framed in such a way as to alert their players about their status in advance: they are artgames, serious games, games for change, games with meaning. As such, they run the risk of privileging their sometimes explicit messages over gameplay.[144] A trio of related games that foreground fun – *BioShock*, *The Stanley Parable*, and *Spec Ops: The Line* – run no such risk.

BioShock, to begin with the now-canonical example, hides its critique of player agency behind triple-A production values and conventional shooter gameplay, two features routinely praised by reviewers for offering their players a sensation of seamless control. Because of this, the game manages to address mainstream audiences that might otherwise leave their relationships to videogames unthought. Game critic Brendan Keogh argues that the 2007 publication of *BioShock* marked a turning point in game design and criticism, an introspective, self-critical moment when the first-person shooter genre became aware of its own limitations and implications.[145] Keogh is hardly the only critic or scholar to place so much significance on Ken Levine's dystopian shooter; books and scholarly articles, to say nothing of popular commentaries, have explored the importance of *BioShock* for thinking through propaganda, dystopia, objectivism, education, capitalism, and medical history.[146] But *BioShock* is most often remembered and discussed for its commentary on choice, which turns on the game's big reveal.[147] As *BioShock* begins, a plane crashes into the Atlantic Ocean. The player character, Jack, swims to a nearby lighthouse, where he finds a bathysphere that transports him to the underwater city of Rapture. A man's voice comes from the side of the bathysphere: "Would you kindly pick up that shortwave radio?" The man identifies himself as Atlas and asks for Jack's help. He has been cut off from his family by the feral, half-human "splicers" who have overrun Rapture, murdering to fuel their addiction to the empowering but destructive genetic serums called plasmids. As the game moves forward, the player learns that Rapture was established by a business magnate named Andrew Ryan, a Randian objectivist bent on liberating himself and others from the "petty morality" of the "small," the "parasites," the "slaves." Some years after its founding, Frank Fontaine, a resident of the city, established a successful biotech company devoted to the manufacture of plasmids. After years of political and economic competition during which biotech abuse led to a growth in the population of the plasmid-addicted splicers, Ryan killed Fontaine. A few months later, a proletarian fisherman – the Atlas Jack meets at the beginning of the game – emerged as a freedom fighter, instigating the civil war that all but destroyed the underwater city.

In the eighth level of the game, the player arrives at Rapture Central Control, where, Atlas tells him, Ryan has barricaded himself: "Now would you kindly head to Ryan's office and kill the son of a bitch?" Jack enters a room where the words "Would You Kindly" are scrawled in large red font on a wall hung with notes and pictures of Rapture's luminaries. Boxes of ammunition are "strewn around the room"; they are, as Matthew Wysocki and Matthew Schandler note, "traditional game signifiers of the difficulty of an impending battle. The player opens one last door," expecting a fight, but:

> The game switches to a cut scene and the player is forced to watch as things unfold. Jack confronts Ryan...Ryan reveals a truth that he has pieced together: Jack was born in Rapture just two years before the start of the game and then genetically modified to mature rapidly. He is Ryan's illegitimate son by an affair with a dancer. When the dancer became pregnant, she had her embryo surgically removed and sold it to the highest bidder. After purchasing Jack's embryo, Fontaine designed him to obey orders that are preceded by the phrase "Would you kindly..." Jack was then sent to the surface to put him beyond Ryan's reach. When the conflict between Fontaine and Ryan reached a stalemate, Jack was sent instructions to board a flight with a package and to use its contents, a revolver, to hijack and crash the plane near the lighthouse, enabling him to return to Rapture as a tool of Fontaine. Ryan demonstrates the power that "Would you kindly?" has over Jack by having him follow some instructions preceded by the trigger phrase. A series of flashbacks reveals the use of the phrase in the game...Finally, Ryan uses the "Would you kindly?" phrase to have Jack kill him, wanting to die on his own terms. During the cut scene, Ryan continues to tell Jack "A man chooses, a slave obeys."[148]

As Ryan dies, Atlas again addresses Jack: "Hurry now, grab Ryan's genetic Key! Now would you kindly put it in that goddamn machine?!" The jig is up: Fontaine never died; he lay in wait and then remerged as Atlas. Throughout the game, Jack has been following his commands, taking actions not because the player wanted Jack to pick up the radio, move through Rapture, or kill Ryan, but because Atlas compelled him to do so. The reveal seems to suggest that the player's agency itself is a lie. Just as

Jack has been unconsciously following a set of hardwired instructions, so too has the player been following the options encoded by the game.

The reveal appears to provide two convincing critiques of control. It first offers an allegorithmic argument, showing the player that any "choice" encoded in a discrete system is meaningless because its outcomes are all known in advance. In this sense, the choice to harvest or rescue the Little Sisters is no more significant than the choice to suspend splicers with a cyclone trap or distract them with an insect swarm. Interpreted this way, the reveal points out something that players might conceivably have failed to notice before, and encourages the player to adopt a critical perspective on their own choices and motivations.[149] Second, on an ideological, narrative level, *BioShock*'s reveal and the events that follow offer a critique of objectivism that doubles as a critique of control in that they demonstrate the murderous and suicidal conclusions of the pursuit of Randian self-interest, a philosophy that perhaps is more guilty than any other of the uncritical valorization of control.[150]

While *BioShock*'s reveal offers at least these two critiques of control, it doesn't really tell the thoughtful player anything new. Players come into games knowing that their choices are not really "free," but they put this knowledge aside in order to immerse themselves in the gameworld. They derive an "illusion of agency" and "the affect of being in control" from this suspension of disbelief, and this is no less legitimate in videogames than any other narrative medium.[151] Additionally, as designer Clint Hocking argues, *BioShock* demonstrates a "ludonarrative dissonance" in the way that it sometimes enables the player to choose between altruism and objectivism, as in the case of the choice to "harvest" or "rescue" the Little Sisters, but at other times railroads the player into a single narrative path, as in the case of the reveal.[152] Moreover, instead of doubling down on its commentary on the player's complicity in Jack's murderous in-game actions by continuing to deprive the player of agency, the player is given the appearance of freedom when Tenenbaum partially reverses the effects of Fontaine's conditioning. The player proceeds to the final fight with Fontaine, and his attempt to use the control phrase in an effort to have Jack commit suicide fails. Narratively, then, the game is claiming to have returned control to the player: they can do as they wish, confronting the man who directly stole their agency away and thereby reasserting their own.[153] At the same time, the mechanics of the game have not changed: the player is still proceeding through the game from one point to another. The player might now experience some *sensation* of "will," but the game's earlier critique of the player's impotence still applies: proceeding to the final showdown with Fontaine is no more an act of free will than murdering Ryan.

The problem here, to be clear, isn't that *BioShock* fails to provide "true" freedom of choice to the player, but that it claims to do so and then fails. Videogames that do not foreground emergent gameplay and storytelling, or videogames that follow a traditional cinematic format, are incapable of providing the player "freedom," at least in the full sense of the word; they leave their players with no choice but to follow a path already laid out. This does not mean that they cannot offer a critique of control by way of a commentary on player complicity, as *BioShock* tries to do, but it does mean that players might bristle at the attempt. *BioShock* attempts to tell the player that they are in some sense responsible for Jack's actions, but they might reasonably respond by laying responsibility at the feet of the designers. They might well want to take actions that are not open for Jack because of the natural limitations on game design and then find themselves frustrated, not so much with that inability as with the game's confused criticism of it.

"Post *BioShock*," Keogh writes, "there has been an absolving of the player's responsibility in gameplay alongside, paradoxically, a determination to hang on to the player's agency. That is, players still demand the ability to make 'choices' but refuse to accept responsibility for those choices."[154] *BioShock*'s "would you kindly?" reveal heralded the beginning of an era of self-aware shooters, but it failed to follow through because of its inability to connect choice to *responsibility*. If a feeling of responsibility is one of the medium's affective affordances, then there should be a sense in which videogames can provide players with an opportunity to feel responsible for the decisions that they or their player characters make.

Since the choices for which players *might* be responsible have effects, many games emphasize the consequences of players' actions. Developers like Bioware and Telltale seem to center their entire catalogues on "meaningful choices," or actions whose effects will ripple out and affect both the gameplay and the story; the watchwords for this choice-responsibility-consequence chain are *The Walking Dead*'s "Clementine will remember that." Many indie games work in similar territory, but *The Stanley Parable* is perhaps the most interesting example, since it combines a focus on choice and consequence with a consciousness of its formal limitations in a mode resembling *BioShock*. A relentlessly ironic work of interactive fiction, *The Stanley Parable* provides the player with a naked decision tree – a series of binary choices that result in a finite number of endings, all of which can be experienced in the game's short run time. The player is presented with these decisions and led to these endings by a male narrator who begins the game by informing the player, who controls a corporate employee named Stanley, that "one day, something very peculiar happened": Stanley stopped receiving instructions. "He got up from his desk and stepped out of his office," the narrator intones, and the player follows suit. "When Stanley came to a set of two open doors," the player is told, "he entered the door on his left." The player then has the opportunity to follow the narration or to break with it; the narrator responds differently in each case, not so much describing Stanley's actions as prescribing them, effectively or not.

Again and again, *The Stanley Parable* calls attention to the fact that it is set up as a series of choices that can, in one sense, be made, but that have, in a more fundamental sense, already *been* made. Examples abound. One of the game's absurd promotional videos promises that it will enable the player to do "literally anything," offering the example of a player "infusing" a bicycle "with the soul of his Great-great-great-Uncle Hermophreles":

> From this point, he might use Hermophreles' ethereal presence to detect nearby mineral deposits, or perhaps he might train the bicycle in the art of undoing temporal paradoxes... Ah: it seems that the player has chosen to use the haunted bicycle to deceive townsfolk as a part of his snake oil salesman ruse. How bold.

In the game itself, the player watches an instructional video apparently from the 1950s that insists that choice is "the best part about being a real person" and that "most medical professionals recommend making at least eight choices per day." If the player repeatedly disobeys the narrator's instructions, the game presents the player with a yellow "adventure line" marked on the floor. The commentary couldn't be any more pointed.

The gameplay of *The Stanley Parable* leads to 18 different endings, many of which continue to comment on choice, responsibility, and consequence. In one, Stanley is welcomed to "Heaven": a white room walled by rotating rings of multi-colored buttons that can be pushed over and over again without effect. Its opposite, the "Museum" ending, might be Hell. The player is about to be crushed to death, but a new narrator freezes the event, plucks Stanley out of the machine, and reflects on his situation:

> [I]t would be just a few minutes before Stanley would restart the game, back in his office, as alive as ever. What exactly did

the narrator think he was going to accomplish? When every path you can walk has been created for you long in advance, death becomes meaningless, making life the same. Do you see now? Do you see that Stanley was already dead – from the moment he hit start?

Addressing the player directly, she begs them to save Stanley and the primary narrator both:

[L]isten to me! You can still save these two! You can stop the program before they both fail! You can push escape and press quit! There's no other way to beat this game! As long as you move forward, you'll be walking someone else's path. Stop now, and make your only true choice! Do choose it! Don't let time choose for you!

For this second narrator, and perhaps for game designer Davey Wreden, the only "true choice" is the one in which the player shuts off the game and returns to a world bounded by death, law, and responsibility rather than the constraints of the game system. In the world of the game, "death becomes meaningless," the second narrator intones; since the gameworld was created long before the player loaded the game and before Stanley stepped out of his office, death in the gameworld is not so much a consequence for which the player is responsible as a mere outcome. Rightly or wrongly, this second narrator interprets the world of the game as an impoverished one, less real than the world in which contingency reigns. In pointing to the disjunction between these worlds and to the player's choice to remain embedded in them both, she is holding the player responsible for the only choice that they *are* making – to continue playing.

The commentary on choice and responsibility offered by *The Stanley Parable* is limited to the question of the relationship between the "real" world and the "game" world. *Spec Ops: The Line* covers similar territory, though it ends by issuing an unrelenting condemnation of the player. For Keogh, who authored a book detailing his experience playing the game,[155] *Spec Ops: The Line* is a reaction to *BioShock*'s failure and an improvement on its formula: "It agrees with *BioShock* that the player...doesn't really make any choices that the game has not already made for them. However, unlike *BioShock*, it insists the player is still responsible for these actions *because* of the one choice the player did make: to play the game in the first place."[156] But *Spec Ops* goes further, undercutting the core power fantasy in a genre characterized more than any other by dreams of literal empowerment.[157] Among its commentaries on the terrible places that the power fantasies of heroism, domination, and so on can lead, *Spec Ops* tells the player that, as lead writer Walt Williams so directly puts it, "you are not in control."[158]

As with *BioShock*, it's necessary to begin here by setting the stage – and it is an absurd stage. *Spec Ops* takes inspiration from *Heart of Darkness* and *Apocalypse Now*, telling the story of the pursuit of John Konrad, the commander of the 33rd Infantry Battalion gone rogue, by three elite counter-terrorism operatives in Dubai. The story is simultaneously absurd and self-serious; it addresses themes of militarism, interventionism, and post-traumatic stress disorder by following the protagonist, Captain Walker, and his fellow Delta Force operatives, Adams and Lugo, into a Dubai half-buried by sandstorms.[159] Initially ordered there to find refugees and evacuate them, the three soldiers soon find themselves embroiled in a complicated conflict between the rogue American battalion, the refugees, and the CIA.[160] The player, as Walker, uncovers the details of the conflict only piece by piece. Because of Walker's ignorance of the situation, and because of his growing obsession with finding Konrad, who saved him on a prior tour of duty in Afghanistan, he ends up radically worsening an already terrible situation.

The game's narrative focuses less on the complexity of the

political situation than on how Walker himself copes with the results of his actions. Those actions grow less and less defensible as the game proceeds. Initially, the game tasks the player with shooting the inexplicably hostile residents of Dubai, who seem to be attacking the 33rd. By Chapter Four, however, events lead Walker and his men into a firefight with the 33rd, who become the antagonists for the remainder of the game.[161] By Chapter Twelve, Walker has dehumanized his fellow American soldiers entirely: "Hey, more target practice." Earlier, though, Walker is less cavalier about the slaughter. The game's turning point, and a key moment for a reading on the nature of choice and control, comes in Chapter Eight, when Walker and his men are approaching a bottleneck between two buildings that they need to capture in order to rescue a group of civilians from the 33rd. Steven Holmes describes the scene:

The plan is to take the gate. After killing a solitary guard, you and your fellow Delta Force soldiers make your way to a high vantage point where you can look out over the army guarding the gate. Stationed nearby is a mortar equipped with white phosphorus ammunition. Staff Sergeant Lugo, your fellow soldier, disagrees with your order to use the white phosphorus ammunition. You have seen what white phosphorus does: hours earlier, you had seen the enemy use it, seen men burning alive as white death rained from the skies. There is no other way to achieve your objective.

Using a targeting camera, you aim the mortar for precise strikes. On your targeting screen, you can see little white dots moving, each white dot a hostile enemy soldier. Of course, it is impossible to see any difference between the dots. You begin firing. Soon your objective is achieved, the white dots are gone and you have successfully taken the gate. You descend down from your vantage to see the charred, burning corpses of the men you have killed. Through the smoke, you walk past the dying and dead soldiers, climbing past a charred foundation with the sculptures of children playing, down to a ledge where one soldier remains. "Why?" he asks. "We were helping." As you look on, you slowly realize that your mortar assault has killed the very civilians that you were attempting to rescue. As you approach, you see forty-seven corpses. Among them, there is a mother clutching an infant child, both dead. The mother's hand covers the dead child's eyes, while the mother herself has had at least one eye seared away from the flames. It is a gruesome image.[162]

Walker's eyes are unreadable, but his response is dispassionate: "We need to keep moving. Reinforcements will be here any second. We need to keep moving." Adams is stunned: "But, Walker...You're not...You're not even..." Walker interrupts: "I'm gonna make these bastards pay for what they've done." It is, somehow, the 33rd who are responsible for the deaths of these forty-seven civilians. Walker refuses responsibility.[163]

It is the character of responsibility and choice in the context of violent gameplay that *Spec Ops* thematizes so well, and its interrogation of these themes crystallizes in the white phosphorus attack. Immediately prior to the attack, Walker explains, to a protesting Lugo, why the attack is necessary:

Lugo: "You've seen what this shit does! You know we can't use it."
Walker: "We might not have a choice, Lugo."
Lugo: "There's *always* a choice."
Walker: "No, there's really not."

This is one of many times in the game where Walker argues that he "has no choice." Keogh convincingly argues that the player is in a similar position: "[t]hrough Walker, the game shows us the choices we refuse to make in our own lives – or perhaps more accurately, the choices we make even while claiming we have no choice but to make them."[164] Just as Walker "has no choice" but to commit atrocities, the player "has no choice" but to follow the path that the game has laid out. Players may well find this seeming lack of choice frustrating,[165] and that frustration can compel players to empathize with Walker, sharing his goals and refusing responsibility. Walker could certainly make another choice – he could turn around and walk away – and in refusing to even acknowledge it, let alone act on it, he becomes responsible for his actions. Just as there is no reason that Walker cannot turn around and leave Dubai, there is no reason that the player cannot shut off the game: "Walker *is* choosing to be in a situation where he has no choice, and so am I."[166]

So, once the player launches the game, they accept a contract that renders their agency illusory. So far, so *BioShock*. But *Spec Ops* offers an additional commentary on the nature of responsibility, and thereby on the subject of videogames and the politics of control. After the white phosphorus attack, Walker begins hearing Konrad's voice over the radio, taunting him, and he turns his efforts to tracking down his former commander. At the end of the game, after killing the remaining members of the 33rd and the CIA, losing Adams and Lugo, and damning the residents of the city to death by destroying tanker trucks full of water, Walker arrives at the Burj Kalifa, ready for a confrontation with Konrad. The scene echoes Jack's confrontation with Ryan in *Bio-Shock*, though the differences are stark.[167] Walker finds Konrad turned toward a painting: it is a depiction of the white phosphorus attack. The camera lingers on the mother and child. Walker accosts Konrad: "You did this." But Konrad protests: "No, you did. Your orders killed 47 innocent people. Someone has to pay for your crimes, Walker. Who's it gonna be?" Moving around the painting, Walker is confused: Konrad has disappeared. "John? Is that you? I'm done playin' games, John." An incorporeal Konrad's reply makes the connection between the player and the player character all but explicit: "I assure you, this is no game."

Walker approaches a figure slumped in a chair, gun dangling from its hand. It is Konrad's corpse, long-dead. The penthouse fades to black, leaving Walker, Konrad's corpse, and Konrad's ghost: "It seems that reports of my survival have been greatly exaggerated." Walker asks how this is possible, and Konrad corrects his question: "Not how. Why." Walker is fixated on causal explanations, but it is clear, by this point in the game, that so much of Walker's experience has been hallucinatory. Konrad reminds Walker that he had no orders to do what he did, but Walker protests:

Walker: "What happened here was out of my control."
Konrad: "*Was* it? None of this would have happened if you'd just *stopped*. But on you marched. And for what?"
Walker: "We – tried to save you – "
Konrad: "You're no savior. Your talents lie elsewhere." [Scenes of Walker killing one person after another are shown.]
Konrad: "The truth, Walker, is that you're here because you wanted to feel like something you're not. A hero."
Konrad: "I'm here because you can't accept what you've done. It broke you. You needed someone to blame, so you cast it on me. A dead man."

Konrad could not be clearer about Walker's refusal to accept the responsibility for his actions, or about the horrifying outcomes of this refusal. At every step, Walker could have turned back, but his refusal pushed him on. Incapable of confronting the consequences of his actions for reasons that appeared to be military but were at root melancholic, he disavowed them.

Even at the end, with the fiction of Konrad's culpability made clear, he continues to disavow: "This isn't my fault." Walker's melancholic disavowal led to the murder of civilians, the killing of soldiers, and the indirect condemnation to death of all the remaining citizens of Dubai. But, as Konrad tells Walker, that's not all: "I know the truth is hard to hear, Walker, but it's time. You're all that's left, and we can't live this lie forever." Walker approaches Konrad, a mirror next to them. Konrad raises a gun, pointing to Walker's reflection. The reflection of Konrad seems to be aiming at Walker himself. The perspective is confused; it's not clear whether the player is looking at the men or their reflections. Konrad tells Walker that he will count to five and then pull the trigger. He counts to one, and Walker reacts with anger: "No. Everything – all this – it was *your* fault!" Konrad: "If that's what you believe, then shoot me!" He counts to two, and Walker reacts with denial: "I didn't mean to hurt anybody." He counts to three, and control is given to the player to react as they choose – perhaps to bargain, to wallow, or to accept the only possible conclusion to Walker's life. Konrad's reflection seems to be pointing its gun directly at the player, implicating them directly, and the player has only seconds to decide. Walker has never been one to choose. Here, at the very end, is the one meaningful choice that the game gives the player, and they are forced to make it under duress. Moving the controller, the player aims Walker's gun. They can point it at Konrad's reflection or away from it, but they can also point it at Walker's reflection; if they do, his reflection holds the gun to Walker's chin.

This is where *Spec Ops* diverges so effectively, and so brutally, from its predecessors. In those games, the player is never given meaningful choice. They can play the game in a range of different ways, but the end, in the case of *BioShock*, or the endings, in the case of *The Stanley Parable*, are always set. In *Spec Ops*, the player makes a single choice that frames their entire experience of the game in terms of responsibility and violence; it reinforces the game's narrative, narrative suggests that the disavowal of responsibility paired with the pursuit of power cannot but lead to the worst forms of violence.[168] In it, the player – the *player*, not Walker – is invited to finally take control and responsibility at the same time. If the player does nothing, Konrad shoots Walker, but a trick of the mirror means that Konrad shoots the player too. The gun is directed at both. Here, Konrad figures both Walker's conscience *and the game itself*, and in his act of shooting Walker and the player, he takes control *from both*.[169] Responsibility lies with Konrad, which is to say with the game, and both Walker and the player "die," neither having accomplished anything but mass murder. Similarly, if the player chooses to shoot Konrad's reflection, Walker refuses the brutal truth Konrad has presented him: he insists that he *does* have a choice, and that he therefore has no responsibility to end his own life. This is, after all, the path that leads to the epilogue, where we see Walker either hallucinating, dead, or the murderer of yet another squad of American soldiers. This is the path down which the denial of responsibility takes him.

If the player commands Walker to shoot his own reflection, something very different happens. Not different in terms of a final death count – Walker still ends up dead – but different in terms of the significance of the choice. When the player commands Walker to shoot his reflection, Walker seems to be listening to his conscience; he seems to be accepting responsibility by finally accepting control. Here, in this moment where he really does have no choice but to take an action that ends in death, he finally stops denying his responsibility for the outcome of his actions, and takes a life understanding full well what the action will mean. It's an awful end, but the only one in which both he and the player take responsibility for Walker's actions and come to terms with their outcome.

Resentment: *Braid*

Design-driven critiques of choice and responsibility like those on offer in the "post-*BioShock*" landscape undoubtedly work as critiques of player control, but they do so very directly. Additionally, they elide the central temporal dimension with which a ludopolitical critique is concerned. Time is just as inextricably linked to issues of game design as it is to issues of control.[170] The dream of perfect control is the logical extension of the power fantasy that games like *Bulletstorm* so explicitly thematize, and it finds expression in almost all videogames because of the way that videogames afford control over time. Player characters have multiple lives; player characters are invulnerable; players can save and reload; players can start and stop a game whenever they like. These are different means of exercising control in a world that otherwise, and fundamentally, offers none: the passage of time is inevitable and the world is unknowable, but videogames present a world that the player can comprehend and relive. Games that do not afford players control over time, or that point to players' unthought reliance on this affordance, are relatively rare. This is a feature that videogames share with technology in general, which tends toward the defiance of mortality and temporality: videogames enable players not only to see, hear, or read about impossible things, but to do them – to fix mistakes, achieve perfection. Many games offer meditations on time or on the player's control over it, but games that really grip their players, compelling them to stay as long as possible, allegorize it more effectively than others.

No game thematizes the relationship between technology, control, and time better than *Braid*, the critically acclaimed 2008 platformer by Jonathan Blow. Popular, too: although *Braid* is an unapologetically artsy indie game, *Braid*'s initial release on Xbox Live Arcade brought it to the attention of a wide range of gamers. This, combined with its universally positive reviews and its presence in 2012's *Indie Game: The Movie*, meant that it was talked about and played more than many triple-A games, and that it continues to receive critical attention nearly a decade after its initial release.

Explicitly nostalgic, *Braid* is a platformer that lifts from *Super Mario Bros.*: the player character proceeds from left to right in search of a Princess, jumping on the heads of monsters that look like Goombas, collecting keys, and dodging traps that look like Piranha Plants. But it twists the traditional platformer genre by introducing a variety of mechanical riffs on the ability to control time. In *Super Mario Bros.*, Mario can die, sending the player to the beginning of the level or to the game over screen. In *Braid*, Tim, the player character, *can't* die. If he falls into a pit of spikes, time freezes, and the game cues the player to rewind. Controlling time is the game's central mechanical conceit. It plays out in different ways as Tim moves through the game's worlds. World 2: Time and Forgiveness gives the player character the ability to rewind time; World 3: Time and Mystery introduces objects that are unaffected by Tim's ability; World 4: Time and Space connects the player character's motion to the passage of time (moving right advances time, while moving left turns it back); World 5: Time and Decision introduces a doppelgänger whom the player controls indirectly; and World 6: Hesitance gives the player a ring that can be dropped in order to create a small bubble where time moves slowly. These mechanics make *Braid* less a platformer than a puzzle game, albeit one that requires a lot of trial and error in order to advance. Moving forward requires the player to continually make mistakes and correct them, slowly figuring out each level's particular twist on the central mechanical conceit.

While *Braid* might look like a simple platformer or a clever puzzle game, it's clear from the beginning that it has more to offer. The game opens on a shadowed figure standing against a burning urban backdrop; the player moves that figure to the right and into a house with five rooms. A door in the first room opens onto World 2, where the player sees six lecterns holding large green books. As Tim moves to the first, text appears on-screen:

Tim is off on a search to rescue the Princess. She has been snatched by a horrible and evil monster.

This happened because Tim made a mistake.

The text continues:

> Not just one. He made many mistakes during the time they spent together, all those years ago. Memories of their relationship have become muddled, replaced wholesale, but one remains clear: the Princess turning sharply away, her braid lashing at him with contempt.
>
> He knows she tried to be forgiving, but who can just shrug away a guilty lie, a stab in the back? Such a mistake will change a relationship irreversibly, even if we have learned from the mistake and would never repeat it. The Princess's eyes grew narrower. She became more distant.
>
> Our world, with its rules of causality, has trained us to be miserly with forgiveness. By forgiving them too readily, we can be badly hurt. But if we've learned from a mistake and became better for it, shouldn't we be rewarded for the learning, rather than punished for the mistake?
>
> What if our world worked differently? Suppose we could tell her: 'I didn't mean what I just said,' and she would say: 'It's okay, I understand,' and she would not turn away, and life would really proceed as though we had never said that thing? We could remove the damage but still be wiser for the experience.
>
> Tim and the Princess lounge in the castle garden, laughing together, giving names to the colorful birds. Their mistakes are hidden from each other, tucked away between the folds of time, safe.

Braid frames the platforming of the first world, where the player first learns to rewind time, with this description of Tim's desire for forgiveness. For Tim, this is not a contrite form of desire, but one accompanied by feelings of injustice: "if we've learned from a mistake and became better for it, *shouldn't* we be rewarded for the learning, rather than punished for the mistake?" Moreover, the game includes the player in those feelings: "What if *our* world worked differently? Suppose *we* could tell her...?" Early on, *Braid* establishes a relationship between the player and the player character, suggesting that the player might see something of their motivations in Tim's.

Braid's mechanics and its narrative dovetail. The former features the ability to manipulate time, and the latter begins with a meditation on regret. As the game proceeds, the player might notice that the mechanical features and the narrative concern resonate with one another more and more. Tim wants to turn back time in order to fix his mistakes – a want that, as the story goes on, becomes a need – and the player has no choice but to turn back time in order to play the game. Dušan Stamenković and Milan Jaćević describe *Braid*'s successful exposition, or the resonance between its mechanics and its narrative, this way:

> [T]he fundamental ideas of *Braid*'s narrative are conveyed to the player metaphorically through the very act of playing the game: Tim's obsessive desire to control the flow of time and make up for his mistakes is mimicked in the player's failed attempts at solving the game's puzzles and his instances of discovering and playing with the rules of time in pursuit of a perfect run through each of the game's levels.[171]

The game compels the player to act in a way that resembles the player character, and from this position of frustration, the player is invited to understand the player character's point of view. The resonance between the game's narrative and its mechanics produces the desire to interpret the narrative, and the richness of this ludonarrative resonance means that there are multiple different ways to carry out that interpretation.

Interpreting *Braid* requires a close reading of its conclusion.

Once the player has completed worlds two through six, a ladder to the attic in Tim's house opens up, inviting him into World 1. Here, in what is, despite its numbering, the game's final world, the gameplay is different: instead of presenting the player with puzzles, the game has them proceed in a series of straightforward platforming levels. In the last, the player sees Tim, at the bottom of the screen, staring up at the top. The Princess is there, asking for help. A burly figure descends from above, attempting to snatch her up, but she escapes. She runs to the right as a wall of fire chases them both from the left, and the two work together to throw a series of switches and avoid the game's final set of traps. At last, Tim climbs up the right side of the screen to her bedroom window – but the screen flashes, the window is replaced by a door, and the gameplay reverses. The music, which had been playing backwards, now plays forwards. The Princess seemed to have been throwing switches to aid Tim, but the player now sees that she was trying to block his path – even trying to kill him. The burly figure wasn't snatching her up; he was pulling her to safety.[172]

Moving back through the door where he first entered the final level, Tim finds himself in the epilogue, a set of ruins in the sky. Lecterns are everywhere, and they tell two stories, from two perspectives. His:

> The boy wanted to protect the girl. He held her hand, or put his arm around her shoulders in a walking embrace, to help her feel supported and close to him amid the impersonal throngs of Manhattan. They turned and made their way toward the Canal St. subway station, and he picked a path through the jostling crowd.

And hers:

> His arm weighed upon her shoulders, felt constrictive around

her neck. "You're burdening me with your ridiculous need," she said. Or, she said: "You're going the wrong way and you're pulling me with you." In another time, another place, she said: "Stop yanking on my arm; you're hurting me!"

By this point, the Princess has become more than a romantic figure: she is a mother as well as a partner, ideal as well as real, an abstract character and an actual human being. Tim, in fact, has become increasingly confused as the levels have gone on, potentially leading the player to wonder whether the Princess ever existed at all.

The ambiguous figuration of the Princess leads to different interpretations of the game as a whole. In one of the most daring interpretations, the Princess is not Tim's former partner, or at least not only this, but is instead the outcome of an experiment into the nature of reality: she is the first atomic bomb. This is an interpretation favored by fans and academics alike.[173] Patrick Jagoda, writing on the significance of *Braid* for understanding the historicity of videogames in general,[174] offers the most convincing argument for this reading. He points to visual and spatial signs that appear before the telling text of the epilogue – a background in which "ashen snowflakes fall," platforms "decorated with outlines of cowboys, astronauts, and corporate executives," and nautical signs warning Tim to stop – and suggests that these "premonitions" have the ability to provoke the same sort of unease in the player that the inhabitants of Hiroshima felt in the days before the bomb finally fell.[175] These intimations are realized in the epilogue. The player reads about Tim's life in "Manhattan," and about the scientific experiments that culminated in a night spent "behind a bunker in the desert." The lecterns, read in a certain sequence, describe the outcome of those experiments. This is how Jagoda sequences the bits of text:

On that moment hung eternity. Time stood still. Space contracted to a pinpoint. It was as though the earth had opened and the skies split. One felt as though he had been privileged to witness the Birth of the World...[1]

Someone near him said: "It worked."

Someone else said: "Now we are all sons of bitches."

She stood tall and majestic. She radiated fury. She shouted: "Who has disturbed me?" But then, anger expelled, she felt the sadness beneath; she let her breath fall softly, like a sigh, like ashes floating gently on the wind.

She couldn't understand why he chose to flirt so closely with the death of the world.

Here we see quotations – the first cited as such, though without an actual footnote to accompany the superscript – from William Lawrence, J. Robert Oppenheimer, and Kenneth Bainbridge, all associated with the Manhattan Project. And we of course see the Princess figured as the explosion itself, "radiating fury," "sadness," and confusion.[176] *Braid*, it seems, is about Tim's pursuit of the knowledge of the atom, and about his regret in finally discovering it.

Jonathan Blow, unlike many game designers, does not shy away from discussing interpretations of his games, or from replying to those interpreters with whom he disagrees. In an interview that questions the significance of the Oppenheimer quotation, Blow suggests that it is certainly "something to take into account when reading the text. But how much does it come into the actual story?" If details like this one count, other details do too:

Nothing in this game is there by accident and that includes all the story pieces. But that's all of them, right? So I feel like when someone takes one of them and decides to say, "This is what the game is all about," they're sort of neglecting a lot of the other ones, which I would not recommend.[177]

So, for Blow, the game is not *only* about the Manhattan Project. (This, to be clear, isn't Jagoda's claim. He notes that "the game cannot be said to be ultimately about the atom bomb or nuclear war," and argues that a second wartime technology is equally important for the structuring and significance of the game: the computer.)[178] In an earlier interview, Blow suggests that the game thematizes the relationship between space, time, agency, and technology, particularly in terms of its contemporary scientific guise; he is interested in the insights that quantum mechanics can provide into the nature of space, time, and agency, and he encodes this interest in *Braid*. There is, as he argues, "no arrow of time at the quantum mechanical level," and there's no scientific reason why "there didn't evolve a mechanism that can remember what happens tomorrow as well as what happens yesterday." If this is true, he intimates, then there is no such thing as free will. And what a terrifying prospect this would be: "[t]he reason [*Braid*] is an exploration of time and space is because there are things that seem to be facts about time and space…that threaten our very existence."[179] For Blow, *Braid* should be understood as a challenge to our existential certainty – to the casual assumption that we are free agents who can act as we choose. It should show us that, despite our best intentions and our most sustained efforts, there is no acting into the future in a way that could not be predicted by the configuration of the past. His follow-up, *The Witness*, might be read in similar terms.

If Jagoda's interpretation is incomplete, then Blow's is problematic, and for a number of reasons that have nothing to do with his ideas about free will. He suggests that *Braid*'s coded rather than textual form somehow makes it immune from "reading" – that code is homologous with the universe, which "is a system," the "truth" of which can therefore be discovered. Moreover, he claims to welcome varying interpretations but suggests that some get closer to his intentions than others, rejecting certain interpretations with which he disagrees (mentioning one that advances a blogger's "feminist agenda" in particular). He rejects critical and literary approaches entirely, in fact, and suggests – in a sweeping and profound misreading of the history of thought – that we no longer need philosophy because "a couple hundred years ago...this thing called science was born": we now can make "observations [about] the universe that are not disputable," and these observations "can be brought to bear on the free will question." In fact, "science" is a prerequisite for any discussion of agency at all: "anyone who's postulating about free will, who doesn't know quantum mechanics, is just talking out their ass. Because they don't have the facts, [and] we have a lot more facts now."[180]

The most significant problem with Blow's scientistic interpretation of *Braid* is that taking it authoritatively might make a reader of the game miss its political and ethical valence. Something similar, in fact, goes for Jagoda's interpretation, despite the fact that Jagoda is working from such a radically different position: reading *Braid* principally as an allegory for the Manhattan Project might lead the reader to miss its more general applicability. *Braid* should not only be understood as a meditation on the relationship between space and time, as Blow suggests, or as an index of the historicity of the contemporary videogame form, as Jagoda argues, but as a reflection of a certain modern triangulation of temporality, technology, and subjectivity, and of the violence that this triangulation entails. The hidden message about the Manhattan Project, for instance, certainly means that *Braid* offers a commentary on how videogames inherited the problems of that period in American history, but it is possible to read it more broadly, or to understand the invocation of the Trinity Test as emblematic rather than exemplary. *Braid* indexes a broad modern attitude configured by technology and oriented toward the control of time, and the Trinity Test is only one outcome, albeit an extraordinary one, among many. That modern attitude should be familiar by now: it takes the world as a standing reserve, understands it as controllable, and, frustrated by its refusal to submit to control, responds with violence. In the case of the Trinity Test, that violence takes ontological and epistemological form, as atoms are divided and existing understandings of the universe are cast aside. In the case of Tim's relationship with the woman whom he figures after the fact as his "Princess," that violence takes a more familiar, interpersonal form. In both cases, the violence proceeds from Tim's regretful, resentful attitude to the passage of time and the irreversibility of his actions, playing out on the one hand in a masculinist scientism and on the other in domestic violence.

There is good textual evidence for the claim that the Manhattan Project and the abuse of a romantic partner have more in common than might at first seem to be the case. Recall Tim's early lament: "Our world, with its rules of causality, has trained us to be miserly with forgiveness. By forgiving them too readily, we can be badly hurt. But if we've learned from a mistake and become better for it, shouldn't we be rewarded for the learning, rather than punished for the mistake?" The "rules of causality" are rules of temporality – the cause always precedes the effect – and Tim resents these rules. *Tim* re(pre)sents *time*: he resents *himself*. Or at least he resents the indelible changes wrought by the passage of time *on* himself, and he wishes to find a way to surpass "time and time's 'It was.'"[181] This, for Tim, would be justice: the proper allocation of rewards doled out to those wise enough to recognize and regret their mistakes and punishments inflicted on those who lack that wisdom.

Now, compare the above with two passages taken from the epilogue that seem to make Tim a scientist:

He worked his ruler and his compass. He inferred. He deduced. He scrutinized the fall of an apple, the twisting of metal orbs hanging from a thread. He was searching for the Princess, and he would not stop until he found her, for he was hungry. He cut rats into pieces to examine their brains, implanted tungsten posts into the skulls of water-starved monkeys.

Through these clues he would find the Princess, see her face. After an especially fervent night of tinkering, he kneeled behind a bunker in the desert; he held a piece of welder's glass up to his eyes and waited.

The second quotation references the Trinity Test, but it is juxtaposed with other, unrelated experiments into physics and biology. This juxtaposition suggests that Tim's actions concern the *general exercise of science*, of experimental research science, rather than of any particular scientific experiment. Moreover, the way that they are described makes clear that this generalized scientific exercise is *violent*: his dispassionate, detached observation of apples and orbs – mere things – extends to rats and monkeys – also mere things – and eventually to people. "She pleaded: 'Look at me!' But he would not see her; he only knew how to look at the outsides of things." This dispassion is in fact founded on a repressed passion, "hungry" and "fervent," for scientific projects designed to rectify his frustration with all the world's injustices.

Tim's frustrated efforts to correct the mistakes that he has made are allegorized in the game's narrative as a scientific enterprise that vivisects rats and dehydrates monkeys just as readily as it observes the effect of gravity on an apple. As allegories, these events did not actually take place in *Braid*'s diegesis; they were imagined, at least in part. Nevertheless, they led Tim to carry out the worst, most unthinkable violence, figured in the epilogue as the detonation of the first atomic bomb.[182]

Tim's resentful attempts to correct his mistakes by correcting time itself take both allegorical and mechanical form. Tim's scientific efforts, for instance, are made mechanical in the various manipulations of time available to the player, which, just like the series of scientific experiments, become more intervention-istic as time goes on. They reach their peak of intensity only in those players who attempt to uncover *Braid*'s last secret. At the beginning of the game, before entering Tim's house, the player might notice a constellation of eight stars. Completionists can collect these stars in the game, thereby lighting up the constella-tion, but most players will never notice that there are stars to be collected at all: they are hidden off screen, usually above. Even learning about the existence of the stars requires curiosity and experimentation. (There are very subtle in-game hints that there is more to the levels than initially meets the eye, like the trace of a platform far out of reach, but there are no obvious ways to get off screen, nor any reason to try to do so.) Then, the player re-quires extraordinary persistence and precision, since acquiring most of the stars requires counterintuitive and difficult feats of platforming and time manipulation. Two go even further. The star in World 2 requires that the player wait for two hours as a cloud that appears to be stationary migrates from right to left, pixel by pixel. The star in World 3 requires the player to collect it before the world has been completed; once the player has locked World 3's painting in place, the only way to collect its star is to restart the game. This is, as Stamenković and Jaćević put it, "a very dramatic instance of mistake correction": the player will "need to annul his or her entire progress and restart the game completely."[183] The game thereby frustrates those completionist players who are compelled to explore and exhaust gameworlds, putting them in a position where they have to perform the most radical act of temporal control in order to truly "finish" the game.

The final star appears during the last level of World 1, during which Tim is pursuing the Princess. Collecting the previous sev-en stars alters the level slightly, enabling Tim to catch up with the Princess. Approaching her – about to finally reach her – she *explodes*: her figure blinks, tracing the pattern of a star just above

Tim's head, and the screen flashes white. The music stops, the firewall and the knight disappear, and time continues to move backwards: monsters and cannonballs move back to their origins rather than away from them. Moving Tim to the right, the player collects the final star, hanging over top of her bead; moving to the left, they leave World 1. Tim returns to the dark, burning scene at the beginning of the game, and sees the constellation now clearly depicted: Andromeda, the woman in chains.

Braid's political and ethical potential stems from its successful employment of the aesthetic affordances of the medium. It delivers its critique of Tim and of the player through ludic mechanisms that do not require the actual reading of text, let alone the work of textual analysis. As Jagoda puts it, citing an example from World 5, "[t]he instrumental act" of sending Tim's doppelgänger to its death "urges the player to think, even if parenthetically, about the responsibility for consequences that such action-oriented games generally bracket or disregard."[184] This is one of several such instances where the game's allegory takes ludic rather than textual form. *Braid*'s most pointed ludic critique is reserved for those completionists who find the game's hidden ending. Here, the "conflation of princess as love object and atom bomb offers the game's most direct statement about the dangers of obsessive, goal-oriented behavior. In the eruption, the game reproachfully upbraids the gamer for a desire for total closure by suggesting a parallel between this achievement and the triggering of a nuclear weapon."[185] This is indeed a critique of "obsessive, goal oriented behavior" as well as a critique of "a desire for total closure," but I would suggest that the near-capture of the Princess needs to be read first and foremost as the impossible desire to turn back time through the technological deployment of scientific rationality. Turning back time, after all, is the means that the player employs to move through the levels, as well as the logical extension of that brand of totalizing, goal oriented behavior that regards objects, animals, and people as mere things.

Additionally, while the alignment of the player's "achievement" and "the triggering of a nuclear weapon" is horrifying, it is perhaps equally horrifying that the Princess, *about* to be caught, seems to opt for self-destruction rather than capture: her explosion could be read as a suicide. After so perfectly exercising control – in Tim's case, so perfectly turning back time and correcting every one of his mistakes, and in the player's case, so perfectly understanding and mastering every nuance of the game – Tim is not actually reunited with the Princess, and the player does not actually witness a "happy" ending. Just the opposite.

Braid's trailer raises the question of the relationship between power, remorse, and subjectivity:

What if you could learn from mistakes...but undo the consequences? What if you could reverse death? What if you could see multiple realities? What if you could warp time? What if...Then what would you be?

It answers this question in its gameplay even more clearly than in its narrative. Controlling time – refusing its passage and repudiating one's mistakes – leads to monstrosity. As a ludic commentary on the ways in which the drive to control time is embedded in the videogame form, *Braid* places the player in a position of complicity that is, at least potentially, self-reflective, self-critical, and attuned to the violence of even the most well-intentioned exercise of technological control.

Exhaustion: *Undertale*

If any single game ties together these observations about choice, responsibility, and time, it's *Undertale*. The game launched in the fall of 2015, and while the fans who had backed it on Kickstarter knew that something brilliant was about to see the light of day, most players were taken by surprise. *Undertale* attracted indie gamers and the critical community who applauded the game for the way that it offered a meta-commentary on videogames in general – on their narrative conventions, their mechanical affordances, and the culture they engender and require. It also managed to achieve popular success, selling 1.5 million copies on Steam alone by the middle of 2016 and another 1.3 million by the following year. The launch of *Undertale* was a watershed for indie gaming.

There are a number of reasons for the game's appeal, not the least of which is its combat system. *Undertale* bills itself as "the friendly RPG where no one has to die," and the ability that it affords the player to show "mercy" to enemies by "sparing" them is indeed one of its core mechanics: the human player character is routinely attacked by monsters in a series of underground caves, and they can attack the monsters in order to gain experience, flee the fight, use an item, or find a way to act against and then show mercy to the monsters, convincing them to leave the player character alone. The latter option is the most challenging, since it prolongs combat encounters during which the player character has to spend more time dodging attacks, and since it leaves the player with an under-leveled protagonist. Additionally, showing mercy to the monsters can be tricky, since different types require different strategies that need to be discovered and then employed.[186]

The mercy mechanic distinguishes *Undertale* from RPGs in which fighting is the player's only option, but it isn't unique on its own. Other games provide violent and non-violent options as well. But when the mercy mechanic is contextualized in terms of the game's narrative, *Undertale* reveals itself as a remarkable commentary on the violence of completionism, both within gameplay and without.

The different ways that the mercy mechanic plays out lead to three different plotlines. If the player kills some monsters but spares others, they achieve the "neutral" ending; if they spare every monster, they achieve the "pacifist" ending; and if they hunt down and kill every monster, they achieve the "no mercy" or "genocide" ending. The player who moves through the game for the first time is most likely to achieve the neutral ending, both because killing is often easier than granting mercy and because the first boss fight gives the player the impression that some fights cannot be avoided.[187] If the player comes back for a subsequent playthrough, which the design of the game encourages, they will have a chance to see what pacifism or genocide yield.

To explain the significance of the game's three endings, I need to go into quite a bit of detail. In the three sections below, I describe the events that the player experiences and then the background that explains them. It's only on this basis that my characterization of *Undertale* as a synthesis of design-based critiques of traditional videogame conventions makes sense.

Undertale begins by describing a war between humans and monsters that led to the monsters being sealed below the "Surface" by a magical barrier. Years later, a human child falls into a cave leading to the monster-filled "Underground." After the player names the child – I saw the ambiguous sprite as a girl, so I named her Maeve, after my daughter – they encounter a smiling flower named Flowey who offers to explain how the Underground works. Flowey asks the child to catch his "love pellets"; when the child touches them, they are reduced to a single hit point as the flower's face turns demonic. He mocks the player: "You idiot. In this world, it's kill or BE killed." Before Flowey's next ring of pellets finishes the job, a maternal goat-like monster appears, knocking Flowey off screen and saving the child's life. Identifying herself as Toriel, she leads the child through the Ruins and to her home, where she offers to keep them safe. When the player guides the child downstairs, Toriel blocks their path, explaining that every other child who has left the Ruins has died. A fight ensues.

After sparing or killing Toriel, the player proceeds through the Underground, meeting a cast of characters en route to an encounter with King Asgore, who, the child is told, awaits them at the barrier they need to cross in order to return home. Over the course of the game, the player learns that human souls are more persistent and powerful than the souls of monsters, and that the barrier between the Underground and the Surface can only be shattered with seven human souls. Asgore, they learn, has been killing human children and harvesting their souls in order to shatter the barrier and return the monsters to the human world. When the player meets him, they learn that he has six already.

At the end of a difficult battle, the player either kills Asgore or spares him; in either case, Flowey appears and finishes the job. Flowey then steals the six human souls and does something unexpected: he *closes the game*, sending the player back to the desktop.[188] When the player relaunches the game, everything is different. The normal introductory crawl is distorted. The player's save file is replaced by one apparently belonging to Flowey. The game window is retitled "Floweytale." The flower himself appears, thanking the player for taking care of Asgore and declaring his intention to take the child's soul in addition to the six he took from Asgore. They will, he says, enable him to become "GOD." The player fights a truly monstrous, screen-filling Flowey, dying again, and again being booted to the desktop. The other six human souls try to help, but Flowey reloads his save file over and over, repeatedly killing the player character.

Eventually, the human souls manage to rebel, stripping Flowey of his godlike ability to save and reload and then defeating him. The player is given the choice to kill or spare the flower; if they spare him, Flowey runs away, uncomprehending. The credits roll, and then one of the characters, the skeleton Sans, calls the child on the cell phone that Toriel provided in the beginning. The monsters remain trapped behind the barrier and Asgore remains dead. Flowey reappears and suggests that the player might move through the game again to get a better ending.

This is just one version of the neutral ending. There are several: the player's choices throughout the game to spare or kill central characters like Toriel, Papyrus, Undyne, and Mettaton, as well as decisions about whom to befriend, change the game's outcome, and the game communicates this to the player in that final cell phone call. This, combined with the player's knowledge that there are other, "happier" endings, and with the comparatively short length of the game, are likely to compel the player to restart.

Players of *Undertale* know, of course, that no monster *has* to die, and they may well have heard that there is a "pacifist route" through the game to its "true ending." If they move through the game without killing anyone, and if they manage to befriend three key characters, the game ends on a very different note. When confronting Asgore, Toriel – who, the player has learned, was the Queen of the Underground before divorcing her husband because of their disagreement over how to handle the barrier – turns up and incapacitates him. After she is joined by the game's central characters, Flowey arrives. Having consumed the six human souls while everyone was talking, he absorbs the monsters' souls as well. Flowey becomes who he was before his transformation into a flower: Asriel Dreemur, the son of Toriel and Asgore. He attacks the child, stripping the player of the ability to save their game but inadvertently bestowing on them the ability to save their friends' trapped souls. The child defeats Asriel, who uses the human and monster souls to destroy the barrier.

Pacifism leads to *Undertale*'s happy ending, though not necessarily to its final one. Having completed the game, some players might find themselves reading about the game's various paths and learning about the no mercy run – about the possibility of killing rather than sparing, thereby learning more about the game's backstory. At the end of the pacifist run, a reformed

Flowey acknowledges that desire, but begs the player to let things be:

> Seems as if everyone is perfectly happy. Monsters have returned to the surface. Peace and prosperity will rule across the land. Take a deep breath. There's nothing left to worry about...Well. There is one thing. One last threat. One being with the power to erase EVERYTHING...YOU still have the power to reset everything. Toriel, Sans, Asgore, Alphys, Papyrus, Undyne...If you so choose... Everyone will be ripped from this timeline and sent back before all of this ever happened. Nobody will remember anything. You'll be able to do whatever you want.
>
> That power. I know that power. That's the power you were fighting to stop, wasn't it? The power that I wanted to use. But now, the idea of resetting everything...I...I don't think I could do it all again. Not after that...So, please. Just let them go. Let Frisk be happy. Let Frisk live their life...But. If I can't change your mind. If you DO end up erasing everything...You have to erase my memories, too...I'm sorry. You've probably heard this a hundred times already, haven't you...? Well, that's all. See you later...Maeve.

Completionists, power gamers, devoted fans, and the simply curious might be tempted to ignore Flowey's plea. These players know, whether by the intuition built up over long years of playing games or by rumours regarding other modes of play, that there is content yet to discover. The game has more possibilities to explore, more narrative threads to reveal – deeper truths. As one of those players, I couldn't resist choosing the true reset. This meant, I thought, that everything would go back to where it had been the first time I played the game. But *Undertale* refuses to let the player break so cleanly with their previous choices. The game remembered that I had reset the game after achieving a "happy ending," and everything after that choice changed.

Undertale's political and ethical force stems from the way that it offers completionist players the temptation of control and then tears it away. To understand how this works, we need to step back from the player's experience of slowly piecing together the plot from their various runs through the game and their reading of fan-made content. What follows is, as near as I can tell, the real story of *Undertale*.

After the war between the monsters and the humans, the first human, Chara, fell into the Underground. Asgore and Toriel adopted Chara, who became close friends with Asriel. Human but thriving in the monster-filled, subterranean environment, Chara gave the monsters hope that they might one day return to the Surface. Learning that the barrier could be crossed with the combination of a human soul and a monster soul but breached entirely with seven human souls, Chara committed an act that might be understood as selfless or insane: they deliberately ingested poison so that their soul could be carried across the barrier by Asriel. Asriel would then retrieve six more human souls and shatter the barrier. Chara's soul entered Asriel's body and Asriel carried Chara's corpse across the barrier, but the humans on the other side, confused and frightened by the monster bearing the body of a human child, attacked. Staggering back across the barrier to the royal garden, Asriel died. Asgore, furious over the murder of his children, declared war on humanity and began collecting the souls of the human children who fell into the Underground. Divorcing the king, Toriel left, bearing Chara's corpse to the Ruins for a proper burial at the place where they had originally fallen down.

As part of his work toward shattering the barrier, Asgore tasked his Royal Scientist, Dr Alphys, with studying souls. Alphys learned that human souls possess an attribute she termed "determination" – the ability to persist after death. Experimenting, Alphys infused determination into a golden flower. The flower, which had blossomed on the spot that Asgore's son had died, was a part of Asriel: awoken by determination – de-ter-minated – it retained his memories but not his soul. Flowey, the failed, soulless experiment, felt nothing for anyone; he ad-dressed Chara, who, in the no mercy run, bears the player-given name: "I just wanted to love someone. I just wanted to care about someone. Maeve, you might not believe this...But I decided... It wasn't worth living anymore. Not in a world without love. Not in a world without you." Committing suicide, Flowey found that, thanks to his determination, he was reborn at a point in the past. He was able to turn back time. "At first," he tells the player character, "I used my powers for good. I became 'friends' with everyone. I solved all their problems flawlessly." Soulless, he interacted with the world soullessly: he was not *friends* with the other monsters, but "friends" with them. He solved their prob-lems without entering into relationships with them, and did so with the perfection granted by the ability to turn back time.

Flowey's fundamental distance, his soullessness, and his lack of investment in the world led to boredom. The companionship of the Underground's monsters "was amusing...for a while. As time repeated, people proved themselves predictable. What would this person say if I gave them this? What would they do if I said this to them? Once you know the answer, that's it. That's all they are." Reduced from personhood to conversational func-tions, Flowey took the next logical step:

It all started because I was curious. Curious what would hap-pen if I killed them. "I don't like this," I told myself. "I'm just doing this because I HAVE to know what happens." Ha ha ha...What an excuse! You of all people must know how liber-ating it is to act this way. At least we're better than those sick-os that stand around and WATCH it happen...Those pathetic people that want to see it, but are too weak to do it themselves. I bet someone like that's watching right now, aren't they...?

Flowey is a rich, complicated antagonist, but he is also a cipher for the completionist player: both are motivated by curiosity and by the desire to see what happens for its own sake; both understand the world and the people who populate it as a set of objects or functions, predictable and without inherent value. And, importantly, *Undertale* is here inviting both the player and the spectator to compare themselves to Flowey. Designer Toby Fox knew that many players would refuse to play through the no mercy route themselves, but would still want to learn about this part of the game's narrative by watching videos or reading fans' accounts of the story. Moreover, Flowey's dialogue here points out the conceit of the completionist player: at least *they* have the *strength* to play through the game themselves!

Bored even by killing, Flowey waited for humans to fall down from the Surface. Six others did, though each time they were rescued by Toriel before making their way to Asgore and their eventual fate. This is where the game begins: the eighth human falls down from Mt. Ebott and is confronted by Flowey. It seems initially that the eighth human is whom the player names, but the pacifist and no mercy routes make the truth of this clear: the eighth human is named *Frisk*, and is only indirectly controlled as a player character; the true player character, the one I named Maeve, is *Chara*. Frisk falls on Chara's grave, awakening them, and Chara, guided by the player, accompanies Frisk as they proceed through the game.

The significance of the confused distinction between Frisk, Chara, and the player becomes clear at the end of the no mercy run, which is a bloody and difficult affair from the beginning. The player moves through the Ruins slowly, pacing back and forth in order to trigger every random encounter and murdering the monsters who turn up until finally they stop. Toriel sees the change in the player character, condemning them with her dying breath: "Now I see who I was protecting by keeping you here. Not you... But them!" Players who fulfill the requirements of the no mercy route ignore the pleas of the non-player characters as the player character – Chara, controlling Frisk – observes them with scorn: "Not worth talking to"; "Forgettable"; "Wipe that smile off your face"; "Looks like free EXP." In the final fight, the skeleton Sans reveals what he knows about the player's abilities to turn back time and reset entire worlds:

> i always thought the anomaly was doing this cause they were unhappy. and when they got what they wanted, they would stop all this. and maybe all they needed was…i dunno. some good food, some bad laughs, some nice friends. but that's ridiculous, right? yeah, you're the kind of person who won't EVER be happy. you'll keep consuming timelines over and over, until…well. hey. take it from me, kid. someday…you gotta learn when to QUIT.

Sans knows about the player's capabilities and their attitude alike: the player's comportment to the gameworld is that of a subject viewing an object, a disposable thing standing in reserve. It is, he notes, reinforcing Flowey's earlier observation, something that the player wants to exhaust simply because they can exhaust it: "you'll just keep going. not out of any desire for good or evil…but just because you think you can. and because you 'can'…you 'have to.'" The player might seem to be amoral, uninterested in good or evil and compelled only by the exploration of systemic possibilities, but Sans characterizes this as a radically unethical position that results in genocide: with total mastery, discrete worlds, and idle curiosity comes violence. Moreover, Sans knows that this attitude and these actions leave the player "unhappy." Happiness, he suggests, requires accepting the end of things without refusing an emotional investment in them. The most "determined" thing the player could do, he says, would be to quit and do anything else.

After the game's most challenging fight, the player character kills Sans and proceeds to the royal garden, where Asgore tells them that a crying flower has just warned him about an approaching monster. Flowey, clearly desperate, pleads with the player character:

> See? I never betrayed you! It was all a trick, see? I was waiting to kill him for you! After all it's me your best friend! I'm help-ful, I can be useful to you I promise I won't get in your way I can help...I can...I can...Please don't kill me.

He offers this plea not to the player, but to *Chara* – to his former sibling. Chara, unprompted by the player, murders Flowey in the last of several instances during the no mercy run where the player loses control over the game. Then, Chara, bearing a star-tling similarity to Frisk, appears at the center of a black screen and addresses the player directly:

> Your power awakened me from death. My "human soul." My "determination." They were not mine, but YOURS. At first, I was so confused. Our plan had failed, hadn't it? Why was I brought back to life? ...You. With your guidance. I realized the purpose of my reincarnation. Power. Together, we erad-icated the enemy and became strong. HP. ATK. DEF. GOLD. EXP. LV. Every time a number increases, that feeling...That's me. "MAEVE."

Power, Chara tells the player, is the increase of a number; it is the ability to eradicate the enemy. This ability is confirmed, made certain, by the discrete, knowable character of the gameworld. Controlling a digital game, particularly a roleplaying game, in-volves the numerically coded acquisition of power permitting the exploration and exhaustion of a system. Chara, like Flowey, is addressing the hidden and problematic motivations of a par-ticular kind of player.

Chara continues: "Now. Now, we have reached the absolute. There is nothing left for us here. Let us erase this pointless world, and move on to the next." They give the player the choice to erase the world or to refuse. If they choose to erase it, Chara states their approval; if they refuse, Chara clarifies the player's relationship to the game: "No...? Hmm...How curious. You must have misunderstood. SINCE WHEN WERE YOU THE ONE IN CONTROL?" Chara slashes the screen, repeated number nines appear, and the game switches to windowed mode, shakes, and closes. Here, *Undertale* points out something obvious that is nevertheless routinely forgotten: since videogames are closed systems, the player is not "free"; nothing truly unexpected can happen. They are therefore not "in control" of what happens to their characters or to the gameworlds they inhabit. In this sense, the game is controlling the player by delimiting the possibilities open to them. In another sense, it is *Chara* who is in control, which is to say it is the player's habits or assumptions – like the completionist's tendency to collect all of the achievements in every game that they play or the spectator's tendency to watch the game play out online.

But the game is not only suggesting that the player is not *free* – it is suggesting that they are not *in control* even in the more limited ways to which they are accustomed. Other games give players who witness "the bad ending" the chance to restart and play through another time, seamlessly altering events and delivering whatever conclusion the player desires. *Undertale* refuses the player that agency, defying the player's expectations. If the no mercy player decides that they want to revisit the gameworld after pursuing genocide, the usual introductory crawl is replaced by a black screen and the sound of howling wind. Nothing happens. After ten minutes, text appears on the bottom of the screen: Chara reminds the player that they caused the destruction of the world, asks the player if they think they are above consequences, and offers to give the world back to the player in exchange for their soul. If the player accepts, the game starts as normal. The player who successfully conducts genocide and then barters away their soul can play through the game again, but the endings are different – forever altered by the player's choices. The pacifist ending that follows the no mercy run shows Chara rather than Frisk: they have killed Toriel and all the others, despite the monsters' successful escape to the Surface. Despite the player's efforts, and in defiance of their expectations of control, everyone has died.

The no mercy ending that follows a previous no mercy run changes Chara's dialogue yet again:

"MAEVE." The demon that comes when people call its name. It doesn't matter when. It doesn't matter where. Time after time, I will appear. And, with your help. We will eradicate the enemy and become strong. HP. ATK. DEF. GOLD. EXP. LV. Every time a number increases, that feeling…That's me. "MAEVE."

Chara, if the point weren't clear enough already, is not a resident of the Underground. They travel with the player from one gameworld to another. Every time the player enters their name in a character creation screen, every time they are hailed by the software, Chara is there, eliciting in them a desire for power. Chara goes on:

…But. You and I are not the same, are we? This SOUL resonates with a strange feeling. There is a reason you continue to recreate this world. There is a reason you continue to destroy it. You. You are wracked with a perverted sentimentality. Hmm. I cannot understand these feelings any more. Despite this. I feel obligated to suggest. Should you choose to create this world once more. Another path would be better suited. Now, partner. Let us send this world back into the abyss.

The player, then, is not identical to Chara, who criticizes them for their "perverted sentimentality." The player simultaneously desires to accumulate and exert power *and* to explore and immerse themselves in worlds. They want to see the story play out. The player might not recognize these as countervailing desires, since most games permit the player to satisfy both, but Chara knows better: mechanical mastery, they suggest, is at odds with narrative immersion. Chara gives the lie to the notion that videogames are somehow "more immersive" than other media because they afford "more interactivity." Games that offer multiple pathways to be explored at the player's leisure, *Undertale* seems to be suggesting, do the exact opposite of immersing the player: they instead establish a fundamental *distance* between the player and the gameworld because the player cannot help but view the gameworld as a toy. This attitude prevents the player from experiencing the degree of immersion that they ostensibly desire and seem to achieve.

Where the player's desire is conflicting, Chara's is uncomplicated. They are free of sentimentality: the increase of number leads to the mastery of games leads to the exhaustion of worlds, one after another. Chara was never, in fact, anything other than this uncomplicated impulse. In the game's narrative, Chara commits suicide in order to cross the barrier, an action inexplicable outside of madness, selflessness, or – the more likely option – the conventions of roleplaying games. The Chara who became the sibling of Asriel saw the barrier as a roleplaying convention: a quest to be fulfilled, a state to be resolved. Chara takes the world of *Undertale* and everything in it – the characters, the dialogue, the combat, the Easter eggs, the plot – as a standing reserve. Everything is there to be consumed. In fact, in Chara, Heidegger's essence of modern technology attains a new extent: it is not only the things of the world that are within their grasp that stand in reserve, and not only the other things that are graspable in principle – the *entire* world is graspable *in practice*. The *whole* world stands in reserve. There is nothing that Chara cannot command. Moreover, it is not only the world of *Undertale* that stands reserved: *all* worlds stand reserved. Chara moves from one to another, exhausting each in turn, granting the player the kind of perfect control that ultimately *turns back on them* – an *autoimmune* control that robs them of what it is that, as *Undertale* would have it, they truly want: to dwell in the worlds that they destroy. *Undertale* makes this explicit by robbing the genocidal player of the ability to change the game's ending – everyone, after the no mercy run, always dies – and it thereby points to the implicit self-destruction that these players enact everywhere they go.

Undertale, Braid, and *Spec Ops: The Line* each point out the destructive and self-destructive character of a certain kind of obsessive gameplay; through their design, they show the player that the same desires that motivate this sort of gameplay also motivate other actions, and that these desires produce outcomes that they would otherwise find problematic. The allegorithm that exhausts gameworlds extends to the exhaustion of the "real world" as well. Completionist gameplay symptomatizes the general desire to know, command, and dispose, and to bring that which cannot be known, commanded, or disposed of into the magic circle through digitization. This is particularly true of the passage of time itself. But different games encourage different comportments to existential constants like time, and therefore different ways of approaching the game. Game design is rarely as effective when it tries to contravene control directly, taking control out of the player's hands, as when it calls attention to the fact and extent of the player's control. When it does so, it can compel the player to experience a range of emotions that are uniquely associated with the medium, opening up the space for the critique of those features of digitality that pose the greatest problems for political and ethical action: its presumptions about the knowability and controllability of people and things, the corresponding need to correct an imperfect world, the frustration that often follows when that need goes unmet, and the resentful politics that issue from that frustration.

Chapter Three

Bastion

When videogames take the form of power fantasies, they give the player the chance to learn and master an algorithm, exerting more and more perfect control. This process is less about winning the game than it is about learning the game's rules. While games in general certainly require a basic understanding of their rules, videogames require that players learn the algorithmic ways that they function. Since videogames are sets of more or less opaque algorithms that govern player action, the power that the player feels derives in part from mastering them. This understanding of videogames suggests that the power fantasy that players are living out arguably has less to do with wielding a big gun, crushing enemies, mastering the globe, or attaining a high score than with achieving an intuitive relation to a set of rules.

While videogames might tend toward power fantasies, they do not necessarily push the player there; they can in fact do the exact opposite, as the last chapter demonstrates, encouraging players to critique the power fantasy entrenched in the code.[189] Even when videogames do contribute to the formation of particular attitudes or understandings, they do not act as agents that inculcate particular attitudes or understandings in and of themselves. Rather, power fantasies in videogames symptomatize power fantasies in society more generally: they illustrate a set of perhaps once hidden, but increasingly explicit, desires. If Wark is right in his description of the intuitive relationship that players develop to videogames and their algorithms, then these increasingly explicit desires are less about the traditional violence of domination than the contemporary violence of digitality. For Wark, the "primary violence" of gamespace "has nothing to do with brightly colored explosions or mounting death counts but with the decision by digital fiat on where everything belongs and how it is ranked...The real violence of gamespace is its dicing of everything analog into the digital, cutting continuums into bits." The challenge of the digital game lies in its proclamation of totality and certainty, and in the promise that it makes to the player: *you can know this world, and then you can master it.* The violence here involves "the expulsion of quality from the world" – the exclusion of the unknown and the exhaustion of the known. And while this exclusionary violence might be "harmless" insofar as it is restricted to the domain of the videogame, it is "extreme" in its aesthetic, epistemological, or ontological force:[190] that is, the algorithmic logic of gamespace allows certain things to appear while disallowing others, encourages the player to understand those things in a particular light, and ultimately bars other things from existing at all. If Wark is right to suggest that gamespace is colonizing the world – that the understanding of the world as fundamentally comprehensible and controllable is shifting from the register of the videogame to the register of the hyperreal[191] – then videogame "violence" is not "harmless."

While the drive toward mastery may be related to the digital game, digitality is not a feature exclusive to digital technologies: it is tied to that attitude wherein all things are revealed as mere means to human ends that stand in reserve and await use and disposal, but it is not necessarily tied to videogames as a particular technological form.[192] In other words, digitality is an important means by which the world is rendered comprehensible, controllable, and disposable, but it has precedents in pre-digital technologies and cultural logics. Because of this, we can find good tools for understanding it in the work of Friedrich Nietzsche: he addresses the political and ethical implications of this digital modality of control more directly than most of the other thinkers mentioned here, making his work surprisingly relevant for the critical analysis of videogames.[193]

In the course of inquiring into the origins of responsibility in his *Genealogy of Morals,* Nietzsche connects the comprehensible and controllable vision of the world (that would later characterize digital ontology) with a comprehensible and controllable human being. For Nietzsche, there could be no promise-making – no certainty with regard to the future, and therefore no trust in and trade with other people – without a predictable human being dwelling in a predictable world:

> To ordain the future in advance...man must first have learned to distinguish necessary events from chance ones, to think causally, to see and anticipate distant eventualities as if they belonged to the present, to decide with certainty what is the goal and what the means to it, and in general be able to calculate and compute. Man himself must first of all have become *calculable, regular, necessary,* even in his own image of himself, if he is to be able to stand security for *his own future,* which is what one who promises does![194]

There can be no "animal *with the right to make promises*"[195] without an understanding that this human animal will dwell in a future that is similar to the present, and that he – "man" – will remain selfsame. Because we can predict how he will act, we can calculate what it is that we should do. And what better way to predict and calculate than to "compute"?[196]

While Nietzsche's genealogical work can be deployed to understand the extent to which slave morality, *ressentiment,* nihilism, and so on map onto contemporary digital phenomena, the question of the political and ethical ramifications of videogame design in particular is best answered by a reading of his doctrine of the eternal return of the same. In what follows, I suggest, with Wark, that videogames present not only the entrenchment of a violent digitality, but the means by which it might be challenged.[197] Furthermore, I argue, with Nietzsche, that embracing this challenge is significant not only for the gamer as a gamer, but for the gamer as an ethical being in the world. While gamers themselves are capable of contravening controlling attitudes no matter the games that they find themselves playing, game designers have a role to play in this attitude as well: they can create worlds in which players live out experiences that contravene control and calculability, even though the players remain in the digital frame that so readily enables these virtues, and they can do so via narrative and mechanics alike.[198] Rather than "expelling quality," game designers can bring it back into the world in a new form, and they can compel the players of their games to experience something of this qualitative vision.

This is what Supergiant Games has achieved with *Bastion*: it contravenes control at the level of its design. And it does so experientially: rather than simply giving the player the chance to read a narrative account of the loss of control – of the desperate attempt to turn back time that *Bastion* thematizes – and rather than giving the player an option to elect that loss, the game puts the player into an experiential position wherein he or she has no such choice, but where that lack of choice seems like a wonderful thing. It teaches the player the love of fate.

Caelondia

An indie game released in 2011 to strong sales and universal critical acclaim, *Bastion* is an isometric action role-playing game, or a brawler, that distinguishes itself from other hack-and-slash games with a distinctive visual and auditory style. Visually, the game is lush: the varied environments and enemies are painted with a vibrant and variegated color palette appropriate to the beauty of the game's general setting – a series of islands in the sky – but standing in stark contrast to the sobriety of the game's central event – an apocalypse that killed off the people and sundered the land. Although the setting is beautiful, it is also devastated and perilous, partially destroyed by the "Calamity" that preceded the player's actions, and constantly threatening the player with death by falling. And not only that: the tiles that make up the landscape do not appear until the player walks toward them, pulled back into place by the geological magnetism of the magical city crest that he wears strapped to his back. The pulling-into-place of the tiles is, as Franklin points out, "a visual metaphor for [the main character] trying to piece his life back together – to get his bearings, to find his stable footing in life." Not only visual, this metaphor is ludic: "[s]ince the floor doesn't appear until you step on it, the player, much like [their character], is uncertain about where to go next, what the proper path is, or how to get themselves out of this situation."[199] The visual style of the game suggests that the player is actively but shakily constructing their world simply by being in it, and the game reinforces this claim with its ludic toolset, putting the player in a position of experiencing the uncertainty that it depicts on the screen.

When people talk about *Bastion*, though, its soundscape is usually what they mention first.[200] The game features a distinctive score that supports its changing moods, and is narrated in a Sam Elliott-sounding voice that accompanies the player wherever they go, describing major plot points and minor mistakes alike. Greg Kasavin's text is written with conviction and economy and Logan Cunningham speaks in a southern-poetic cadence, with his narration sounding out over the top of the gameplay rather than interrupting it. The narrator himself plays a central role in the plot, meeting the player's character – whom the narrator dubs "the Kid" – at the end of the game's brief first act, and then guiding him through the game's events.[201] His voice provides an accompaniment to the player's actions that is simultaneously masculine, melancholic, and warm. Long before the end of the game, he feels like a friend. This connection between the player and the narrator makes the complications of the narrator's involvement in the Calamity – and his later-revealed desire to literally turn back time – all the more affecting.

As the Kid moves through Caelondia, the narrator gradually explains the events that brought him there. Before the Calamity, Caelondia was a rich, industrious city-state populated by the technologically-minded Caels. They made a gear their city crest, while their dark-haired neighbors, the Ura, represented themselves with a spade. The Caels generally distrusted the Ura, so they protected themselves by purchasing their land "on the cheap" and by erecting the Rippling Walls. The Walls offered Caelondia protection from a nebulous set of external threats, as the narrator notes: the Walls "kept Caelondia safe from whatever's out there. The elements, the Ura. You name it." As the City expanded, the Caels terraformed the surrounding wilds and built a rail line to the east, but the rail disturbed the underground-dwelling Ura, and the two city-states found themselves at war. The colonizers' technological superiority led to their eventual victory and an unsteady peace: the Ura retreated to their Tazal Terminals, but the Caelondian rulers ordered that those Ura who had taken refuge in Caelondia during the war were to remain. The xenophobia of the Caels compelled them to fortify the City, both by building the Walls and by attempting a pre-emptive "securitization" of the Uras' home: the Caels developed a weapon that would let them "seal the Ura tunnels shut... in a flash." The attempted genocide backfired when one of the engineers associated with the project pointed the Caels' weapon to Caelondia itself. The resulting Calamity fractured the ground and killed nearly every one of the city dwellers, vaporizing them or turning them into columns of ash.

At the beginning of the game, the Kid seems to be the only one left alive. He wakes up to discover the devastation and makes his way to the Bastion. The highest point of the City, the Bastion was the place "where everyone agreed to go in case of trouble." There, he finds only the narrator, whose name is Rucks, who tells him that everyone else seems to have died in the Calamity. Rucks also tells him that the Bastion is more than just a sanctuary: if its construction could be finished, it could "undo the Calamity," "fix everything," and "make it like it was before." At the time, Rucks does not specify exactly how it is that the Bastion could put things aright, only saying that it is in a state of terrible disrepair, its Core broken into pieces and scattered across the ruined landscape. So, in traditional roleplaying game style, Rucks tasks the player with going out into the wilds and retrieving the fragments of the Core. From here, the game progresses in a familiar fashion, with the player exploring the land, acquiring and upgrading weapons, meeting and saving two Ura "refugees," and gradually restoring the Bastion to its former functionality. *Bastion*, in other words, operates in much the same way as any other power fantasy, offering the player the chance to learn and master the game. But *Bastion*'s ending – among a number of other iconographic and metaphorical features – demonstrates just how different its operation is.

The Eternal Return of the Same

The game's ending can be understood in terms of Nietzsche's philosophy, the heart of which is the eternal return of the same.[202] Nietzsche's most succinct definition of eternal recurrence can be found in his notes from August 26, 1881, where he describes it as the "desire to experience it all once again, an eternity of times."[203] He articulates it in *Thus Spoke Zarathustra, Beyond Good and Evil, Twilight of the Idols*, and his autobiography,[204] but the first published reference to it is made in *The Gay Science*. Here, he describes a demon who "[steals] after you in your loneliest loneliness and [says] to you: 'This life as you now live it and have lived it, you will have to live once more and innumerable times more.'" How would you react to this statement, Nietzsche asks?

> Would you not throw yourself down and gnash your teeth...? Or have you once experienced a tremendous moment when you would have answered him: "You are a god and never

have I heard anything more divine." If this thought gained possession of you, it would change you as you are or perhaps crush you. The question in each and every thing, "Do you desire this once more and innumerable times more?" would lie upon your actions as the greatest weight.[205]

In *The Gay Science*, then, the eternal return of the same is figured as a terrible existential challenge. Could you relive your life? Could you meet each event – each decision made, each chance encounter, each twist of fate – with levity and affirmation? Even the worst terrors and injustices: could you embrace them?

The challenge makes sense in the context of Nietzsche's confrontation with nihilism. While nihilism appears at the center of many of Nietzsche's writings – perhaps most concisely in *The Will to Power*, where the nihilist is described as "a man who judges of the world as it is that it ought *not* to be, and of the world as it ought to be that it does not exist"[206] – he articulates it in the context of the eternal recurrence in *Thus Spoke Zarathustra*. In the parable of "The Vision and the Riddle," Zarathustra relates the tale of his ascent of a mountain in twilight, in which he struggles against "the spirit of gravity" personified as a dwarf clinging to his back. The two climb their way to a gateway marked "Moment" from which one path stretches infinitely into the past and another stretches infinitely into the future:

> "Observe," I continued, "This Moment! From the gateway, This Moment, there runs a long eternal lane *backwards*: behind us lies an eternity.
>
> "Must not whatever *can* run its course of all things, have already run along that lane? Must not whatever *can* happen of all things have already happened, resulted, and gone by?
>
> "And if everything has already existed, what do you think, dwarf, of This Moment? Must not this gateway also – have already existed?

"And are not all things closely bound together in such a way that This Moment draws all coming things after it? *Consequently* – itself also?

"For whatever *can* run its course of all things, also in this long lane *outward – must* it once more run! –

"And this slow spider which creeps in the moonlight, and this moonlight itself, and you and I in this gateway whispering together, whispering of eternal things – must we not all have already existed?

"– And must we not return and run in that other lane out before us, that long weird lane – must we not eternally return?" –[207]

Growing quieter, Zarathustra hears a dog howling. He notices that the dwarf, the gateway, and the spider are gone, and finds himself "in the dreariest moonlight." The moonlight reveals a young shepherd lying nearby, choking on a black snake; the snake has crawled into his mouth and bitten fast. Zarathustra attempts to pull the snake from the man's mouth, but fails. Zarathustra then cries out, urging the shepherd to bite off the head of the snake. The shepherd bites it and springs up, "[n]o longer shepherd, no longer man – a transformed being, a light-surrounded being, that *laughed*!"[208]

The vision of the shepherd and the snake figures the eternal return and the confrontation with nihilism. The shepherd is incapacitated by the snake's bite: he cannot speak or move – he is lying, not standing – and neither he nor anyone else can pull it off of him. The snake is "all that is heaviest, blackest"[209] – the *ressentiment* that is the worst tendency of "Christian man." In Heidegger's reading of Nietzsche, the meaning of the snake is indisputable: "[t]he black snake is drear monotony, ultimately the goallessness and meaningless of nihilism. It is nihilism itself."[210] Like the insinuations of the ascetic priest, the snake has stolen upon the shepherd while he was sleeping and taken hold, preventing him from contemplating anything other than the snake itself, and compelling him to see it with "disgust and pallid horror."[211] But the snake does not kill him or inject him with a tranquilizer, biting from the outside; it works its way *inside* the shepherd, *incorporating* itself into him. So, instead of falling asleep and dreaming of a world free of pain, or longing for an afterlife where his sufferings will be compensated, the shepherd wakes up and confronts his fear.[212]

The shepherd's confrontation with nihilism is not a destruction of it. It does not come from the outside, and it never can,[213] since there is no overcoming finitude, whether construed as one's own end or as "the history of the oblivion *of* being and the abandonment *by* being," as David Farrell Krell puts it.[214] For Nietzsche, nihilism is a basic condition of human existence: "how could there be an outside-of-me? There is no outside!"[215] Because there is only this world, and because we are always already losing it, there can be no ultimate, decisive destruction of nihilism – only an identification with it (the awakening to the horror of the "*it is all alike*") and a crossing over it (the transformative convalescence that follows the sickness). Zarathustra, then, is "Zarathustra the Godless" because he wants to live without appeal to a foundational outside, "cheerfully" confronting the vicissitudes of fate. If he is "the advocate of life, the advocate of suffering, the advocate of the circle,"[216] this is because it is only by electing suffering – over and over again – that he can elect life. This is what the shepherd does when he bites off the head of the snake: he embraces existence without denying its suffering. He becomes "a transformed being, a light-surrounded being, that *laughed*"[217] by rising to the demon's challenge with gaiety and affirmation.

Safe States

The eternal return of the same can be characterized in a range of different ways – as a doctrine, as a thought experiment, as a myth, as a cosmology, and so on. Considered in ethical terms, it can be characterized as a *challenge*: it demands that its subject develop an attitude of equanimity and moderation, or the acceptance of existence as it is – an *amor fati*[218] or even an *ishvara pranidhana*[219] – even when that means accepting its end. It is a confrontation with finitude that demands joyful resignation and promises radical transformation. *Bastion* can be understood as a ludic instantiation of this ethics of the eternal return. Although it eventually situates the player in a position where they have no choice but to affirm eternal recurrence, it first demonstrates the extraordinary dangers of doing the opposite.

At the end of *Bastion*, the game presents the player with two binary choices. The second of these involves the Bastion itself. In the final act of the game, Rucks tasks the Kid with retrieving the final Shard from the Ura. As the Kid goes about retrieving it, Rucks fills in some background detail: not only was he the architect of the Rippling Walls – he was the architect of the Bastion itself. When the player returns with the Shard, the narrator announces that the Bastion is complete. He invites the Kid into its "heart" and provides him with a choice: the Bastion can be used – as Rucks has insisted throughout the game – to restore the Old World, "undo[ing] the Calamity here and now." But it also has "another function, strictly speaking":

If ever the Monument blew out and we couldn't repair it, we could still... evacuate. First we'd round up as many folks as we could carry. Next we'd detonate the Cores...and we'd take off. Away from here. Of course that would mean no going back. Ever. But then again, that way all of us could leave the City – together.

The choice, then, is between Restoration and Evacuation, and Rucks leans hard toward the former, asking the Kid – and the player – to set the world aright. Rucks is not alone in this ambition, either: the game itself has been working to ensure that the desire that Rucks and the Kid feel for the Restoration option is shared by the player. The glimpses that the player catches of the Caelondia-that-was reveal it to have been a stunningly beautiful place, even idyllic, and the player might very reasonably want to try to save the untold number of people who died in the Calamity.

Restoring might seem, at first, like an embrace of the eternal return: the player would be electing to relive the past as it happened before, answering the demon's challenge with the certainty of a binary choice. But the choice to restore the Old World, returning to the Caelondia-that-was, is the opposite of an affirmation: it is a denial that this moment – the moment of the choice, which is a moment of radical uncertainty in the face of finitude – be lived again and again. In seriously considering Restoration, the Kid is casting about for security and assurance in the midst of his "loneliest loneliness," witnessing the devastation wrought by the Calamity and fervently wishing that it might be avoided. He is expressing the impossible longing to return home – a *nostos algein* for a reality that never was – deploying technology in order to establish a post facto security in a world where that dream was killed long ago.[220]

This existential security crisis generates immensely problematic political effects. From the beginning, Rucks – the architect of the Rippling Walls – was working to safeguard Caelondia from the ravages of the wilds, and after the war, Caelondia set him to work providing a safeguard against the Ura: "At the heart of the Calamity was a simple idea: we never wanted to go to war again. Wanted to rule it out." The intention was to write political contingency out of the picture, making uncertainty impossible by ordering the world in such a way that nothing – and particularly no external population – could threaten it. This intention is, for Nietzsche, ignorant of the actual functioning of politics and destructive of its practitioners and their worlds: "A legal order thought of as sovereign and universal...a means of *preventing* all struggle in general... would be a principle *hostile to life*, an agent of the dissolution and destruction of man...a secret path to nothingness."[221] No surprise, then, that this technological attempt to create the perfect legal order – the goal of a certain branch of political theory dating back to Hobbes' nominalist dream of a safe state[222] and stretching forward to Foucault's description of the state racism of biopolitics[223] – backfires.

Rucks, as it happens, feels partially responsible for the Calamity: "We put a lot of folks against that problem – scientists, soldiers, spies. Even me." A guilt-wracked narrator as well as an unreliable one, Rucks desperately wants to undo his mistaken contribution to the Calamity, and in that desire to undo it, he claims to feel no concern for the beasts and the people who need to die because they are in the way. The colonial violence of this attitude is clearly demonstrated by Rucks' comments on the animals of "the Wild Unknown." Although they are only setting up their own homes, they are standing in the way of radical renewal – so they can be ethically destroyed. In fact, killing them is *good* for them:

> The creatures of the Wild...they've been building a Bastion of their own. [But the] best thing we can do for those beasts right now is put them down quick and clean. Look at it this way: it's either them, or us. There's only one kind of mercy left these days. Takes a lot of convincing, and our mortars have to do the talking. But if we win, they win too. Our Bastion is everybody's gain, not just our own. Unfortunately, there's no explaining that to a simple beast.

In this narration, the game is giving meaning to the killing of enemies – a set of actions so commonplace in brawlers as to be meaningless.[224] Because the Bastion will fix everything, giving even these beasts a better life, this slaughter can be coded as laudable. It works in the service of life. Rucks knows, though, that certain listeners might have differing opinions on this bio-political project. After the Kid puts down the last of the animals barring his path to one of the shards, the narrator reassures his interlocutor and himself: "He's done what's best for them, don't you worry. Don't you worry." The parallels to settler attitudes to indigenous populations – the need and the ability to rationalize slaughter; the giving to oneself of a superior intellectual and ethical position; the disregard for alterity in the extraction of world-improving resources – are clear.

The colonial violence of the Kid's actions is even more obvious from the murder of the Ura warriors – committed using a miniature version of the very device that caused the genocide called the "Calamity Cannon," of all things, that both kills the warriors and destroys their homes. As with the beasts of the Wild, however, the game directly and indirectly comments on the problematic character of what is being done. At the end of one of the final sections, the Kid brings home an Ura child's drawing, and Rucks demonstrates that he feels qualms about the murders: "I don't need to see what happened to the Ura. I'm trying to undo it, remember?" When the player takes down an Ura warrior, their body remains lying on the ground, suggesting that the Kid distinguishes human from animal, and that he is particularly bothered by what he is now being required to do. That Rucks' calamitous desire to "fix things" is not restricted to the Calamity itself is apparent from another extended quotation, voiced as the player is committing this reluctant slaughter:

Things will go back to the way they used to be. That's the power of the Bastion. This whole place is a living record of the times before the Calamity. The way things were before this story. Good times, right? You'd be your old self again. Think of all those times that didn't go your way. All of life's little setbacks – imagine if you could have another go at them. No mistakes. Anyone you've ever hurt...everything you've ever done...you could do it over. And wouldn't that be grand? Well...I guess there's nothing more to say.

The fantasy of Restoration begins with the desire to prevent the Calamity, but extends to "all of life's little setbacks" – all of those moments of imperfect control – and its fantastic quality doubles down on its nihilistic coding. Even if the Bastion were to work as Rucks hopes, enabling the nostalgic return to a glorious past by way of a technological abrogation of the devastated and devastating present, it would still entail the devaluation of this present. Rucks' desperate desire to fix the past – articulated during a portion of gameplay in which "the world as it is" is literally falling to pieces underneath the Kid's feet – shows that Rucks perfectly fits Nietzsche's description of the nihilist as the "man who judges of the world as it is that it ought *not* to be, and of the world as it ought to be that it does not exist."[225] Worse, Rucks knows it. He delivers some of his lines – "Good times, right?" – with a heavy dose of irony, and others – "Well...I guess there's nothing more to say" – with weary exhaustion.

Rucks is clearly all too aware of the pointlessness of his enterprise,[226] but unable to stop himself from pursuing it, or from attempting to convince the Kid to complete his designs and correct his mistakes. In these attempts at conversion, he resembles the ascetic priest whom Nietzsche describes in the *Genealogy of Morals*: a resentful shepherd attempting to convince his flock to do his bidding by installing a fictional but superior reality in place of an existing but dissatisfying one.[227] And the scope of this mission is immense: Rucks wants to answer a failed technological attempt to securitize the City with an even grander technology – one that would sanitize not a people or a species, but a time.[228]

Save States
One of the principal themes of *Bastion* is the complicated rela-

tionship of people, games, and nation-states to temporality. At the beginning of the game, the first words of the narration are these: "A proper story's supposed to begin at the beginning. Things ain't so simple with this one." From the beginning, the game foregrounds the complicated character of its temporality. That this point of narration refers to the game seemingly beginning *in medias res* is the least of its complications. If the player chooses to use the Bastion to restore Caelondia to a time before the Calamity, the game ends with a picture of the characters fading from view in front of a world swirling with green energy, apparently putting itself back together and erasing them from history. Rucks' last words to the player are explicitly nostalgic: "Caelondia, we're comin' home." His penultimate words, however, are: "So long, Kid. Maybe I'll see you in the next one." The player is then given the option to try a New Game +,[229] which starts off – differently than the first time – with a distorted echo of the "see you in the next one" line sounding in the background. As the player moves through the game a subsequent time, the narration changes slightly. When entering the Sole Regret, Rucks experiences déjà vu: "He sets foot inside one of Caelondia's famous watering holes. Wait – haven't I...? Anyway, Rondy's place just brings back memories." When first encountering one of the Ura survivors in the Hanging Gardens, the original narration is replaced with, "Something so familiar about that man." And when moving through the dangerous Urzendra Gate, the narrator says, "It's strange – feels like I told this part a thousand times." The game strongly suggests, then, that Restoration fails to prevent the Calamity. The Bastion can indeed rollback time, but the events that led to the Calamity will ultimately play out in the exact same way.

The temporal structure of *Bastion* is therefore cyclical, but not simply so. To begin with, there is no repetition during the first play through: each line of narration is spoken only a single time, and each area, with the exception of the optional training grounds, is visited only once. And the game's save itself is not under the player's control, or at least not the extent that it would be were this a game that featured regular saving and reloading, let alone multiple save files: there can only be one playthrough happening at a time. If the Kid's life is cut short, the game sends the player back to the beginning of the level. Not an instance of the game being restored, *Bastion* rationalizes death as a narrative tangent or a mistaken recollection on the part of Rucks.[230] The only control that the player can in fact exert over *Bastion*'s temporality is in the choice between Restoration and Evacuation. And – vitally – this choice is precisely about the *relinquishment* of control rather than its exercise. When the player chooses Evacuation, Rucks expresses dismay while a picture of the Bastion untethered from its former moorings and drifting off into the sky is displayed: "You want to stay? In a world like this?" His dismay turns to admitted confusion – "I gotta admit, Kid, I ain't put much thought in that idea. Of carrying on. With you here." – and then to something in between resignation and excitement: "We can't go back no more. But I suppose we could go...wherever we please."

Evacuation, then, frees Caelondia's survivors from the impossible fantasy of returning to a better time. It grants them freedom by depriving them of control. As Chun argues, the fiction of "the Internet" brought with it a set of axiomatics, including the notion that freedom and control are synonymous.[231] There is, however, a greater sense of freedom to be found in the embrace of vulnerability. The fact that this is a claim commonly made in this digital era[232] suggests that there might be a tendency operational in the technology, but the fact that a similar answer was given well over a hundred years ago by Nietzsche – for vulnerability and *amor fati* might not be far from one another – suggests that the problem to which this answer is given predates contemporary technology. Freedom becomes control by way of protocol,[233] but this was a shift we might have noticed long ago.

We only see the problem in such stark relief now because protocol is so readily comprehensible. As Frederic Jameson puts it, "the technology of contemporary society...seems to offer some privileged representational shorthand for grasping a network of power and control even more difficult for our minds and imaginations to grasp: the whole new decentered global network of the third stage of capital itself."[234] Relatedly, but perhaps more profoundly, contemporary technology enables us to more easily discern Heidegger's *essence* of modern technology. In this context, *Bastion*'s final decision is one of the sites in which the ethical and political stakes of this tendency become apparent.

Where Restoration signifies the denial of the eternal return, wishing that things could be other than they are, Evacuation signifies its acceptance. When the player decides to move on, they choose to accept their fate, acknowledging that they do not in fact have a choice. So, while the game does not *enforce* Evacuation over Restoration, I want to suggest that the Evacuation ending is the canonical one. It is an ending proper. Restoration only ever ends in Calamity, but Evacuation moves the survivors into an uncertain, imperfect future. Insofar as the game *guides* the player to an eventual Evacuation, it mirrors life itself – striving for control and seeming to attain it for a period, but then facing a situation that demands its relinquishment. The game manages to coax the player's hand without moralizing, unlike other games that do something similar. *Bastion* does not claim that the player is a bad person for playing the game or desiring control, and it refuses to openly castigate Rucks for his nostalgic and disastrous pursuit of a world that probably never existed. Player character and non-player character alike are treated with understanding and empathy even while being criticized, and the game does not insist that the player make "the right" choice – at least not in that very moment. It models in gameplay the sort of forgiveness of the unforgiveable and acceptance of an uncertain future that the storyline presents.[235]

The Twilight of the Idols

Along with the eternal return, the confrontation with nihilism, and the ineluctable danger of nostalgia, *Bastion* drives its thematic focus home with another Nietzschean set of concepts: groundlessness, *ressentiment*, and forgiveness. We see these concepts in the ludic metaphor of the game's difficulty system and in the complicated narrative deployment of the two Ura refugees.

Bastion is, as I noted before, literally groundless: it is only through the magical invocation of the technology of the city crest and something like a conative drive to exist, or a will to power, that the Kid can pull the world back together. But the game is also metaphorically groundless in that Caelondia seems to have been abandoned by its gods. Early in the game, when the Kid travels to Pyth Orchard, a place built for the bull god of commotion and order, the narrator says the following: "No use praying to the gods these days. No time for it, either...[the] gods are long gone now." But "Kid says a little prayer anyway. Couldn't hurt, right?" Returning to the Bastion with a miniature bull-shaped idol, the Kid builds a shrine to the gods and slots the miniature Pyth there. From here on in, the player can choose to invoke the gods, selectively adding difficulty to the game in exchange for improved rewards, but the player is most likely to start invoking the idols only in their second run through the game, when they have mastered the controls and want to challenge themselves. As a Cael, the Kid invokes the gods without compunction. His attitude is simultaneously instrumental and pious: he disrespects the gods by praying to them for some particular outcome, or by asking for favors, but he respects them by acknowledging their lingering power.

If the player invokes the gods during a New Game + run, which is the most likely time that they will seek additional challenge, the Kid is placing his faith in the gods after his faith in technological renewal via Restoration has been shattered. We see here the swing from one extreme to another that Nietzsche describes in *The Will to Power*.[236] Losing faith in the gods, the Caels lost faith in the meaning of things as such, but then placed their faith in technology; losing faith in technology, they place their faith back in the gods – but without conviction. This nihilism is "incomplete" insofar as the Caels have not renounced *all* values, and this poses a problem for Nietzsche since it results in the entrenchment of nihilism, this time taking the form of a pendulum swing between extremes. Partly aware of and unsettled by their reluctant apostasy, the Caels attempt to escape their old religious commitments, but do so by making an appeal to alternative categories of reason (or faith) that remain within the sway of the old metaphysics. When they – and they are we – attempt this escape from nihilism "without revaluating our values so far," we "produce the opposite [values], make the problem more acute."[237] Our "awareness" of nihilism, partial and reactive as it is, does not help us to escape from this swing between extreme commitments; it only accentuates it.[238]

Deprived of a ground, the Caels cast about for a firm footing; playing through the game for a second or subsequent time, the player casts about for additional challenge. Again, *Bastion* makes use of its ludic language to the same effect as its narrative message. The player who has tried to restore the Old World knows that the gods have abandoned Caelondia and that the Calamity will take place no matter what. Just as the player knows that their invocation is purely ornamental – that it will not change the world – the Caels know that they have lost something that once gave the world meaning and stability: "Pyth stood for something once. Something real. In time, though, the Bull stopped being a symbol, and started being a decoration." This attitude stands in contrast to the attitude of the Caels' enemies to the east: "The Ura feared the gods. We turned them into toys – put them on our walls." Both the player and the Caels know that this is the twilight of the idols, but that does not stop them from offering half-hearted worship at the Shrine. The game redoubles its claims about nihilism by impelling the player to act nihilistically.

The Caels are not the only ones who have lost faith, however. In the aftermath of the Calamity, the Ura also have to confront the abandonment of the gods. Their responses to the Calamity are represented in very different ways by the two Ura survivors, Zia and Zulf. The Kid meets the latter in the Hanging Gardens, where he sees Zulf standing and staring into the sky, an expression of horror on his face – "as if the gods would answer him." Returning to the Bastion, Rucks and the player learn his backstory. An orphaned child, Zulf survived by pickpocketing until he was caught by a Caelondian missionary living in the Tazal Terminals. The missionary took him in, teaching him "theology, history, and mercy." When the missionary died, Zulf took up his message of forgiveness and tolerance, preaching first in the Terminals and later in the City. There, he proposed to a Caelondian woman, and she accepted – but then the Calamity happened, taking her and leaving him. Back in the Bastion, Zulf is soon joined by another Ura refugee: the Kid finds Zia in Prosper Bluff by following the sound of a beautiful, mournful song back to its source. Where Zulf's story begins in forgiveness, hers begins in betrayal. After the War, her then-young father was taken in by Caelondia as an orphaned refugee; born in the City, Zia was raised a Cael but never allowed to forget the white of her skin or the black of her hair. A young man curious about her Ura heritage befriended her but betrayed her and her father, who was then compelled to work for the Caels in exchange for her freedom. When she arrives in the Bastion, she brings with her his notebook written in the Ura language.

Zulf and Zia figure different responses to the Calamity and attitudes toward life. Zulf is a figure who raises questions of vengeance and forgiveness. The "tolerance" he learns in his early life is tested by the Calamity and after it. Zia cannot read the Ura language, but Zulf can, and after reading her father's notebook, he learns the truth of the Calamity: not a random accident, it was the result of Caelondia's plan to wipe the Ura from the map. Appalled by the machinations against his now-peaceful compatriots, and conscious of the role that Rucks played, he vows revenge: "The Calamity failed, but I will not." For the remainder of the game, Zulf plots against the Bastion and its survivors, carrying out an agenda fueled by a sense of deep injustice and a desire to prevent the Caelondians from carrying on with what he perceives as their genocidal mission. He leads his "countrymen" to the Bastion "to take revenge"; some of them take Zia away, and then the rest start "digging their holes."

After the Kid dispatches the invaders, he pursues the remaining Ura back to their homeland, and as the casualties mount, the Ura turn on Zulf and put him down. The Kid finds his badly beaten body lying on the ground, and the player faces the other binary choice that the game provides: they can either move on, leaving Zulf to his fate – which is perfectly rational, since, as the choice puts it, "Zulf's situation is hopeless and a distraction," and since he "deserves" death anyway – or they can pick him up and carry him, dropping the battering ram that would otherwise protect the Kid on his way through the last gauntlet of Ura warriors. The player is given the choice of a pointless and possibly fatal forgiveness, since Zulf's body will prevent the Kid from fighting back, or of a rational and calculated abandonment. If the player leaves Zulf, the Kid fights his way through the remaining Ura, killing them all, and reaches the end of the game. But if he takes Zulf, everything changes. The music switches from the usual aggressive soundtrack to Zulf's melancholic song, and the Kid wades into the gauntlet. This is the first time in the game that he interacts with his enemies with anything other than murderous aggression. He walks slowly over the ground, suffering a stream of arrows, but they eventually come to a stop: the Ura warriors only stand and watch. One impossible forgiveness gives rise to a second.

Although Zia's reaction to the Calamity could not be more different, she is not the forgiving female counterpart to Zulf's male vengeance – nor a mother, sister, or lover. Zia's alternative response to the Calamity is not forgiveness, but *terror*. This is clearest from her song.[239] If the player ignores its lyrics, focusing only on the melody, they might miss its threatening message:

I dig my hole, you build a wall
I dig my hole, you build a wall
One day that wall is gonna fall

Gon' build that city on a hill
Gon' build that city on a hill
Someday those tears are gonna spill

So build that wall and build it strong
'Cause we'll be there before too long[240]

The threat is issued on two levels. The first is clear: the Ura consider themselves to be oppressed, and they intend to destroy the source of their oppression by literally undermining the security apparatus of the Caelondian state. The second is more oblique. A threat spoken not by the Ura or by Zia but by existence as such, it reminds the Caels of their finitude: no matter what they do, they will die. This threat, however, is accompanied by a promise: "Gon' build that wall up to the sky / One day your bird is gonna fly." Again, the promise is sung in two registers: the Ura captives of the Caelondian state will escape, and so will the repressed potential of the Caels themselves, whether they like it or not. Nietzsche would recognize his own judgment of Europeans in Zia's judgment of the Caels: "Here precisely is what has become a fatality for Europe – together with the fear of man we have also lost our love of him, our reverence for him, our hopes for him, even the will to him. The sight of man now makes us weary – what is nihilism today if it is not *that*?"[241] Fear and hope are twins, and both Zia and Nietzsche know it. The pointless denial of mortality results in the repression of natality as well. The terror that Zia inspires in the Caels is less about the threat to the Rippling Walls than the threat to the false sense of security, the perverse satisfaction, that Rucks finds in his weary nihilism. Zia as an existential terrorist, then: a damsel who distresses.[242]

Bastion has Zia deliver her message in a positive form as well as a negative one, however. She is an agent who willingly faces the horror of the post-apocalyptic world. When the Ura come to the Bastion, she is not kidnapped – she goes with them willingly because she wants to know the truth about the Calamity. Toward the end of the game, she takes this understanding and challenges Rucks, who talks down to her: "You're wondering if there ain't some other way out of this mess...But why would you even want another way, unless...unless you wanted to stay here – with us? That's sweet and all, but I don't know that I can stick around." He replies to her "sweet" suggestion with a masculine adoption of responsibility that covers over the uncertainty that her question makes him feel: "The weight of the Calamity...it's on our shoulders." At the very end, while Rucks pushes for Restoration, she raises the possibility of Evacuation. She does so in her own undemanding voice, making this the first time in the game that the player hears a voice other than the narrator's, and the first time they have not been urged to choose Restoration. Asked about Evacuation, she says the following: "If I could be anyplace I wanted, I'd stay right here. We could go anywhere in the world." And: "Any moment I'd want to live again happened after the Calamity, not before." Where Zulf is too mired in his own desire for vengeance to consider eternal recurrence, and where Rucks is too guilty and melancholic to rise to its challenge, Zia embraces it with a superhuman gaiety.

Evacuation, Not Escape

Bastion offers the player an experience rich with metaphor and laden with difficult questions about the ethics of living in a finite world. Even the small things of the game reinforce these questions. When the player finds the Bronze Spyglass out in the Wilds, for instance, Rucks' and Zia's comments on it express conflicting answers to the question of eternal recurrence. When the player offers the Spyglass to Rucks, he says, "We could always see the stars – we could just never reach 'em. No matter how high we built." An indirect commentary on the futility of building one's way out of a political mess or out of the complexity of interpersonal relations, it is also a commentary on the desire to escape choice, politics, and (ultimately) finitude by way of technology. In seeing the stars, the Caels think they can see the moment when they committed a great wrong, and this sight makes them think they can build back to it. The stars are the burst of the Calamity, and the Bastion itself is the edifice built up to get there. Zia, however, offers a different perspective: "Sure the world's all gone t' pieces farther than the eye can see...but leave it to this gal to point out the amazin' view." Zia, a figure of transformation, willingly ignores the fantastic return to the moment of choice in order to inhabit the world around her. Where Rucks wants to build up an edifice that would allow people to alter their fate by taking back a calamitous choice, Zia wants to move forward.

But how does this desire to move forward not fall back into the fantasy of escape? In choosing to Evacuate, how is the player *not* expressing yet another fantasy – this time, the nostalgic fantasy of establishing a fresh beginning? As the Bastion sails off into the sky, away from the thousands of Caels, Ura, and animals that Rucks and the Kid have murdered, how could it be that the player is *not* disavowing responsibility? From a narrative perspective, the answer is fairly straightforward: all four survivors are living in a broken world where the ashes of the dead still remain in the air, and they know it. They have all lost loved ones, and three of them have blood on their hands. The survivors are willing to acknowledge the loss of the dead and the persistence of their memory.

This thematization of loss plays out in the different ways that *Bastion* concludes. In the Restoration ending, the player is treated to pictures of the survivors before the Calamity: Zulf gazes lovingly into the eyes of his fiancée; Zia plays her instrument in front of an audience; Rucks pores over blueprints in front of the Bastion's Monument; and the Kid works with his hammer on the Walls: all of them lead the same lives that led up to the Calamity. In the Evacuation ending, however, the pictures express a different set of attitudes. More mournful than melancholic, Rucks and Zulf – the figures of *ressentiment* – have begun to process their loss. Zulf is shown preparing a meal in the galley, thoughtfully reflecting on something, and Rucks stands proudly, no longer obsessing over his architectural design. Zia the "Yes-sayer" stands at the bow of the ship, smiling out at the horizon and seeming to have moved beyond mourning and melancholia both: "[l]ooking away" from the Calamity is her "only negation."[243] Unable to live in the Tazal Terminals with the Ura for fairly obvious reasons, and lacking both the colonial technologies that would enable them to make a home in the Wilds and the will to displace the animals yet again, the survivors do the only thing that they can: they sail away. This is a new beginning, but it is not necessarily the fantasy of a fresh start in the state of nature. The Calamity destroyed the security state of Caelondia, but it left the rest of the world untouched, with all its history and complications – and the survivors have to live in that world.

Chapter Four

Play against Control

Good game design can foster good gameplay, whether that means gameplay that's interesting, compelling, addictive, exciting, critical, or whatever else, but it doesn't necessarily do so. Likewise, good gameplay doesn't require good game design, since creative players can get just about anything out of any given game. This is partly because games, like all other cultural objects, are always interpreted from several points of view regardless of the intentions of their authors, but it's also because videogames are *played*. As interactive objects, they lend themselves to all sorts of use and abuse: they are modded, hacked, and speedrun; they are anticipated, discussed, and critiqued; they are the materials for the creation of films, comics, and other games. In these uses and abuses, they extend beyond themselves and the subcultures that play with them, acting as allegorithms for computational culture,[244] rites bounded by circles that are equally messy and magical,[245] and player-produced metagames that, as game designer Richard Garfield puts it, "interact with life."[246]

Because videogames don't end with their design, any reflection on their political significance needs to consider the ways that their cultures and their players make use of them. There is no such thing as a game in itself; there are only ever games in social context, games with history, games-in-play, games that generate other games.[247] All games are already metagames. While metagames can be "games about games" or "the games we play in, on, around, and through games or before, during, and after games," they are, as Stephanie Boluk and Patrick Lemieux put it, "for all intents and purposes...the only kind of games that we play."[248] Moreover, as such medial objects, metagames are the locus of a critical, creative potential that indirectly involves the political valence of contemporary technology. Thinking and playing through metagames turns our attention from the relatively static object of the videogame to:

> alternate histories of play defined not by code, commerce, and computation but by the diverse practices and material discontinuities that emerge between the human experience of playing videogames and their nonhuman operations. Metagames transform videogames from a mass medium and cultural commodity into instruments, equipment, tools, and toys for playing, competing, spectating, cheating, trading, breaking, making, and ultimately intervening in the sensory and political economies of those technologies responsible for the privatization of play. And although the term *metagame* has been used within many wargaming, roleplaying, and collectible card gaming communities for decades, since the turn of the millennium it has become a popularly used and particularly useful label for a diverse form of play, a game design paradigm, and a way of life occurring not only around videogames but around all forms of digital technology.[249]

Thinking and playing through metagames makes it clear how the relatively "static" "object" of the videogame is anything but.

Consider Penn and Teller's *Desert Bus* (1995), reputedly the worst game in the world. Created by the comedian-magicians in the early 1990s as a rejoinder to Janet Reno's suggestion that videogames should be less violent and more educational, the game provides a thorough and thoroughly tedious education in what it's like to drive the straight line from Tucson, Arizona to Las Vegas, Nevada at 45 miles per hour in real time. Nothing much happens during the eight-hour journey: the player nudges the bus back onto the road as it lists slightly and constantly to the left, a bug hits the windshield about halfway through, and the player receives a single point when they reach their destination.

That's it.

Desert Bus provided the material for a metagame by sketch comedy group Loading Ready Run. The group wanted to find a way to raise donations for the charity Child's Play, so they decided to put on a telethon: they would play "this horrible, horrible, horrible game for as long as people were willing to pay us to do so. And it turns out this is a very long time."[250] The first telethon was broadcast out of a basement in Victoria, BC in 2007, and it went on for four days during which the members of Loading Ready Run became increasingly sleep deprived and profoundly bored:

> The thing with *Desert Bus* as a game is that it is so boring that I can't imagine anyone wanting to sit and watch it, or watch someone play it, for any great period of time. So what made *Desert Bus* interesting was what we were doing, because we were incredibly bored as well and [were] trying to pass the time. So we started giving people challenges, saying, Okay, give us something that you want us to do – play upside down, play with a costume on, play with our feet, do something else – and, you know, make a donation and we'll do it. And that became sort of a thing; that's sort of become what it is all about...Year One *Desert Bus* was weird.[251]

The group raised nearly $22,000 in its first year, and has raised more than $3 million more in the years since. The charity is only one of the ways that Loading Ready Run *made use* of the game for other ends – one of the ways that the group turned *Desert Bus* into the material for making other games. The fact of filming and broadcasting the game in the first place was itself a form of metagaming, even before the addition of the alternative modes of play, the singing and dancing, the interaction with viewers, the preparation that goes into the event, and the press that covered it. *Desert Bus* was and is the center around which these alternative and playful modes of sociality arose, modes that were loosely connected to the game's ruleset but were governed far more by *paidia* than *ludus*.

Although alternative modes of sociality like these contravene the norms of single-player games, many of them, like the filming and broadcasting of gameplay, have now become commonplace.[252] Nevertheless, critics, designers, and players too often forget that these metagaming practices are normal and ubiquitous, and that they signal something about the relationship between games and culture. Play can mount an effective challenge to control.

Play and Counterplay

Different practices of play appeal to different kinds of players. A player needs to willingly follow the rules of a game in order to move toward its objective, which generally involves adopting an inefficient means: using feet instead of hands, or jumping over obstacles, or actually playing a videogame instead of just cheating in a new high score. These features make up the heart of Bernard Suits' definition of gameplay: it is the "attempt to achieve a specific state of affairs [prelusory goal], using only means permitted by rules, where the rules [lusory means] prohibit use of more efficient in favor of less efficient means [constitutive rules], and where the rules are accepted just because they make possible such activity [lusory attitude]." Playing a game is, in short, "a voluntary attempt to overcome unnecessary obstacles."[253] These features also provide Suits with a typology of player types: "triflers recognize rules but not goals, cheats recognize goals but not rules, players recognize both rules and goals, and spoilsports recognize neither rules nor goals."[254]

The trifler/cheat/player/spoilsport typology has the distinction of paying close attention to those elements of gameplay that cause videogames to resonate so strongly with computational culture: rules, goals, and what Suits describes as "the institution of the game." It also resonates with Johann Huizinga, known in game studies for his foundational description of the magic circle that bounds and enables play. Whether demarcated literally or metaphorically, the magic circle is a separate and limited space and time in which players freely obey "an absolute and peculiar order."[255] It's an essential concept for understanding the relationship of games to culture, and one that game studies scholars often reference without analyzing. Of particular importance in *Homo Ludens*, especially in the context of this chapter's concerns with unconventional forms of play, are Huizinga's comments on the importance of rules and their relationship to different sorts of players:

> All play has its rules. They determine what "holds" in the temporary world circumscribed by play. The rules of a game are absolutely binding and all no doubt. Paul Valery once in passing gave expression to a very cogent thought when he said: "No skepticism is possible where the rules of a game are concerned, for the principle underlying them is an unshakable truth..." Indeed, as soon the rules are transgressed the whole play-world collapses.[256]

The "truth" of the game is "unshakable" in a way that the truths of the world never are, since play would be impossible without the security that this truth imparts and requires. Trespassing against the rules, as with cheating, means the breakdown of play, and signals the presence of a non-player.[257] Huizinga goes on:

> The player who trespasses against the rules or ignores them is a "spoil-sport." The spoil-sport is not the same as the false player, the cheat; for the latter pretends to be playing the game and, on the face of it, still acknowledges the magic circle. It is curious to note how much more lenient society is to

the cheat than to the spoil-sport. This is because the spoil-sport shatters the play-world itself. By withdrawing from the game he reveals the relativity and fragility of the play-world in which he had temporarily shut himself with others. He robs play of its *illusion*…Therefore he must be cast out.[258]

In breaking the rules, the cheat at least acknowledges their importance to the "institution" of the game, recognizing that the game could not exist without a general faith in those rules. The spoilsport, on the other hand, has no interest in the rules of the game or in the existence of the game at all. Because of this, the spoilsport not only "collapses" the play-world – they *shatter* it.

Huizinga's principal argument – that play not only models civilization but founds it – suggests that the rules of a game are akin to the laws of a society. Just as a game breaks down in the absence of an agreement to its "truth," so too can society break down given the presence of people who refuse to obey its laws or respect its ideals: "[i]n the world of high seriousness, too, the cheat and the hypocrite have always had an easier time of it than the spoil-sports, here called apostates, heretics, innovators, prophets, conscientious objectors, etc."[259] In refusing the legitimacy of God or State or any other instrument of political theology, these spoilsports destabilize the societies in which they live.

More than that: spoilsports threaten civilization itself. Huizinga's player-citizen metonymy extends to the international system, where bad states operate in the same way as bad players, refusing to follow the rules of the geopolitical game.[260] Here and elsewhere, and in sharp distinction to Suits,[261] Huizinga makes clear his allegiance to those Enlightenment political philosophies according to which all of humankind is progressing toward some natural endpoint. And he expresses his fear that this progress could be held up: "[t]he cheat or the spoil-sport shatters civilization itself. To be a sound culture-creating force this play-element must be pure. It must not consist in the darkening or debasing of standards set up by reason, faith, or humanity."[262] On the basis of his concern for progress, his alarm at the rise of National Socialism, and his disinterest in that fourth, unthought player type, the trifler, Huizinga registers his desire that play remain "pure."

Cheats, spoilsports, and triflers relate differently to rules and goals, but they share a common ability to destabilize game-worlds. And while cheats and spoilsports can "collapse" or "shatter" these worlds through their disregard for rules and goals, particularly when this disregard takes the antisocial form of counterplay,[263] the rule-abiding triflers also act as forces of destabilization, though of a different kind. When rules are bent far enough, they may be as good as broken. Moreover, these acts of destabilization or destruction are often acts of creation as well. Huizinga: "[i]t sometimes happens...that the spoil-sports in their turn make a new community with rules of its own."[264] This double role – destructive and creative – means that cheats, spoilsports, and triflers are all creatures of the boundary: they question it, test it, cross it, refuse it – and they *enact* it.[265]

The relation of cheats, spoilsports, and triflers to gamespace seems to mirror the relation of trickster to the world. As Lewis Hyde notes, while trickster – whether Coyote or Hermes, Eshu or Loki – is routinely described as a boundary *crosser*, "there are also cases in which trickster *creates* a boundary, or brings to the surface a distinction previously hidden from sight."[266] Gods of the threshold and heralds of contingency, tricksters are feared for their "disruptive behavior" but also "honored as the creators of culture."[267] Although they most often act out of selfishness or caprice, tricksters nevertheless create new institutions – new worlds – that benefit others. Even when they stop short of creating those new worlds, their "seemingly asocial actions" nevertheless benefit those worlds that already exist: they "continue to keep our world lively and give it the flexibility to endure."[268]

Triflers might seem like the tricksters of the digital age. Bored with the goals that games offer up, they probe their boundaries, discovering their limitations and imperfections. They struggle "to escape boredom and produce difference," or to create new worlds, and while they find that "this too has its limits" – that gamespace remains a rulebound place offering only an imperfect freedom – they thereby come to an understanding of the ways in which games and gamespace alike are constructed.[269] They reveal the non-necessity of its construction, and they create new, equally non-necessary, equally unfree worlds.[270]

But taking Wark seriously means distinguishing between the trifler and the trickster. If the latter is the god of the threshold, then this is because *there is* a threshold between the earthly and the divine; one can pass from here to there, provided that one knows the way. No such passage is possible for the trifler because there is no threshold and no other world: "[t]he game has not just colonized reality, it is also the sole remaining ideal."[271] In Wark's *Gamer Theory*, the platonic cave, out of which emerges the enlightened philosopher, becomes The Cave™, at once an entertainment space, a game system, and an allegory for the postmodern condition – something that cannot be escaped. Which is not necessarily a problem. Rather than trying to escape, the gamer becomes a trifler, "playing with style to understand the game as a *form*" and trifling "with the game to understand the nature of gamespace as a world – as *the* world."[272] The trifler is uniquely equipped to understand both the totalizing extent of gamespace and the failure of gamespace to totalize: in trifling with individual games, they "discover in what way gamespace falls short of its self-proclaimed perfection."[273] Their work on the game's algorithm is an allegorithm for the nature of what used to be known as reality; it is a metagame proper.

Speedrunning *Super Mario Bros.*

Triflers understand how gamespace works because they practice its dominant form – process, algorithm, code. This enables them to critique it, illuminating its conditions of possibility, its history, its technical limitations, its failures, and the implications of following it to its logical conclusion. This is all well and good, but it's also decidedly abstract.[274] What does it look like in practice? What does the gamer theorist *do*?

Player practices are as diverse as the skillsets that players bring to the games they play. Artistically minded players make machinima, short films that repurpose the assets of a videogame to dramatic or comedic effect. Socially inclined players stream or create let's plays, text- or video-based playthroughs of games that let the player demonstrate their mastery, offer commentary, highlight little known details of a popular game, or bring an unpopular one to light. Investigative players explore games in order to write walkthroughs or discover ideal routes, overlooked combinations, or hidden exploits, and players concerned with efficiency use these discoveries to optimize play. Technically proficient players modify existing games, whether to tweak minor details or to create completely new games out of this old ludic material. Players on the mischievous-to-misanthropic spectrum engage in everything from espionage to social engineering to player-killing.

While each of these practices offers is worth studying on its own,[275] the ur-form of trifling is perhaps the speedrun – a practice diverging from regular play just enough to make its differences worth studying. In a speedrun, a player attempts to reach the end of a game as quickly as possible through game knowledge, manual dexterity, and any other means that the game provides. Speedrunners aren't supposed to cheat (by, say, splicing individually perfected segments together to create the illusion of a perfectly executed overall run), but they can do everything else: glitch through walls, manipulate the randomness of numbers, boost through otherwise unavoidable cutscenes, abuse temporary invincibility, perform credits warps and other forms of sequence breaking, and on and on. Because skilled speedrunners have learned to make use of these kinds of strategies and tools, they can complete glitchy games in a fraction of the time that it would take even a very good player.

Take the most iconic console game as an example. A skilled player can beat *Super Mario Bros.* in under 7 minutes, using the warp zones in worlds 1-2 and 4-2 and avoiding death entirely. A speedrunner can beat it in five. In 2004, Scott Kessler set the world record at 5:10:00. Trevor Seguin unseated him, hitting 5:06:00, and then Kessler reclaimed the title, shaving a second off Seguin's time. That year, Andrew Gardikis, then 14, started speedrunning the game. By 2007, he had discovered and learned how to consistently employ a range of glitches and techniques that let him cut off five seconds, hitting 5:00:60.[276]

The techniques employed by *Super Mario Bros.* speedrunners are phenomenally precise.[277] Simpler techniques are feats of skill and technical literacy: jumping backwards from a standing start in order to gain momentum; knowing when to stop holding right in order to avoid losing time by hitting the edge of a block; performing a wall jump on the edge of a green pipe by hitting a single pixel; avoiding the conditions that would trigger the time-consuming end-of-level fireworks. Advanced techniques are more demanding in every way. The best players can slide through solid bricks, pass through the flagpole without lowering the flag, and even change the destination of the green pipes that Mario descends.

The discovery and exploitation of these techniques are equally important. Take the "wrong warp" glitch, which speedrunner Darbian explains in a helpful tutorial video:

There's [only] one spot in the game's memory that tells the game where to send Mario if he takes a warp, [that is] climbing a vine or going down a pipe...There [are] some levels where there [are] multiple warps, such as [4-2], where you have a vine here and just to the right you have a pipe. So that value in memory has to get updated at some point, and the developers chose to use the screen's position to determine when that value gets updated.[278]

In 4-2, players usually want to hit the hidden coin blocks that let them climb up the vine to the warp zone leading to 8-1, but, as it turns out, this is suboptimal. Speedrunners who descend the green pipe just to the right can get to the warp zone faster, providing they're able to prevent that global memory value from being updated so that the pipe leads to the warp zone rather than the usual coin room. So how to prevent that memory update?

There just so happens to be a way to push Mario ahead on the screen. Right now, [my x-position is] 112 pixels; well, I can push him further ahead on the screen, and what that allows me to do is reach the warp pipe before the screen has scrolled as far as it normally would...The way you do this is to do backward jumps against blocks, like this. Every time I do one of these, Mario's x-position goes up. So now, his x-position's at 138: I pushed him 26 pixels ahead, and you can visibly see that he's now under the "W" in "WORLD" and no longer under the second digit in the coin counter. By getting this far ahead I've now reached this pipe before the screen has scrolled far enough ahead to update that value in memory.[279]

The wrong warp glitch requires that the player be able to perform backwards jumps against blocks, but it also requires that they know a host of things: they need to know how to keep track of Mario's x-position, that jumping against blocks modifies Mario's x-position, that modifying his x-position will prevent that value in the game's memory from being updated, that this will send Mario into the warp zone rather than the coin room, and that doing all of this rather than just ascending the vine will save the long five seconds that it takes to watch the vine slowly creep its way up into the next screen. This is how Andrew Gardikis took the world record so decisively in 2007.

Saving five seconds is obviously worth the hassle and risk, but where to go from there? Seven years after Gardikis first introduced the wrong warp, he had pushed his time to 4:58:09. By 2016, Blubbler, Kosmicd12, and Darbian had achieved times in the range of 4:47:194 to 4:57:69 – differences now being measured in milliseconds, and achieved thanks to a combination of new discoveries and a mastery of the controller inputs required to exploit them. In October of 2016, after 21,000 recorded attempts, Darbian broke the 4:57:00 barrier: he hit 4:56:878 and set a new world record by successfully executing the flagpole glitch, a frame- and *sub*pixel-perfect trick that had previously only been achieved with the assistance of replay tools, twice. Here are a sample set of instructions for how to perform the glitch in World 1-1:

> Step 1: Jump and land on the first pixel of the 2nd stair from the top. You must NOT be holding B when you land.
>
> Step 2: At this point, press Right + B for exactly two frames. These first two steps manipulate your x-subpixel and your x-speed subpixel to a value that allows Mario to clip into the flagpole block.
>
> Step 3: Do a full jump and do the inputs for [the] flagpole glitch. On [frame 1341], apply these inputs: 1st frame: Left; 2nd frame: Left; 3rd frame: Left; 4th frame: Left + A.[280]

In the highly-viewed video where Darbian achieves the new world record,[281] he replies to a viewer of his Twitch stream asking about his success rate with the glitch. "It's about 10 percent." After executing it in World 1-1 and 4-1, he reacts: "It's a go." His heart rate, which he monitors and displays on his Twitch stream, climbs from the 80s into the 90s. Executing the wrong warp, he moves through 8-1 and into 8-2, where he skips through the flagpole using another glitch involving Bullet Bill. "This is legitimately serious." His heart rate climbs: 115; 120; 130. By the end of Bowser's Castle, it hits 161. "That was it! That was it!"

Speedrunning is a form of what James Newman refers to as "superplay" – "a generic term that describes a range of gaming practices that differ significantly in their execution and implementation but that are bound together by a common desire to demonstrate mastery of the game through performance."[282] Not just one form of superplay among many, speedrunning "represents the ultimate expression of gamers' mastery of the system and of playing with videogames."[283] Nevertheless, it is not only "about" the mastery of individual players. As Newman points out, speedrunning and other forms of superplay are only possible on the basis of collaboration and the productive of collective knowledge. Darbian could not have set his *Super Mario Bros.* world record without the previous two decades of record attempts, code scraping, glitch hunting, and conversation. Post-facto viewer commentary and annotation were vital aspects of the speedrunners Newman studied in the mid-2000s, when speedruns were almost always unadorned gameplay videos accompanied by a textual explanation.[284] Early speedruns relegated the actual speedrunner to that text, and even there, runners tended to frame their success in terms of the work done by previous players.[285] While things have changed since the mid-2000s, with players' faces (and heartbeats) embedded in live streams and video records, community is no less important in 2017 than it was then. Runners like Darbian continue to namecheck their predecessors, and they do new things, too: they interact with viewers, publish speedrunning tutorials, gather in conventions, and respond to the press. Their interactions refigure the objects and practices they touch; even the games change, turning from single-player experiences into massively multiplayer online environments.[286] Speedrunners might not exactly be in the limelight, but YouTube and Twitch have brought them a lot more publicity than they ever enjoyed before.

So speedrunning remains a social practice. It involves the attempt to exercise perfect control, but it couches an individual runner's attempt in the speedrunning community. Additionally, and vitally, it engenders an understanding of the fallible, imperfect nature of videogames and the digital systems on which they rely. Runners rely on bugs to perform their runs, and they find themselves at the mercy of fickle, imperfect systems. Newman notes by way of example that Bill Carlton's attempt to claim the world record for *Missile Command* by playing the game for two uninterrupted days was foiled by cabinet resets or freezes – problems predictable enough for old arcade hardware, but that crop up on modern systems as well.[287]

These aspects of speedrunning – its situation in a community on the one hand and its simultaneous reliance on and susceptibility to bugs and breaks on the other – mean that speedrunning can be counted as a contravention of the usual exercise of control. If videogame control is something that an individual player exercises over a digital system, then speedrunning is a practice that transcends it. Seb Franklin: "speedruns place technical virtuosity and the will to distort software's intended use at the heart of a mode of gameplay that pushes beyond...If code takes the place of the referee that stops athletes profiting from running off the track, or the police that prevents drivers from ignoring red lights, the speedrunner's practice is to become nonexistent to this code."[288] Speedrunning is a "minor practice" that unsettles the perfection of the computational context in which it takes place. The speedrunner-as-trifler understands that rules are imperfect and systems are violable, provided that enough people come together to break them apart; their entire practice depends on this knowledge. Because speedrunners recognize video-games as ambivalent cultural artifacts despite our collective tendency to regard them as perfect digital systems, the "mastery" for which they strive is one that recognizes that ultimate mastery –

total and final control – can't be attained.

Datamining *Undertale*

Speedrunners aren't the only ones who recognize that video-games are ambivalent cultural artefacts. The biggest fans – the kind who obsess over small details or fantasize about characters – valorize their chosen games even while repurposing them. In fans like these, we see the obsessive tendencies of completionism channeled in novel directions – theorycrafting, datamining, fiction writing, and more, including, importantly, the creation of new games that draw from, acknowledge, or parody old ones. Games are, as Boluk and Lemieux argue, tools with which to create other games; metagaming and trifling practices are ultimately creative endeavors.

Undertale is as good an example of these creative endeavors as any. Interested in *EarthBound*, a quirky Japanese roleplaying game that was relatively unpopular in North America, and in *Homestuck*, a webcomic with a large and fanatical fanbase, Toby Fox spent his teenage years creating ROM hacks for the former and music for the latter. This prefigured the work he would later do on *Undertale*, an endlessly self-referential, self-critical game very clearly aware of the generic conventions of the RPG. Fox's work as a fan led to the creation of a game that engendered even more work by fans: artwork, webcomics, fonts, remixes, fanfic, slashfic, fan theories, cosplays, game mods, engine mods – Fox's game stretched well beyond the game itself. God even took an interest: Matthew Robert Patrick of YouTube channel The Game Theorists, chosen to represent content creators to the Vatican, gave the Pope a copy of the game (and made a video about the experience).[289] While any of these fan labors would make for an interesting case study, I want to focus here on fans' efforts to uncover and explain what might be *Undertale*'s biggest secret – the existence and significance of a character named W. D. Gaster. The means by which they discovered him involved practices similar to those employed by *Super Mario Bros.* speedrunners and the glitch hunters on whom they rely, but put to very different ends.

Most players of *Undertale* won't come across any evidence of Gaster's existence, since signs pointing directly to him only appear in the game 2.8% of the time it's played.[290] In most games, the player will only notice one faint, indirect clue – the River Person saying the following: "Beware the man who speaks in hands." Since no character in the game could be said to speak in hands, interested players dug for evidence: they looked at the game's filenames and figured out the dates that they were added; they read through dialogue in the game's code; they puzzled over the hints that Toby Fox left on social media; they edited the game to manipulate key values; they created reddit-based communities to communicate with one another and resources like the game's unofficial Wiki where the data that they were gathering could be collected and scrutinized. They used tools and techniques ranging from spectrograms to digital forensics to handwriting analysis not to win records or accolades but to explain a tiny but tantalizing mystery.

An exhaustive explanation of the Gaster mystery or the means by which players have arrived at their conclusions would be impossible here, but I will highlight a few of the most important aspects of both. It's in the combination of technical endeavor and fan theorizing that *Undertale* shines as an example of creative, non-masterful player practices. Different data gathered at different times through different means or through different lenses led fan theorists to propose different ideas for Gaster's genesis, from the wildly speculative to the carefully grounded.

Take Tidazi's "f/Fun" Theory: it made sense of Gaster by suggesting that he was partially responsible for *Undertale*'s messy timeline, and it did so through a careful interpretation of the capitalization of a single variable in the game's undertale.ini file. Initialization files like this one contain plain text that sets the parameters for a program. Because they're frequently used in videogames, triflers interested in looking closer at the game opened up undertale.ini very quickly after its release. Here's the undertale.ini file for a character partway through a no mercy run:

```
[Sans]
M1="1.000000"
[Toriel]
TK="1.000000"
Bscotch="2.000000"
[Flowey]
Met1="1.000000"
truename="1.000000"
alter2="1.000000"
[reset]
reset="1.000000"
[General]
fun="63.000000"
Name="Groark"
Love="10.000000"
Time="270416.000000"
Kills="60.000000"
Room="131.000000"
Gameover="2.000000"
[Papyrus]
M1="1.000000"
PK="1.000000"
```

The file will be longer or shorter depending on the player's accomplishments, and variables like "Love" and "Kills" will change as the player murders monsters. In addition to straightforward variables like these, however, there is "fun." Randomly set to a number between 1 and 100 at the beginning of a game, the "fun" value alters small and sometimes significant parts of a playthrough. Certain ranges of "fun," players soon discovered, would cause telephone calls to take place during particular moments in the game, the appearance of certain items to change, or non-player characters to appear.

The changes associated with different "fun" values were mostly innocuous, but there were a few that helped explain the mystery of Gaster. When the "fun" value was set to 61, 62, or 63, one of Gaster's "followers" appeared when the player reached Hotland. Pale gray, almost ghostly, they differed sharply in appearance from the other monsters in the area. They differed in conversation, too: they referenced Gaster himself, the "old" Royal Scientist who "fell into his creation." He "shattered across time and space," they reported, when one of his experiments "went wrong." When the "fun" value was set to 66, a new hallway with a strange gray door appeared in Waterfall, and one out of ten times the player entered, they might see an NPC named "Mystery Man" before he disappeared – an NPC whom the player base has agreed must be Gaster himself.

In the release version of the game, however, these events, and others believed to be associated with Gaster, would never occur on their own. They would only take place if the player modified not only the "fun" value to 61, 62, 63, or 66, but if they capitalized it as well: "Fun." Tidazi, the theorist of "f/Fun," explains:

There is a distinction between the two. I have good reason to believe that this was not an error, a typo, or a mistake of any kind. I believe that "Fun" is an acronym, specifically one like Love. At the end of a neutral run, Sans explains the misleading nature of the acronyms "LOVE" [which stands for "Level of Violence"] and "EXP" [which stands for "Execution Points"]. LOVE is also found under the [General] section of the ini, listed as "Love". Only the "L" is capitalized, not the whole word. The fact that new and different events are accessible only when "Fun" is capitalized is important. Building on this, the very nature and tone of the events that are accessible with a "Fun" value are distinctly different than those you can get with the default "fun". By capitalizing "Fun", you are acknowledging the fact that it is an acronym and identifying it as such.[291]

"Fun," then, would be "Fork Unification Number," Tidazi speculates – an index of the parallel universe in which the player character finds themselves. "Under this interpretation, the value of 'Fun' acts as the bridge between two branches, or forks, of the original convergence point in the timeline: Frisk's arrival in the Underground. If your current position in the timeline is near enough to the relative position in this fork, it establishes a point of convergence between the two timelines. This allows you to observe people and places that no longer exist in your timeline" – that is, Gaster's followers, and Gaster himself.

It's significant that the player needs to edit the name of the variable to turn it into something resembling acronyms like Love/LOVE. Only a few of the characters in *Undertale* are aware of the temporally confusing nature of their world, and only a few of these can manipulate it. Flowey, for instance, is conscious not only of the existence of multiple timelines, but of the fact that *Undertale* is a game with a save file – something that he can destroy: "Forget about escaping to your old SAVE FILE. It's gone FOREVER." Sans, for his part, knows not only that Frisk has or has not been violent, but that their violence can be quantified: "You will be judged for every EXP you've earned. What's EXP? It's an acronym. It stands for 'execution points.'" Sans has direct, intuitive access to Frisk's EXP and LOVE; he, like Flowey, seems to be able to read the game's files. Tidazi draws on this extra-diegetic awareness to speculate that Gaster and his followers are only *supposed* to show up when the player modifies the save file – that save file modification is part of the game's canon.[292] The player needs to manually re-introduce the "Fork Unification

Number" by capitalizing the "F" in "Fun" in order to bring Gaster, "shattered across time and space," back into the game.

Tidazi's theory is inventive and expansive, but it's probably wrong. A few months after they penned it, Toby Fox updated the game from version 1.00 to version 1.001, introducing a change to the "fun" value in the process: the player no longer needed to capitalize it in order to encounter the Mystery Man, Gaster's followers, or any of the other previously "Fun"-specific events. Meticulously researched and conceived, it only took a small change to a single data point for the "f/Fun" Theory to collapse.

Manipulating the "fun" value in undertale.ini allowed the player to interact with key figures in the Gaster mystery, but certain other Gaster-related events could only be accessed through more complicated means. Deeper investigations, like the use of the game's debug mode or a hexadecimal editor, yielded more information on Gaster, including the revelation of Room 264. Here, the player sees a confusing crawl of hieroglyphics – the Wing Dings font: ☜︎☝︎✌︎☹︎☹︎ ☝︎✝︎☜︎✞︎☞︎☜︎☜︎ ◆︎☜︎✝︎☞︎☜︎☝︎✌︎☜︎☜︎✌︎. "ENTRY NUMBER SEVENTEEN," it reads when converted to a normal typeface:

DARK DARKER YET DARKER
THE DARKNESS KEEPS GROWING
THE SHADOWS CUTTING DEEPER
PHOTON READINGS NEGATIVE
THIS NEXT EXPERIMENT
SEEMS
VERY
VERY
INTERESTING

WHAT DO YOU TWO THINK?

During a pacifist playthrough of the game, with which any play-

er going to these lengths will already be familiar, Frisk enters the
True Lab, learning about the experiments that led to the creation
of Flowey through a series of diary entries. Entry 17, however,
is missing. Here, after save editing and translating, the player
sees that it was written by someone else – "Wing Dings Gaster,"
the fans agree, the "man who speaks in hands." Other connec-
tions became clear when fans looked into other technical details,
like the names of the sprites used in-game; the weapons used
by Sans in the final fight of the no mercy run, for instance, were
called "Gaster Blasters." Still further information only appeared
when the game was updated, like the speculative connection between Sans, Clam Girl, and Gaster, or when Toby Fox updated
his Twitter account with old artwork.

Many fans speculated on what breadcrumbs like these might
mean, but a few went further. On Underminers, the subreddit
devoted to *Undertale* datamining, Karibil_Watar purported to
have "solved Gaster":

Tobyfox needed a reason to explain how Sans would suddenly be ridiculously overpowered and understood time travel,
and so he developed Gaster late in the game development
to explain it. Most of the appearances of him are mysterious
and creepy in game in order to provide Tobyfox an outlet
on which to add more content later if he wanted. Therefore,
attempts to connect him with the main plot of the game are
pointless.[293]

They had come to this conclusion by painstakingly putting together *Undertale*'s timeline – not the timeline of in-game events,
but the timeline of the game's development. Watar was able to
establish what they took to be a definitive development timeline because they could point to the dates during which different parts of the game's content were added. The community at
Underminers had extracted several lists of that content – Rooms,

Battles, Monsters, Music, and Objects. However, as Watar notes, "[c]ontent[s] within these lists are not uniform in their order": the place that an item occupies up or down any given list would not necessarily be an indication of when that item was created. Watar compared the Monsters and Battles lists, which stored their contents as arrays and therefore could not be easily reordered, and arrived at what they described as "a fairly stable way by which to judge Tobyfox's order of creation as he was much less likely to reorder them due to the difficulty." Cross-referencing the Battles and Monsters lists with significant in-game events and locations, Watar then demonstrated that all of the Gaster-related content was developed *after* the vast majority of the game. "Gaster never appears or is referenced in the game files until very late. The first place where he is ever referenced is at the very end of the Truelab implementation, when Sans' rooms were added to the game. He disappears from development until the very end of the Genocide Bosses with the Sans fight, which was after Tobyfox programmed the pacifist run and every other genocide run boss battle." The "mystery," according to Watar, had been solved.

Perhaps because they rested on scant information, theories like Tidazi's engendered lengthy and often complicated speculation. Theories like Watar's made reference to many more data points, and, in their seeming certainty, were brief; they felt less like theories than assemblies of facts. Other theories – an incredible range of them – proposed meanings for Gaster that ran the speculative gamut. While their plausibility might be important for some fans, the question of whether they hold water isn't significant in the context of the ludopolitical questions under examination here. Instead, the emphasis should be placed on what the game's fans have *done* with their theories, and how those accomplishments have reframed the relationship between designer, player, and meaning. Digging up data and assembling it into more or less plausible narratives, *Undertale*'s fans have created an expanded universe for the game that may as well be legitimate. Expanded universes in large franchises like *Star Wars* usually consist of official releases, but in *Undertale*, the "property" of a single, open-minded creator rather than a massive corporation, the canon is flexible. So we might say that *Undertale* has no single story – but this wouldn't be right. Rather, we should say that the *Undertale* canon *consists of* its fan theories. It stands to reason that Toby Fox, coming of age on *EarthBound* and *Homestuck* forums, would place more significance on the works of fans than a corporation like Lucasfilm would do, and this is apparent in his lax approach to fan-made merchandise ("if hand-made and few, it's OK," reads his blog; "I really don't want to stop fans from having fun or expressing themselves"), his general refusal to comment on fans' interpretations of the game, and the game's embrace of multiple, non-exclusive timelines. Fans of *Undertale* haven't needed to wrest creative control from the game's originator in order to do their work. They've done it in tandem.[294]

Although *Undertale* refuses to let the player treat its world cavalierly, it embraces a multiplicity of interpretations, timelines, and outcomes. Why *couldn't* it be the case that Gaster is the brother of Sans and Papyrus, or that Gaster split into Sans and Papyrus, or that Gaster and *Yume Nikki*'s Uboa are the same character, or even that Sans is *EarthBound*'s Ness? Toby Fox's *Undertale*, however that might be defined, is neither complete nor authoritative. Put differently, just as there is no *Undertale* without Toby Fox, there is also no *Undertale* without its fans – and not only because they backed the project on Kickstarter. It's the fans who give coherence and meaning to Gaster, which means that it's the fans who make *Undertale* into something more than the short experience that it otherwise might be. Gaster enriches the game. While the details of the individual meanings that fans ascribe to him might differ from one interpretation to another, there is a meaning that obtains across all of their interpretations. Gaster signifies a fandom significant in itself – not significant as an addendum to the original, authoritative creation, but as the condition for the act of creation. It complicates the usual conception that readers have concerning the authority of the author, namely their univocal control.

Player involvement can change the meaning of the game for the developer, too. Toby Fox is notoriously reluctant to do interviews or discuss *Undertale*, but other designers often comment on this process. Developer commentary at speedrunning marathons and on Twitch streams, for instance, is frequently punctuated by exclamations of surprise and appreciation. Derek Yu, the designer of the roguelike cave exploration game *Spelunky*, was similarly delighted by what players managed to make out of an apparently meaningless item: he had inserted the useless and fragile eggplant and a related Easter egg into the game at a whim fairly late in the game's development cycle, and had then thought no more about it. Players, however, were intrigued. The eggplant was difficult to lug around, which made navigating the challenging platformer even harder than before, but players nevertheless experimented with it shortly after the game's initial console launch, trying to do different things with it in order to make something happen. Nothing worked. Once the game was ported to the PC, however, they discovered a texture file for an eggplant monster that looked a little like the game's final boss. After some experimentation, they figured out how to make the eggplant work: when they brought it all the way to the boss and hit him with it, his head turned into a giant eggplant. The eggplant run was born.

This was the point where Yu's relationship to his game changed. Players first achieved the eggplant run legitimately in multiplayer, with one player carrying the eggplant and the others protecting them. Soon, though, the *Spelunky* community started to speculate about a solo eggplant run. One player managed it, and sent a video of the run to Yu:

It completely blew my mind. It involved so many tricks and glitches and stuff like that that were put together separately by different players, even. It just makes *Spelunky* feel like so much bigger for me, like all of a sudden *Spelunky* for me is now this new world, and I feel like a stranger in it. Which is just a great feeling.[295]

The designer sets a fairly careless challenge; the players meet that challenge; the players exceed that challenge, and in doing so, they reframe the game, expanding its worldly boundaries for player and designer alike. In taking control from the designer, they illustrate the interestingly generative ways in which the designer never had complete control in the first place.

Games can be communally produced objects to play *with*, not just finished commercial products to play. Major studios want to maintain control over their products, however, which Yu understands: "I think especially with a big budget game, they want to have a lot of control. You don't want to leave things to chance, you don't want to have glitches, and you don't want the players doing unexpected things. You worry about whether the player is going to get from beginning to end." Confusing games don't test well with focus groups, so profit-maximizing developers insert signposts to ensure that players don't get lost; inconsistent or glitchy products don't review well, so the same developers take pains to avoid them (even if they sometimes fail to do so). Smaller studios, less concerned with profit maximization than with simply making a reasonable profit at all, don't need to worry so much about maintaining that level of control over players' actions. When developers struggle less to control the players' actions, they can create much more compelling gameplay. This, Yu suggests, is what is "real," "immersive," and "fun" about games: "discovering things on my own, making my own mistakes – that's what gives the games meaning. When I feel like someone just has their hand on my shoulder...I just feel like I'm losing a lot of the meaning of games, which is that joy of discovery."[296]

Mythologizing Twitch Plays Pokémon

As an everyday practice – speedrunning, streaming, remixing, shipping, theorizing, and so on – trifling often either goes unnoticed or becomes part of mainstream gaming culture. But there are exceptional instances of trifling, too – times when the trifler's ability to define new boundaries and create new worlds is on display. One such instance begins on Twitch. In August 2014, Amazon spent nearly $1,000,000,000 on what was then a relatively new platform devoted to live-streaming videogames. On Twitch, viewers tune in to see people playing through games, with live video of the players usually accompanying the gameplay. The move caught a few mainstream media commentators off-guard, some of whom had never heard of the site. David Carr of the *New York Times*, for instance, seemed incredulous: "After surfing around for 90 minutes, I couldn't help asking, is this really a thing?"[297] But most market watchers were unsurprised. Twitch has been extraordinarily successful since its launch in 2011:[298] in 2013 it was attracting 45 million unique visitors per month, and by 2014 that number had more than doubled. By the beginning of 2015, 100 million people were logging on every month to watch other people play videogames.

But numbers don't tell the whole story – and its growth isn't the most interesting aspect of Twitch. The platform owes its success to many things, not the least of which is its sociability: the viewers sprawling on the "infinite couch" are watching, but they are also chatting, *seeing themselves* chatting, and occasionally *hearing the streamer* chat *back*. If it's true that there's nothing quite like the experience of hearing your name on television, then there must be some similar magic in hearing your name directed – albeit from a slightly different screen – at you. Twitch is a social experience, but it is also a profoundly self-conscious one.

At the beginning of Bill Wasik's *And Then There's This: How Stories Live and Die in Viral Culture*, he describes one of the conditions that distinguishes viral material from pre-internet fads:

> If there is one attribute of today's consumers, whether of products or of media, that differentiates them from their forebears of even twenty years ago, it is this: they are so acutely aware of how *media narratives themselves* operate, and of how their own behavior fits into these narratives, that their awareness feeds back almost immediately into their consumption itself.[299]

Twitch viewers know that they are viewing someone else doing what they could do; they know that they are part of a miniature media ecosystem; they know that the player knows about the importance of their role; they feel that what they are doing, inconsequential, passive, and cloistered though it might appear, is somehow significant; and they may even know that they know all of these things. Embedded in game culture in general and the niche cultures of individual games, genres, or movements in particular, they are conscious that they are engaged in something that still perplexes the mainstream. It takes a "gamer" to appreciate all of those informal features that lie outside of the game itself: livestreams, forum threads, Let's Plays, machinima, walkthroughs, and so on. This appreciation is the hallmark of the insider: it's what defines whatever's left of "gamer culture."

How does this rhetoric of reflection – a consciousness of and attitude to subjectivity that characterizes modernity as such[300] – relate to the problem of control? And what does the self-consciousness that helps sustain services like Twitch have to do with unconventional modes of play like trifling? What, that is, can the self-conscious use of Twitch tell us about the self as it is situated in algorithmic culture?

In the spring of 2014, tens of thousands of people began to play a single copy of *Pokémon Red* at the same time. An anonymous Australian programmer had developed code to emulate the Game Boy game on modern computers, parsing input from Twitch chat ("a," "b," "up," "down") and assigning it to the corresponding key presses, and players had descended on the new channel to contribute. *Pokémon Red* is a relatively straightforward game involving map navigation and turn-based battles; a normal player can beat it in 26 hours. But because the thousands of players of Twitch Plays Pokémon were effectively fighting for a single controller, they took a lot longer than that. Here's an example of the text from Twitch Chat over the course of five seconds during the morning of February 17, 2014, four days into the social experiment, that might explain why:

<skillat> left
<xtagtv> up
<sapphiresin> up
<extraspectre> GIVE START BACK
<risfayne> down
<startsomethingg> up
<chairs9816> up
<kalamara61121> up
<diogritor> down
<lakek_> up
<mormonofdeath> b
<mrwetball> up
<torpidwaters> up
<ogszyphent> yp
<itsjoshmate> up
<kawfii> up
<transall> up
<xxdelkarxx> ╭ʊ ☐_☐╮ʊ USE HELIX ╭ʊ ☐_☐╮ʊ
<pexy94> B

<kevinro> right
<phallotismo> select
<mountainmanjed> dpwn
<razrvg> up
<napalm985> up
<snubz221> up
<spiderman97828> up
<hero88go> right
<helokity> up
<kingwampy> PRAISE LORD HELIX
<beerisgood69> downdown
<theresmoretothemap> up
<thecrimpdude> up
<brunotheminer> UP
<rislyeu> down
<masterhack91> select[301]

The text parser would crawl through this mass of text, periodically collecting a command, and then apply it to the game in a process that was by turns captivating, frustrating, hilarious, and rewarding. The protagonist, Red, would spin in a circle rather than advancing, continually and pointlessly open the menu, or repeatedly save. Sometimes, there was just enough consensus to move the protagonist forward.

The first Twitch Plays Pokémon social experiment successfully concluded after 16 days of continuous play during which players, trolls, and the programmer reacted to one another in a series of provocations and adaptations. When Red entered an area featuring cliffs, for instance, a certain set of trolls would instruct him to jump off of them, wasting time. The same group would pause the game by pressing START over and over again, frustrating any attempt at gameplay. Even those players attempting to beat the game had a hard time collectively navigating its more challenging sections, like the mazes and corners where Red could easily get stuck. The principal programmer and a group of active users responded to this tragedy in the commons by throttling the START command, creating a script to hide commands from Twitch Chat in order to facilitate coordination, and coding in a "democracy" mode to complement the "anarchy" that had preceded it, allowing the protagonist to follow orders from the most popular command given during a brief period rather than the most recently collected command.

These technical adaptations complicated and enriched the player narrative that was emerging from the chaos of the gameplay. The actual story of *Pokémon Red* took a backseat to the ongoing story of the players' attempt to coordinate with one another and beat the game (along with the trolls who were attempting to thwart them), but the original game's narrative elements played a mythological role in the world of Twitch Plays Pokémon. More than that: their narrative, assisted by an avalanche of brilliantly irreverent fan art to which no textual description could do justice, *made* the world. In the chatlog above, players write "USE HELIX" and "PRAISE LORD HELIX," for instance; these are references to the Helix Fossil, a mostly-useless in-game item that the protagonist repeatedly pulled out of their pack and examined thanks to the mess of player inputs. The Twitch Plays Pokémon community agreed upon a meaning for these actions: uncertain about what to do, Red was "consulting" the Helix Fossil; a totem that gave advice, it became something animate, prophetic – "a tribute to the power of anarchy and a symbol of what thousands of people can accomplish by almost working together to achieve goals they sort-of share." As game reporter Sam Barsanti put it:

[T]he Helix was promoted from "magic advice giver" to "messiah," which is certainly a reasonable leap to make. Cries of "Praise Helix!" arose from the chat whenever things went well, and it became so integral to the adventure that some people thought bringing the fossil to the Pokémon Laboratory was more important than actually beating the game. After 11 straight days of lugging around a useless rock, Twitch Plays Pokémon reached the lab and earned its Omanyte. He was proclaimed Lord Helix, god of anarchy, and there was much rejoicing.[302]

Taken together in the context of the Twitch Plays Pokémon metagame, Helix and a small cast of associated characters – Flareon the False Prophet, Dome Fossil the anti-Helix, Pidgeot the Bird Jesus, ABBBBBBK) the Charmander, AATTVVV the Venomoth – played out a dramatic narrative intimately associated with the game's structure. Helix was praised because the chat continued to examine the Fossil, and Helix became the God of Anarchy because the chat valorized its non-democratic origins.

Twitch Plays Pokémon's mythology, then, was shaped in concert with its technical affordances, but it was also shaped by its meta-narrative. There is no Twitch Plays Pokémon without the *story of* Twitch Plays Pokémon – the story told by reporters and archivists and fans and people looking back on the event with fondness and nostalgia. Twitch Plays Pokémon exists now not as the play experience, or even as a playback of the play experience (which, at 16 days, can't be experienced again), but as the dozens of reports about what it was like and what it signified. For *Ars Technica*, for instance, the social experiment was about human struggle:

Twitch Plays Pokémon is a bleak-but-perfect summary of the human condition – a group of people unified behind a common cause that struggles and fails to accomplish even the most basic tasks. We ostensibly want the same thing, yet we expend Herculean amounts of effort only to end up right back where we started – at best. And that's the case even without considering the people who are only out for themselves.[303]

For *Game Informer*, it was about the creation of meaning:

> In many ways, the development of Twitch Plays Pokémon...
> can be seen as an allegory for much of how civilization works.
> We assign meaning to what was once meaningless. We create
> symbols and attach characteristics to these symbols to un-
> derstand them. We create stories not only to make sense of
> our past, but also because it's fun and entertaining to do so.
> These fundamental aspects of human existence are what has
> led to mythologies and religions being formed. Twitch Plays
> Pokémon is no different in this sense; the narrative surround-
> ing it all comes from a love and a need to tell stories.[304]

Commentaries suggesting that the meaning of Twitch Plays
Pokémon was meaning as such make good sense, and they provide the reader with another layer of meaning: Twitch Plays
Pokémon was significant because of the way that it encouraged
reflection on its own significance.

This isn't just a function of the passage of time. Twitch Plays
Pokémon has in a sense only ever existed in this self-referential
context. The early days of the event saw a little bit of reporting
and some tentative commentary; as it trickled out, it attracted
new viewers and new players: six thousand, ten thousand, twen-
ty. Stories appeared on mainstream gaming sites like *Destructoid*
as soon as two days after the whole thing began, and those stories fed back into the play experience.[305] Twitch Plays Pokémon
was mediated by the players' implicit understanding that they
were engaged in an act of myth-making and that they were creating something they would look back on later through the lens
of the reporter and the critic. It was always a story for the players
of Twitch Plays Pokémon and for the audience observing it from
a distance, a story about temporal disconnection and narrative,
about observation and mediation, and about the mostly-uncon-
scious self-reflection that accompanies any act of communal cre-

ation. Twitch itself hailed the players' accomplishment, citing the work of "Bird Jesus, ATV, Double-A Jay, Air Jordan, King Fonz, O Master Helix, and you."[306] Whether an expression of earnest appreciation or a cynical act of corporate capitalism, Twitch was speaking to the players of the social experiment in their own terms.

With Twitch Plays Pokémon, then, community is self-evidently important as the self-reflective condition of play. In this state of self-reflection, Twitch Plays Pokémon, for all of its technical brilliance and memetic currency, seems to reveal itself as a distinctly *modern* phenomenon – something that might have emerged at the end of the nineteenth century, had the technology and the culture been ready. It indexes what Elizabeth S. Goodstein calls a "rhetoric of reflection" on subjectivity, a self-conscious rhetoric that emerges alongside the democratizations of leisure, skepticism, and boredom that characterized late modernity.[307] This skeptical ennui and an associated feeling of unfreedom stretch today into the subject itself and thereby encourage a rhetoric of *reflection* on the subject.[308] Modernity involves a critical but frequently disempowered way of feeling about the subject, "or more precisely, a form of reflective distance that becomes a new attitude toward experience altogether."[309]

Goodstein's critique of this reflective distance is useful for understanding modern subjectivity in general and mediated subjectivity in particular. Today, leisure, skepticism, and boredom appear nowhere more clearly than in the aimlessness of internet browsing: swinging between interest and boredom, browsers periodically find themselves lifted out of their stupor by the realization of the futility of it all – a mostly useless realization, since it generally doesn't do much to change the browser's behavior.[310] Unable to interact in any meaningful fashion, the browser remains temporarily stuck in a comportment to the world characterized by the complete lack of control and perhaps by a quiet frustration with that fact. The browser, in other words, remains governed by control, even in absence.

Twitch Plays Pokémon, as an emblematic internet phenomenon, might seem like a simple extension of this bored, browsing state, but there is a significant difference between the distanced and reflective "man without qualities" whom Goodstein takes as an emblem of boredom on the one hand and the engaged and reflective player of Twitch Plays Pokémon on the other. Rather than pulling a viewer out of their stupor and then depositing them back in it, powerless to change their state and frustrated by that fact, Twitch Plays Pokémon trifled with the usual modes of viewing and browsing alike, encouraging viewers to play and frustrating players from taking their customary control. In doing so, it provided its viewer-players with a different way of acting in the world. Learning the structure of the site and the original game, Twitch Plays Pokémon's designer took advantage of the rules that governed each in order to create something new and weird – something that, in its strangeness, *required* explanation. Twitch Plays Pokémon required a mythology. The reflection that was prompted in this state was accompanied by the need to make meaning out of something wonderful and confusing. The reflection of the participant was a reflection conscious of the structure of the game, of the culture, and of their situation in both. Powerless to affect the game, they instead created a culture.

Trifling and Time

Myth-making, datamining, and speedrunning seem like three disparate forms of trifling, joined together by their interest in games' rules and their disregard for goals but little else. This lack of focus seems to distinguish them from the clear focus of the previous chapters, in which examples of game design directly thematized temporality: a responsibility for previous actions in *Spec Ops: The Line*, the resentment of an unchangeable past in *Braid*, the irreversibility of one's actions in *Undertale*, and the importance of embracing the eternal return in *Bastion*. Each of these design-based contraventions of control was tied closely to the need to come to terms with finitude. But here, in these player practices, we also see three examples of player practices that are joined in their relationship to time, if a bit less centrally.

Speedrunning places a new emphasis on time, making it the center of gameplay rather than an incidental framework. It might seem like the attempt to get it in hand is a controlling one, but this isn't right: speedrunning is a hobby characterized principally by practice and failure and only rarely punctuated by the accomplishment of a personal best, let alone a world record – and even then, players know that their times will not stand forever. New techniques can be discovered, improvements made. In replacing the comparatively easy pleasure of playing a game *well* with playing it *perfectly*, which is to say in the fastest time possible, speedrunners are substituting the sensation of mastery achieved with its mostly fruitless pursuit. This is a reframing of control associated with a differently situated time.

Datamining, at least in the context of *Undertale*'s devoted fan community, reveals the ways in which narratives are never absolutely or finally authored and are never the product of a sole creator. The practices examined here collapse the distinction between the world of the game and the world beyond, and by de-centring the act of creation, the game unsettles the concept of foundation as such. The usual conception of authorship connotes commencement and commandment, an originary point at which the world begins to take shape and time begins to unfold.[311] The unfinished world of the *Undertale* fan community denies the ultimately originary character of that first line of the pen or click of the keyboard, giving weight to the importance of the experience even after its apparent completion. It complicates the temporally linear character of control by complicating the point of origin.

Myth-making is already a temporal concept, oriented as it is toward a fictional but necessary past. It too is thereby connected to the subject of political order: the projection from the past to the future entails a delimitation of the events that proceed along the way. In the case of Twitch Plays Pokémon, though, this familiar form of temporality was replaced by something different. The social experiment witnessed the same complication of diegetic and non-diegetic elements as *Undertale*, reframing the past, but it reframed the future as well: the project took place in a future perfect tense addressing a future that will have been, a time in which the actions taken then will have retroactively made sense. The meaning that players and commentators made out of Twitch Plays Pokémon arose in their present, but it made sense in a context informed by memories created for and from the future.

Player practices are, of course, too multivalent to truly center on a single set of thematic or political concerns; saying that the three described here hold significance for the form of temporality that accompanies the usual understanding of technological control – that is, that they complicate or contravene it – would be correct, but it would also ignore the many other layers to the practices themselves. The same can be said of tool-assisted speedrunning, the subject of the next chapter: it is a rich, complicated player practice that cannot be reduced to a single analytical framework. At the same time, the attention that it pays to what Hansen calls the "non-phenomenological" temporal scale of new media, or to the non-human speeds at which it takes place, means that it most directly exemplifies the broader concerns of this book. There is no way of thinking about a medium in which events unfold in time other than technically, and no way of thinking technology without also thinking temporally.

Chapter Five

Pokémon Plays Twitch

In February 2014, Twitch played *Pokémon*. In January 2015, *Pokémon* played Twitch.[312] At an annual speedrunning marathon called Awesome Games Done Quick, a team of speedrunners plugged an assemblage of custom hardware called TASBot into a Super Game Boy, an adapter cartridge that allows Game Boy games to be played on a television screen through a Super Nintendo Entertainment System. They started a new game of *Pokémon Red*, the same game that had been collectively played on Twitch earlier that year, and TASBot began "playing" the game, feeding a script of commands from a carefully written computer file into the console through a standard SNES controller. A live audience of hundreds gathered in the conference hotel and a home audience of hundreds of thousands watching live on Twitch waited patiently for what happened next. The setup was slow and a little strange: bizarre symbols appeared in the game's Pokedex, and TASBot threw item after item away. This, one of the TASBot team members explained, was a means of manipulating the game's memory, and preparing it to do something unusual – something that wouldn't be fully explained to the audience until long afterwards.[313] After a brief pause, a jumble of text and emotes began scrolling rapidly down a screen that no longer bore any relation to the user interface of *Pokémon Red* save the font type. The word "Chat" appeared in the bottom right. Text scrolled by for over two minutes while the team wondered aloud about the connection and the replay, and then it resolved:

dajahvis: gooteks?
anondl: que?
glass1212: wtf

G OR ***
able: Down6
rm_midnyt: b
tart9
brettaroo: DOWN
itch??
cubanoman: doritos
mellondog: this sure is fun
quickshot20: BOT DIED

Scrolling up, the text was now recognizable as the rapid-fire banter of the marathon's official chat stream. "Twitch Chat," the marathon's host intoned, "say hi to the couch." The room burst into applause; one of the TASBot team members started laughing; messages from Twitch Chat acknowledging its appearance on the main marathon screen began to appear in *Pokémon Red's* font, somehow making their way from internet to TASBot to Super NES: "HI MOM," "HI COUCH," "Wait WHAT," "There is no way!" The TASBot team waved, Twitch Chat made references to Twitch Plays Pokémon ("Helix!"), and the camera panned over the audience in the conference room as it rose in a standing ovation. The team's spokesperson summarized what had just happened: "We just did a triple total control. We took over *Pokémon Red*. Then we took over the Super Game Boy. Then we took over the entire Super Nintendo. *Then* we started streaming Twitch Chat directly through the controller cables. And yes, we did add emotes."

What the assembled speedrunners and viewers had witnessed was an example of tool-assisted speedrunning, albeit a strange one. In a conventional tool-assisted speedrun, or TAS, the runner acts like a programmer, putting together a precise series of key-presses that are executed in sequence, enabling them to create a perfectly optimized run. In the process of creating these perfectly optimized runs, tool-assisted speedrunners, or

TASers, regularly discover and exploit a game's glitches – errors and elisions overlooked by the game's original programmers that can produce system crashes, shortcuts, and stranger things. The ADGQ performance was an example of a glitch repurposed to do the latter. The phrase used to describe this variety of run is telling: it is a "total control." In these creative and pointless pursuits of novelty, TASers use their superior knowledge of their games to completely repurpose them, turning consoles into platforms and games into operating systems. The total control is a means of making things into means.

Speedrunning is an attempt to exercise mastery that nonetheless issues in an immanent critique of control. Tool-assisted speedrunning, or TASing, takes both claims further: the TASer is not out for a close approximation of mastery, but its actual achievement. At the same time, the TASer is even more attuned to the problematic tendencies of control; the performance of total control can militate against the technological ideal of control itself. How does this work? How is it that an attempt to exercise total control can constitute a ludopolitical rejoinder to the ethos and logic of modern technology?

Tool-Assisted Speedrunning

A TAS is a sequence of key-presses that can be executed by special software to simulate the performance of a videogame. Written by human runners using emulation tools either adapted for TASing or built specifically for the practice, these sequences are exceedingly precise, enabling (and requiring) the runners to program input in every single frame – one key-press every 0.033 or 0.0165 seconds, depending on the hardware in question. These key-presses come together to form a "movie file," a sort of script that can be played back in the game to simulate and record a perfect run, that is usually hosted online. "Using these tools," as TASVideos, the internet's biggest TASing website, puts it, "we overcome human limitations to complete games with extremely high precision, entertaining our viewers as our players tear through games at seemingly impossible speeds." Although the extraordinary videos that are the outcome of a TAS might appear to be the product of cheating, "[t]he end result of this process is simply a series of key-presses which may be performed on the original hardware." TASers do not break any rules; their performance works within the terms of the game's code. It stays inside the magic circle. "Some of these tricks we use make the games look broken. But we are not breaking the games, we are just breaking your notion on them."[314]

Normal speedruns of the sort described in the previous chapter are referred to as "real-time attacks," or RTAs, and they can require thousands of hours of dedicated practice. Tool-assisted speedruns, or TASes, are no different: recording one is usually a serious commitment of time, requiring research into previous work (on the videogame, the platform, or the emulator in question), the innovation of new methods for speeding up the run (reverse engineering, glitch hunting, discussion and teamwork), the painstaking process of recording tens of thousands of key-presses, and the eventual release into the wild – not the friendly and informal Twitch stream of the RTA speedrunner but the regimented judgment of TASVideos.org, the online archive that has become arbiter, repository, resource, and forum.

While TASes might take just as much of an investment of time as RTAs, they require a completely different approach to the game. The implementation of key-presses is slow and methodical instead of fast and twitchy, and the majority of the work is cognitive rather than physical. If RTAs are feats of skill, then TASes are feats of engineering. At a minimum, they require a working knowledge of emulation software, a thorough knowledge of the game being played, and a familiarity with the TASing community and its technical and social protocols. More often, though, they demand an exhaustive understanding of these subjects – the sort of familiarity that enables runners to find and exploit glitches that have in many cases gone undiscovered for decades. It's not an exaggeration to say that the players responsible for the most impressive runs know their games better than the games' programmers did.

The appeal of TASing lies partly in the display of this technical achievement, of course: it's delightful to see an unmodified, familiar game completed in an impossibly fast time frame, especially when the runner has abused bizarre glitches to do so. In the TAS of *Mega Man 2*, coming in at a total time of 23:48.51, Mega Man uses power-ups called Items to clip into and through ceilings and walls, zipping through whole rooms and even entire sections. The game seems to recoil in protest: the latter half of the Quick Man stage is played in complete darkness; the fight with Bubble Man takes place outside of his room; and the Woodman stage is skipped entirely, with Mega Man zipping straight to the fight with the robot master. The Wiley stages are treated with similar disregard. It's impressive. But another part of the appeal of TASing, and one to which I will return, is the viewer's first discovery of the hobby and the process of exploration that follows. When casual gamers stumble across RTAs of their favorite games, TASes are often only a click or two away – and from there, it's just another small step to tasvideos.org. At the same time, TASing is still a comparatively minor practice, with videos like the *Mega Man 2* run described above gathering only a few thousand views. This, combined with the technical know-how required to appreciate them, let alone design them, lends TASes a certain geeky mystique. The discovery of such a strange niche hobby as TASing naturally leads to a curiosity about what, why, and how it's done.

The pleasure taken in technique and discovery begins to point to the broader significance of the hobby. TASing is "an exploration of the inner-life of video games," as games writer Steven Messner puts it;[315] according to scholar James Newman, it "showcases the potentialities of the game and game system, revealing new possibilities and highlighting the malleability of the game, its openness to different 'playings' and the sheer number of imperfections that go unnoticed during normal play."[316] As an idiosyncratic technical and cultural practice pursued by a very small number of dedicated players, TASing is a privileged site for thinking through digitality. It is a computational hobby bent on control and mastery that somehow sublates them. It both indexes and challenges the ludic and computational character of the times.

Appreciating the broader significance of TASing requires understanding how they work in detail both technical and historical. The beginnings of the practice can be traced to the late 1990s, the heyday of classic first-person shooters like id Software's *DOOM* and *Quake*. This was a time when players competed with one another in multiplayer deathmatches, first over local-area networks and then over phone lines. Soon, they competed in single player as well. id Software had provided players with a simple way to record game sessions in its proprietary .dem file format, tracking all of a player's inputs so that they could be played back in the game engine, perfectly recreating everything they had done. Additionally, each game included a static screen at the end of each level listing statistics – something Newman describes as "a powerful device that urge[d] reflection on the performance and encourage[d] replay so that performance may be honed."[317]

The combination of the statistics screen, the ability to record a performance, and the availability of a network to share them naturally led to competition, but it also led to modification. In 1998, a player-programmer named Andy Kempling altered *DOOM*'s source code, enabling players "to record demos in slowmotion and in several sessions"[318] – what the website Doom World called "tools-assisted speedruns." The demo files that *DOOM* and *Quake* provided could only be played back by players within the games themselves, making them relatively difficult to share with other interested viewers, and of course they didn't help players of other games. But the 1990s also gave rise to software emulators that could replicate the functioning of videogame consoles within DOS, Windows, and Linux. Nintendo games could now be played using emulators like iNES, released in 1996; with a tiny bit of tinkering, these emulators could be made to play those games at different speeds or in single pieces, or to record their gameplay for video output. In the early 2000s, an emulator featuring just these sorts of tools, Famtasia, enabled a Japanese player named Morimoto to create moSMB3.wmv, a viral video that appeared in late 2003. LeMieux describes its initial appearance on Western websites this way:

Not long after .GIFs of dancing babies (and dancing bananas and dancing hamsters) colonized Geocities websites in the late nineties and "all your base belonged to us" in 2001, a serial Mario meme spread across the Internet alongside Star Wars Kids and Badger Badgers in 2003. Titled moSMB3.wmv, the 18.4-megabyte Windows Media Video file was traded via torrents, uploaded to university accounts, and, of course, exhibited on eBaum's World as "Super Mario 3 beat in 11 minutes."[319]

The video itself played out like this:

After downloading the file (for what might have been hours) and getting the video to play (after also downloading the proper codec), Morimoto's speedrun begins with the faint sound of the start screen of *Super Mario Bros. 3* accompanied by a white overlay with two lines of green, right-justified text: "super mario bross3 [sic] / time attack video." As the overlay dissolves into the World 1 map screen, the first stage is quickly selected and Mario glides through Level 1-1 with mechanical precision. The tiny, four-tone sprite scrolls right at a constant rate of 3.5 pixels per frame, effortlessly avoiding obstacles and bouncing off enemy after enemy before reaching his goal in the first three stages of Grass Land. After two minutes of gameplay and two warp whistles, Mario has already entered World 8 and is nearing the end of his quest to rescue the princess. Instantly transported from the pastoral fields and benign obstacles of World 1 to the dark, industrial hell of what is ostensibly Bowser's home turf, Mario starts to really show off. The final world of *Mario 3* begins [with] three "autoscrollers" – levels in which the screen moves at a fixed rate to simulate the procession of wooden tanks, ships, and planes that make up the Koopa King's army. Since speed is constrained to the slow panning of the stage, rather than simply pressing his nose against the rightmost pixel of the frame, Mario bides his time by bouncing acrobatically from bob-omb to bob-omb to cannonball and back, racking up thousands of points and extra lives. Whereas the streamlined speedrun through the first three levels seemed practiced, Mario's death-defying antics and carefree hot-dogging at the end of the game are downright superhuman. The first stage of the Dark Land is completed with 79 lives. The entire game is over in eleven minutes, three seconds, and ninety five milliseconds – exactly 39,837 frames – and fades to another white slide with green credits: "played by もりもと / @やるきなす / http://soramimi.egoism.jp/ / http://homepage3.nifty.com/nura/."[320]

This sort of optimized gameplay has become commonplace, but in the early 2000s, it was astounding. Viewers had a hard time believing their eyes. TASVideos, which accords the video a special place in TASing history, accounts for the reaction: "since few people knew how the video was made, it was widely believed that it was played in real-time by an extremely skilled player...During this time, the concept of tool-assistance was still mostly unknown, and people even went as far as claiming that Morimoto had constructed the movie in several years' time by performing video editing on every single frame of the WMV."[321] LeMieux notes that viewers of Morimoto's work, perhaps familiar with speedrunning websites like Speed Demos Archive but unfamiliar with tool-assistance, were initially "dumbfounded." Soon, however, they moved on to "disbelief," "antipathy," "skepticism," "sarcasm," and "overt racism" – typical reactions to "techno-Orientalist anxieties."[322]

This is a good point at which to add a demographic note to the technical and historical context at hand: speedrunners, whether of the RTA or TAS variety, seem to be largely white and male. Reactions like the sort that LeMieux notes above suggest that their viewers are similar. There are non-white boys and men among speedrunners, but not in representative proportion. Although gaming has become demographically diverse, non-white runners are so comparatively rare that they will sometimes note their non-white status in their names, as in the case of TheMexicanRunner. Likewise, there are also girls, women, and trans people in the speedrunning community, but not in representative proportion, and non-male or non-straight runners routinely face sexist or homophobic reactions and harassment, as with Narcissa Wright, the co-founder of SpeedRunsLive. This chapter is not intended to lionize the work of a few clever white men, but all of the runners named are indeed white and male. This doesn't mean that they necessarily fall prey to the "techno-Orientalist anxieties" on show in the reactions to Morimoto's work, or even to outright sexism or racism, but it doesn't mean that they always avoid these anxieties, either.

Some of the viewers who were less inclined to an Orientalist reception of moSMB3.wmv understood the technical magic behind it, and they took Morimoto's work as something of a rallying cry. Joel "Bisqwit" Yliluoma recoded Morimoto's low quality .wmv file as a smaller, better quality .avi file, and hosted it on his

183

website, NESVideos.[323] Bisqwit published more of Morimoto's work that year, and then others' submissions in 2004. When he began publishing more and more videos for games on platforms other than the Nintendo Entertainment System, he changed the site's name to TASVideos.

TASBot

The initial publication of the Morimoto video, the formation of websites like Speed Demos Archive and TASVideos, the advent of the BitTorrent file format in 2001 and its subsequent widespread adoption, the creation of video sharing sites like YouTube in 2005 – all of these factors combined to help popularize speedrunning and to begin moving its tool-assisted variant into the light. The next decade saw the awareness of both practices grow. In 2010, Speed Demos Archive hosted the first Games Done Quick (GDQ) speedrunning marathon, a charity event during which speedrunners played game after game on a live internet stream while soliciting donations from viewers, donations that have gone to organizations including CARE, the Prevent Cancer Foundation, the Organisation for Autism Research, and Doctors Without Borders. The first GDQ, "Classic Games Run Quick," became "Awesome Games Done Quick" the next year; that summer, Speed Demos Archive also ran "Summer Games Done Quick," and the alternation of AGDQ and SGDQ has now established an annual rhythm in the world of speedrunning.

Originally, the GDQ events focused only on RTAs. At SGDQ 2011, TASing made its debut with "NESbot," an Arduino-based device built by Peter "micro500" Greenwood for the purposes of "console verification," or ensuring that a TAS could be played back on real hardware as well as on an emulator.[324] That exhibition took place during the marathon's infancy, in front of a mere 1500 concurrent viewers; TASing next appeared at the marathon during AGDQ 2014, by which time viewership had increased to more than 63,000.[325] This undoubtedly had to do with the growing popularity of the marathon and with Twitch, but it was also because the TASBot block was such an unusual showcase. Most GDQ performances feature a runner and a friend or two sitting on a couch in front of a console; viewers at home see the couch and the audience in the background on one side of their monitors and a feed showing the runners' screen on the other. In the AGDQ 2014 TASBot block,[326] the runners took backseat to a modified Nintendo Robotic Operating Buddy (ROB), a robotic accessory for the Nintendo Entertainment System manufactured and sold in the 1980s that was capable of "playing" two games, *Gyromite* and *Stack Up*. Made of the same off-white and gray plastic as other NES peripherals, ROB was nevertheless designed to be friendlier: in addition to its familiar name, it was anthropomorphic, with two eyes, two arms, a rotating torso, and a base. When the modified ROB appeared at AGDQ 2014, it was propping up a Raspberry Pi (an inexpensive computer built on a single circuit board useful for robotics) and an adapter board (at first the NES/SNES Replay Device created by a programmer who goes by the name of true, and in later marathons a replay device built by Greenwood)[327] that buffered between the Raspberry Pi and a console. Its hands held a modified NES controller that flashed lights instead of pressing keys. This was TASBot. The TASBot team had written movie files for four games – *Gradius, Super Mario Kart 64, Super Mario 64,* and *Super Mario World* – and it fed this data to TASBot through the Raspberry Pi. TASBot then "played" the games, sending key-presses to actual consoles – NES, Nintendo 64, and Super Nintendo. Most TAS movie files were fed into emulators, but TASBot was playing them live.

Allan "dwangoAC" Cecil, TASBot's spokesman, explained what was happening. TASBot played *Gradius* in the background while Cecil described how TASBot was built and what exactly "he" was doing. Cecil had to pause repeatedly for laughter and applause as Andrés "adelikat" Delikat's speedrun showed off extraordinary things: "I shouldn't even talk. This is just too awesome to watch." Then, a minute-and-a-half into what was supposed to be an 11-minute run, the player's ship exploded. "Oh my goodness, we desynced!…Okay, could somebody go get my NES?" The error, Cecil hypothesized, had to do with minor differences between particular consoles: despite standardized industrial production routines, no two Nintendo Entertainment Systems were exactly the same. Cecil had only tested the *Gradius* movie file on his own NES, failing to anticipate the problem. The team tried to run *Gradius* again later in the showcase, and it again succumbed to hardware desynchronization.

Unexpected errors have become a standard feature of TASBot presentations, and both their commonality and the TASBot team's responses to them are worth discussion. I'll return to them later in the chapter. The desynchronization was hardly the most notable feature of the TASBot block at AGDQ 2014, however. The block ended with TASBot making "seemingly random, completely intended" moves in the first level of *Super Mario World*, as another couch commenter, TheGreekBrit, put it. Mario hatched multiple Yoshi eggs and spawned multiple one-up mushrooms; Yoshi ate and released Koopa shells without apparent rhyme or reason, blowing fireballs across the screen; Mario hopped off an invisible Yoshi over and over, and Yoshi fell through the landscape and off the screen. TheGreekBrit explained:

What he's actually doing is spawning tiles in a specific order. There's this thing called the OAM [Object Attribute Memory or Map], which is just a table which contains all the physical, graphical properties of all the tiles on screen. The p-switch is really the key factor here; what he just did, *right here*, he stunned one of those flying item boxes, which basically means that he makes it act like a Koopa shell, and then he…

The screen froze, broken sprites appeared all over, and the game cut to black. "LOADING GAMES…1 of 2" appeared in green, and then a simple menu:

AGDQ 2014

Pong
Snake
THE END

Mario's head appeared between two paddles made out of textures from *Super Mario World*, and TASBot played *Pong*. Then it played *Snake*. Then the human players took over, challenging each other to a game of *Pong* built using assets from *Super Mario World* inside of *Super Mario World* itself. The crowd, astounded, cheered.

TASBot had somehow programmed *Snake* and *Pong* on the fly using only key-presses from the Super Nintendo controller. Well, from eight Super Nintendo controllers passing input simultaneously through a "multitap" peripheral – but still, key-presses alone. The TASBot team had, in its terminology, taken "total control" of the game. Kyle Orland, a writer for *Ars Technica*, provided a simplified explanation of what had taken place:

Suffice it to say that the first minute-and-a-half or so of this TAS is merely an effort to spawn a specific set of sprites into the game's Object Attribute Memory (OAM) buffer in a specific order. The TAS runner then uses a stun glitch to spawn an unused sprite into the game, which in turn causes the system to treat the sprites in that OAM buffer as raw executable code. In this case, that code has been arranged to jump to the memory location for controller data, in essence letting the user insert whatever executable program he or she wants into memory by converting the binary data for precisely ordered button presses into assembly code (interestingly, this data is entered more quickly by simulating the inputs of eight controllers plugged in through simulated multitaps on each controller port).

...[T]hese memory-corruption efforts are [usually] used to simply jump the game's state to the "ending" movie, thereby "completing" it in a much shorter time than is usually possible. This new *Super Mario World* TAS sets itself apart by using its total control of the system to actually program a new game on top of the existing one.[328]

Orland's explanation accounted for the fact that *Super Mario World* could be hacked with controller input alone, but how had the movie file's author programmed "a new game on top of the existing one"? And who was responsible, anyway?

Arbitrary Code Execution

During the relative chaos of the TASBot block, Cecil had forgotten to mention the name of the runner responsible for writing the *Super Mario World* movie file, a programmer named Masterjun. In the same year that the first GDQ charity marathon took place, 2010, he had begun experimenting with TASing. This was also a period of time during which there was an initial wave of discoveries in the speedrunning community related to extreme glitch abuse. The period kicked off accidentally, with a Canadian streamer named raocow stumbling upon what would become known as the "null sprite glitch" in 2009 during a let's play of a *Super Mario World* ROM hack called *VIP 4*.[329] The glitch wasn't understood at first; it took several players several months of experimentation to document its properties. Normally, the sprites that appear in the item box at the top of the screen in *Super Mario World* refer to a particular portion of the game's code, the Object Attribute Memory (or Map) table; under certain circumstances, however, the item box can "point" to another portion of code. When this happens, a "null sprite" appears in the box, a sprite outside of the OAM; it takes the visual form of an unrecognizable mess of pixels, and it can lead to the arbitrary execution of code. This is what took place in raocow's video, and it's also what took place in Masterjun's movie at AGDQ 2014. The replay board designer, true, explained what happened succinctly:

> All the events leading up to the game looking like it was freezing were intentional and were used to set up a spawn of an invalid item, which resulted in a jump to memory to execute the controller button status as instructions. Obviously manipulating the buttons at this point results in arbitrary code execution. Code for the loader/controller handler was then sent, then the game code was sent and jumped to.[330]

The null sprite glitch, discovered accidentally in 2009 and then reverse engineered for months, was the key to writing arbitrary code into the game using only standard controller key-presses – a clear example of trifling with the game, not cheating.[331]

The *Super Mario World* total control was one of the first instances of "arbitrary code execution," or ACE, within the speedrunning community. (The first ACE was bortreb's "glitch-fest" of *Pokémon Yellow*.)[332] The term can refer to a general feature of software that accepts external inputs, namely its vulnerability to attacks that can grant the attacker a substantial degree of control over the victim's system, but its connotations in the world of TASing are more anodyne, since runners have so far only implemented ACE for entertainment. Masterjun's ACE was built on the back of the research done by glitch hunters including nathanisbored, bahamete, Mister, antaasas, and Jordan "p4plus2" Potter; the latter two were particularly important, since they had first figured out how to perform a credits warp in the Yoshi's Island 3 level of *Super Mario World* using only controller inputs. Masterjun made use of the same principles as the credits warp, but used the location of the sprites onscreen to write new code rather than simply executing the existing code that would have taken Mario to the credits – something he had figured out how to do earlier. The TASBot team used Masterjun's movie file, only completed the night before the TASBot block at AGDQ 2014, to illustrate to the broader speedrunning community the unexpected results that can come from intimate knowledge of a game's code.

AGDQ 2014 was just the beginning. At the following AGDQ events, the team performed new and more ambitious exploits. During AGDQ 2015, TASBot's first feat was familiar, starting from a new movie file for *Super Mario World*, again coded by Masterjun, with help from p4plus2, a student at Cal State East Bay: Mario ran around on the screen, again in an apparently random fashion, setting up the conditions to take control of the game. Cecil, explaining succinctly, described the process as "corrupt[ing] the Object Attribute Map, the OAM, so everything you see is just positioning things correctly." Greenwood talked through the remainder of the setup until the glitch took place and the screen went black. In the ensuing silence: "Hopefully it'll work." Then, *Super Mario Bros.* – the *first* game of the series, played in North America on the NES – appeared where *Super Mario World* had been moments before. An 8-bit Mario started running right, through an almost perfectly rendered World 1-1. The sounds were taken from *Super Mario All-Stars*, and there were some strange visual artefacts – quarters of Goombas flashing on the screen, pipes painted half-white instead of all green – but TASBot had successfully executed another ACE, programming a completely playable *Super Mario Bros.* inside of *Super Mario World*. "[O]nce total control was achieved," as Orland writes, "the team decided to code in a fully functional copy of Super Mario Bros. onto the Super NES through faster-than-human button presses, essentially writing the game to the system's 128KB of RAM in real time at a rate of 384 bytes per frame (23 KB/s)." Only a warm-up to the triple total control of Pokémon Plays Twitch described above, the "Super Mario Inception" was still impressive.[333]

The TASBot block at AGDQ 2016 was no less so.[334] TASBot played a few games "normally," without executing any arbitrary code, though even these allowed the TASBot team to show off its members' superior understanding of the games that had become their artistic medium. *Brain Age,* for instance, normally requires the player to sketch the answer to simple mathematical questions using the Nintendo DS's touchscreen or stylus, drawing an 8 when the game asked the player the answer for 7+1; TASBot sketched pictures that appeared to bear no relation to the shape of the number in question, but the game nevertheless accepted a picture of the Nintendo ROB as the answer for 2+5, the AGDQ 2016 logo as the answer for 4+3, and the word "HYPE" as the answer for 4x7.[335] Then, the team welcomed to the stage Mitch-FlowerPower, a *Super Mario Bros. 3* speedrunner, who commented on TASBot's run of *Super Mario Bros. 3*: although it appeared like a normal playthrough leading to a wrong warp, the pipe that usually leads to the end credits instead led to a screen reading "Super Mario Bros. 3 Back Door." TASBot then ran a version of the children's game *Color a Dinosaur,* which gave way to a heavily glitched version of *Super Mario Bros. 3* in which Mario cycled through power-up stages that don't exist in the normal game – a total control by Lord Tom. Cecil handed MitchFlowerPower the controller, demonstrating that the game-within-a-game was, as usual, playable.

Again, though, this wasn't the main event. Cecil was joined on the couch by p4plus2 and Weatherton, as well as Alex "PangaeaPanga" Tan, a ROM hacker and speedrunner known for successfully playing through *Super Mario World* blindfolded, and SethBling, a popular YouTuber known earlier for his extraordinary work with the redstone programming language of *Minecraft* and then for his feats of skill in the overlap between RTA and TAS communities. TASBot appeared in front of the couch holding four controllers, as usual, but he was relatively difficult to make out. It was a different feeling than the previous two years; the TASBot block had become one of the marathon's main attractions, and the excitement in the room, packed with 1400 conference attendees, was palpable. Cecil played coy about the game the audience was about to see, but not about the method: "This is a total control run of *something*." *Super Mario All-Stars*, a collection of Mario games for the SNES, appeared on the screen, and TASBot selected *Super Mario World* from the available options. After Cecil credited Masterjun for the following portion of the showcase, the total control began. Mario icons appeared at the top of a black screen, accompanied by text: "SUPER MARIO MAKER ALL STARS."

This was January 2016, and *Super Mario Maker* had been released for the Wii U console only months before; the game allowed players to make, play, and share their own Mario levels, drawing on the resources of Mario games old and new. The game had enjoyed considerable popularity on Twitch and YouTube, as skilled players competed to create and run through unbelievably challenging levels. Panga was responsible for many of these. *Super Mario Maker* wasn't included in *Super Mario All-Stars*, of course – it didn't exist – so the audience now had an idea of what they were in for. Panga took over the commentary as TASBot began painting the black background with tiles from *Super Mario World*, explaining that he had written the movie file that TASBot was currently executing and that his level copied one of SethBling's designs for *Super Mario Maker* that had been run earlier in the marathon. Once the level was complete, Cecil invited dram55, a speedrunner, to take the controller and play the level, demonstrating that it was completely functional.

But TASBot wasn't done. After several minutes of partially explained fiddling on the part of p4plus, he said, "Let's see it Twitch." Cecil and p4plus2 watched the laptop screen, waiting to see Twitch take control. After several more minutes of technical difficulties, the TASBot team finally succeeded in giving control over to Twitch Chat: by typing in words that would be recognized by the internet relay chat interpreter as console input commands (*up*, *down*, *left*, *right*, *x*, *y*, *a*, and *b*), they were able to collectively – anarchically – change the level's design, placing four pre-selected blocks and moving the cursor. The name of the AGDQ event changed from "SUPER MARIO MAKER ALL-STARS" to "TWITCH PLAYS MARIO VERY BADLY." For some reason, the interpreter initially collected movement commands almost exclusively, so the cursor moved, stuttering, to the right. Then, something bizarre happened: the gray blocks that had made up much of the level's design glitched out, and then the rest of the level joined them. The screen became a riot of purple, pink, and neon green cross-hatching, and then a flashing black and white; there were recognizable shapes at first, but they quickly gave way to chaos. Parts of the screen resolved back into recognizable sprites. The event changed names again: "TWITCH BREAKS MARIO." "*Oh* my *goodness*," Cecil exclaimed, bursting out laughing. The audience cheered. "The best part – it hasn't even crashed. You know what's actually happened?" p4plus2 asked. "They wrapped around the level enough times vertically, they're just writing garbage into VRAM. This isn't going to crash the game – it's just going to get better." The TASBot team took control back from Twitch and gave dram55 the chance to play the now heavily glitched level. And it worked. Cecil: "You can break this game *so badly* and still play it! I've never seen anything quite like this." Finally, the game crashed.

Glitch

Crashes upon crashes: during every TASBot block, something fell apart. In AGDQ 2014, the use of a different NES console led to the *Gradius* desynchronization; in 2015, the metal rolling cart stopped *Super Mario World* halfway through and then led to bizarre visual artefacts during the total control; and in 2016, "TWITCH BREAKS MARIO" became an almost-impenetrable glitchfest.

Every TASBot performance was characterized by technical wizardry peppered by unpredictable malfunctions, and each case delivered a window into the runners' understanding of the games and the hardware that TASBot was playing. Cecil's comments about the minute differences between individual NES consoles in 2014, for instance, revealed something that runners know, but that most others fail to appreciate: the products of even the most sophisticated post-industrial manufacturing processes are non-fungible. They seem identical, but they are never quite the same. This lesson should resound in the context of contemporary technoculture, a context in which fungibility is held aloft as both the ground for digitization and as its justification: if the objects of the world cannot be straightforwardly encoded and reduced to a series of bits – if the principle of digitality never ultimately or perfectly translates into practice – then there will always be elisions and escapes. Imperfections are unavoidable in the production of transistors, even when the principal means of manufacture is both metaphorically and literally sunlight.

While the non-fungibility of consoles seemed at first to be the problem, video review revealed that the issue lay elsewhere. During the rushed setup, unshielded microphone cables had been casually draped over unshielded controller cables. When the microphones registered a loud noise – the audience reacting to something TASBot was doing – they inadvertently communicated, as it were, with the controllers. Although the amount of electromagnetic interference was quite small, it was enough to disrupt the script that TASBot was running: inputs were provided during the wrong frames and TASBot entered them anyway, resulting in the ship in *Gradius* crashing – a conveniently literal representation of the effects of desynchronization.

The differences between one console and another, or the significance of the electromagnetism that any charged wire gives off, might be invisible to both the naked eye or even to standard electronic quality control protocols, but they still register at the micro-temporal level at which TASBot operates. The glitch that caused *Gradius* to repeatedly crash pointed to the very existence of the micro-temporal level. The entirety of tool-assisted speedrunning attests to that level, in fact: the practice calls attention to the speed of the computer, or at least to the speed at which humans can be expected to have some minimal degree of control – 30 frames per second or 60 frames per second, depending on the hardware in question. The practice is a reminder that computers, as media theorists from Kittler to Hansen argue, operate at a non-phenomenological level, or that they put into play processes over which we have no meaningful control. This is something that a media theorist learns, but that a runner *apprehends*.

Admittedly, however, the runner needs to learn this lesson too, at least insofar as they need to become intimately familiar with the hardware and software that enable their hobby. The technical minutiae that explain some of the glitches TASBot has encountered over the years are as fascinating as they are frustrating. During 2016, for instance, the TASBot team was trying to perform an ACE in *Donkey Kong Country 2* for the SNES. The code worked well on the emulator, but refused to work consistently on any of the consoles that they employed for testing. The problem, it turned out, had to do with the material used to manufacture the sound processor on the SNES: while the clock of the main CPU is a very reliable crystal oscillator, the clock of the sound processor is made of cheap ceramic. The imprecise sound processor was slightly out of sync with the precise CPU even when the SNES was new; 25 years later, the problem was worse. It's a problem that has almost no noticeable effect on typical gameplay, but it does affect the frame-perfect gameplay of a TAS because the two processors rely on one another: in some games, the CPU will not allow the player to advance forward until the sound processor indicates that an effect has finished sounding. In the case of a TAS, this might mean waiting several frames longer than expected, resulting, again, in desynchronization. As Cecil put it in a forum post:

> For my console, the 24.576 MHz crystal is clocking more like 24.573 MHz likely due to age and being a cheap part to begin with. Why does this matter? If the sound board takes the wrong amount of time to play certain sounds the SMP will spinlock against the main CPU and the result will be a different number of frames to perform certain actions, i.e. it will cause a desync.[336]

In the case of the *Gradius* crashes at AGDQ 2014, the problem was simple enough to fix: use shielded cables instead of unshielded ones, and keep controllers and consoles away from sources of electromagnetism. In the case of *Donkey Kong Country 2*, however, there was no solution. Because the ceramic oscillator of the sound processor was inherently unpredictable, it produced non-deterministic behavior, rendering the game inappropriate for marathon performance.[337] This sort of non-determinism might seem like an exception to the normal functioning of electronic hardware, but it's perfectly common – it's just that it takes place at an electronic and temporal register to which we can only indirectly and occasionally relate.

A similar set of problems took place during the "inception" of *Super Mario Bros.* in 2015 thanks to normally-hidden properties of hardware and electricity. When the game broke the first time, the couch commenters explained the problem:

> Cecil: I broke the cardinal rule: I ran a wire over a wire.
> Greenwood: It can randomly do this.
> Weatherton: So, when you're running on actual hardware, things can get a little interesting, 'cause you're dealing with real physics, in terms of electrical interference. Things

outside the game can actually interfere with the movie.
Greenwood: I've had refrigerators mess with it.[338]

Even equipped with this understanding of the possibility of electromagnetic interference, the team had chosen to place TAS-Bot on an electrical rolling cart; unfortunately, it "acted like a giant antenna funneling EMI right at our unshielded cables."[339] And the team members were unprepared for the exact problems that the EMI would cause. When the game displayed flashing quarters of Goombas laid on top of the normal level, Cecil was surprised: "In all of our testing, I have never seen it flash like that, ever."

Here, the unpredictable effects of EMI point to another feature of console hardware, and electronic devices in general, that also goes underappreciated: zeros are only imperfectly divided from ones. LeMieux, describing the way that the NES works, explains:

Press "START." Sixty times a second an electrical impulse is sent from the Nintendo Entertainment System (NES) to the sixth pin of its first controller port. From port to plug to cord to controller, the signal travels down one of five colored wires to the NES-4021, an 8-bit, parallel-to-serial shift register housed within a standard controller. After receiving a high pulse for 12 microseconds from the orange wire connected to pin six, the 4021 "latches" the state of the controller's eight buttons and immediately sends a single pulse of electricity back to the NES along the yellow wire, pin seven. This pulse represents a single bit of serial data. An absent or "low" current pulse (i.e., 0V), is interpreted as a 0 by the NES's central processing unit (CPU) – a modified version of MOS Technology's popular 6502 processor called the Ricoh 2A03. A "high" current pulse (i.e., +5V) is registered as a 1. Although digital media are never quite digital, the infinitely individuated physical attributes of electrical current are measured, sampled, and abstracted into serial units by mechanisms like the flip-flop circuits of the 4021 and the semiconductor arrays of the 6502's input/output registers. As Matthew Kirschenbaum confirms in *Mechanisms: New Media and the Forensic Imagination*, "while bits are the smallest symbolic units of computation, they are not the smallest inscribed unit." Serial communication, however, privileges the discrete, repeatable bit over the continuous flows of electricity. Surges, spikes, static, and other forms of interference are either ignored by the processor, translated into bits by the processor, or crash the processor – there is no middle ground.[340]

The transistors that make up a processor send electrons along one of two channels that are interpreted as a zero or a one depending on the voltage of the electronic pulse, but this voltage is not restricted to two values; it varies between and beyond them. When it varies beyond its normal range thanks to unexpected electromagnetic events like the sort that took place during the 2015 TASBot block, the resulting bits of information can end up garbled. They might crash the processor, or they might do the sorts of things that TASBot's audience saw. In either case, they demonstrate that the ones and zeroes that represent the work of transistors do their work imperfectly. The symbols fail to accurately describe the real. "Digital media are never quite digital," as LeMieux writes; they "cut continuums into bits," as Wark puts it, but they do so imperfectly. We mostly operate according to the symbolic fiction of the sharp cut, but we need to recall that it is a fiction, since the fantasy of digitality's perfection, of its absolute division, is part of the symbolic scaffolding of the fantasy of control.

Despite their attempts to achieve perfection, TASers understand full well the impossibility of their endeavors. It is *because* of these attempts, in fact: armed with a thorough knowledge of the imperfections of hardware, they expect the unexpected, and they play and perform ready to react to uncertainty. This does not stop them from being surprised, delighted, or frustrated by the particular forms that it takes, of course, but it does mean that they operate in a state of anticipation of the glitch.

Indeed, their whole hobby is predicated on the uncertainty and imperfection of hardware and software alike. On the software side, TASers – particularly those hunting for hidden glitches or aiming for total control – need to become intimately familiar with the ways in which games handle things like memory management. Becoming so familiar with subjects like the OAM often means that the runners understand portions of the game's code better than the original programmers did. This was the case in AGDQ 2016, for instance: the TASBot team had hoped to allow the player to select sprites from all of the games included in the *Super Mario All-Stars* package, but, as Orland notes, they were unable to do so because of "sloppy coding on Nintendo's part more than two decades ago":

> The TASBot team originally planned to let the editor use graphics and items from all five of the *Mario* games on the *SMAS+W* [*Super Mario All-Stars + Super Mario World*] cartridge. But "it turns out [all the *Super Mario All-Stars* games], when they ported them over, they did a pretty haphazard job and barely got them working," Cecil told Ars.
>
> This haphazard coding means the *SMAS+W* cart uses some inconsistent memory management for the in-game sprite tiles, putting enemies and objects in highly unexpected places in the code. "They're unstable...there were a lot of hacky nuances where they had really unusual spaghetti code," Cecil said. "They just threw things at the wall and hoped it would stick."[341]

The game's programmers reasonably expected that their code

would remain hidden and that their players would only inter-act with their games through harmless key-presses. Even if the programmers had foreseen the possibility that hackers would one day reverse engineer their code, they couldn't have possibly expected that they would do so through the key-presses them-selves, or that they would turn them to such absurd ends.

Total Control

In the TASers' perspective on hardware and software, then, we have the beginnings of an answer to the ludopolitical paradox of total control. TASers might be attempting to wrest control from the games and consoles in which it is conventionally understood to reside, but: 1) they use their relative mastery to unexpected ends that do not conform to the normal channels of play, 2) their total controls are explicitly non-utilitarian even though control is otherwise associated with efficiency and purpose, and 3) they adhere to an interpersonal ethic of collaboration and citation that places the locus of agency in interpersonal relations and history rather than the masterful individual. They repurpose control in such a way that it militates against the ontotheology of code.

Normal players, following Suits, obey the rules and aim to win. As triflers, TASers pursue completely different objectives, although they often satisfy normal victory conditions at the same time. Those objectives might be as general as uncovering new knowledge about the game or as particular as constructing a new credits warp that can be achieved in an RTA; regardless, they're usually fun to watch. Indeed, "entertainment" is one of two reasons that TASVideos lists for creating TASes. The other reason, and the one most relevant in the context of the ludopo-litical paradox of total control, is the following: "we are curious how far a game can be pushed. The process of creating [TASes] is also a form of problem-solving and challenge to our intellect and ingenuity." The TASVideos page goes on:

If a child receives a box containing an expensive toy as a birthday present, it's possible that he'll enjoy the box more than the toy. This is creativity. We're doing the same for these games. Instead of walking on the paths created for us, we create our own paths, our own legs and so on. And we're not listening to people who say "you can't do that!". Just like children.[342]

Elsewhere, TASVideos describes TASing as "an art form" and "a craft."[343] In the TASBot block at AGDQ 2017, Cecil described "everything we do at TASVideos [as] art: it's just a form of taking the original game that the developers created and making something new out of it." In addition to this technical understanding of the "art" of TASing, I want to add a conceptual interpretation: the hobby is artistic insofar as it unsettles expectations and frames of understanding and gives form to the technological unconscious, changing our assumptions about what is possible, both within the magic circle and without.[344] Indeed, TASing expands the bounds of the magic circle itself, altering our understandings of "play" and "rules" by adopting new objectives and new methods. The circle seems all the more flexible when these objectives and methods are as extraordinary as they are in the sorts of total controls performed by TASBot. Insofar as the rule-bound institutions of the "real world" operate according to principles that are ludic and computational, the boundary-pushing, relativizing artwork of the TAS functions as an aesthetic means of politicization.

And it is indeed difficult to separate game from reality – hence Wark's "gamespace," and hence my second note on the ludopolitical paradox of total control: although both TASers and captains of industry employ the language of "optimization," TASers generally have a non-utilitarian understanding of their work. Acquisition, production, securitization, consumption, and all the other outcomes associated with technologized neoliberalism have nothing to do with the hobby. It can certainly be argued that the skills being learned by TASers can be translated to capitalist ends, but this is not their primary purpose. The replay board's designer, true, made a comment on *Hackaday* that illustrates both points:

> matt: This is rather impressive. I wonder what these guys could do if they applied themselves to a project which had a[n] actual useful purpose.
>
> true: I designed the bot used in this run. I do apply myself to projects which have actual useful purposes. This one is no exception. Perhaps you have a more strictly un-fun, strictly capitalistic view of "useful." I had fun, and I have console verified other games (like Zelda on NES), so I think what I did was useful.[345]

In this understanding, "usefulness" means pleasure taken in the activity for its own sake. It might lead to something else – console verification, raising money for charity, projects "which have actual useful purposes" – but it does so only incidentally.

The fact that the runners are there for the games is apparent when extreme frivolity, excess, and communal spirit are on display, as with TASBot's live performances. In these moments, the liberalism that is often inherent to hacking, with its emphasis on values like access, freedom, and production, can fall away. E. Gabriella Coleman, writing on the free and open source software community, describes the ways in which even this liberal, production-oriented practice can sometimes exceed it:

> In pushing their personal capacities and technologies to new horizons (and encountering many frustrations along the way), hackers experience the joy that follows from the self-directed realization of skills, goals, and talents. At times, hacking provides experiences so completely overpowering, they hold the

capacity to shred self-awareness, thus cutting into a particular conception of the liberal self – autonomous, authentic, and rational – that these hackers otherwise routinely advance.[346]

Even if TASers' explicit disinterest in utility did not distinguish their outlook from those of their more production-oriented compatriots – even if, in other words, we threw out their assertions about "entertainment," "art," and "fun," and asserted in turn that the majority of their work was ultimately productivist in character – we should be inclined to look on events like TASBot's performances with an eye to the ways in which it might "cut into" the ideals of liberalism, control very much included.[347]

If the liberal self involves autonomy in addition to authenticity and rationality, as Coleman glosses it, then a practice that questions or rejects autonomy would also be a practice that rejects certain vital components of liberalism. The valorization of control is associated with the valorization of an autonomy based on a willing, rational individual – a relatum that precedes and produces his relations. This Hobbesian vision of the subject's place in the world is familiar from the impoverished models of neoclassical economics and realpolitik, but it completely fails to describe a lived experience characterized by being in the world *with others*, others beyond our control, others who are the very condition for the emergence of the new.[348] TASBot seems to be the product of such an understanding: its *performances* of total control militate against the *ideal* of control not only in their ends-agnostic ludic structure and their rejection of productivism, but in their valorization of community and collaboration over autonomy and authorship as well.[349] These values are on continual show at the TASVideos forum and in Twitch streams, YouTube videos, and GitHub code repositories, places where the identities of individuals are obscured by pseudonyms and where their work is always situated in a communal context. Here, the technical structures of the websites and programs in question, as well as the remarkable complexity of the games being played, are key to the values in question. Forms of communication of the sort that take place among these technically-minded players solidify communities and establish order within them.[350] The production and publication of a single movie file at TASVideos, for instance, typically requires the runner to interact extensively with the community, making use of its formal written resources and its less formal forum. In instances where a new runner submits an imperfect movie file without the usual degree of interaction, the site's moderators point them to a range of documentation and then demand that they seek the feedback of the community before submitting again. This sort of interaction is designed to lead to an understanding of the community's key players, its conventions, and its history, since the community is the repository of the deep technical knowledge required for the production of a run. Online collaboration only rarely turns into in-person meetings of the sort that take place at AGDQ, but the fact that it mostly takes place at a distance does not mean that it is not absolutely vital for the work that TASers do: the techniques, tools, and exploits that are central to the hobby depend on both the technical and the social affordances of the internet.

The TASing community's valorization of community and collaboration is particularly visible in its citation practices – the different ways in which runners credit one another for their contributions to particular runs and to the hobby in general. This is a practice that dates back to the early days of speedrunning. In the early 2000s, RTA speedrunners routinely practiced citation in the write-ups to demos and video files, explaining how they had achieved their latest records by making explicit reference to the runners who had gone before, to the techniques that others had discovered, to the family members and friends who had encouraged them to pursue the challenge, and so on.[351] Because these explanations took written form during a time when it was relatively difficult to add commentary to videos and when sharing videos at all was still new and challenging, one might expect that the success of sites like YouTube and Twitch might have made these practices of citation a thing of the past. This is indeed the case for some RTA speedrunners (although many popular runners still go out of their way to cite prior record holders and the techniques they employed), but written citation remains perfectly common among TASers; their completed runs are the culmination of weeks or months of work rather than the routine output of streaming RTAs, and their emphasis is almost always on gameplay and technical explanation to the exclusion of commentary. These citation practices might remain rigorous even if there were no centralized website like TASVideos, given the precedents set by other speedrunners and the characteristics of the medium, but TASVideos ensures it: all published videos are accompanied by explanations authored by the runners, usually lengthy and technical ones; they include justifications for publication written by the site's administrators; they connect to automatically generated forum posts so that community members can discuss the run with the runner and each other; and in instances where the run has "obsoleted" a previous movie, that movie is linked. Authorship is never in doubt, but the community takes center stage.

When the medium for TASing changes from a formal submission to something else, the method of citation changes as well. During TASBot's AGDQ performances, Cecil always mentions the contributions of individual community members to the various aspects of the performance. He repeatedly names the TAS-Videos website as well, taking care to distinguish representative runs like *Gradius* from the strange arbitrary code executions that so often began in *Super Mario World*. SethBling's work in this area is even more interesting. A popular YouTube personality known increasingly for his work in TASing, he, like Cecil, is careful to cite his fellow runners. In a 2016 video describing ACE in *Super Mario World*,[352] for instance, he begins by noting the importance of a "route" discovered by a runner named Jeffw356; the name appears in large font in the middle of the screen as SethBling says it, and he repeats it later in the video. He gives p4plus2 the same treatment, calling him "the real brains of the operation," and notes that MrCheeze discovered the "arbitrary code execution setup that made this whole code execution possible." As a YouTuber with nearly two million subscribers, SethBling is no doubt conscious of the importance of these citations: they give credit where credit is due, calling attention to the otherwise invisible work performed by runners who are known only as faceless pseudonyms when they are known at all.

But the simple fact of citation is far from the most interesting thing about this particular video. In it, SethBling performs an ACE *by hand* – the same thing that TASBot did during AGDQ 2015 with the help of a pre-scripted movie file passing through eight SNES controllers linked together by a multitap. He explains:

> I used a series of *Super Mario World* glitches to inject 331 bytes of processor instructions into system RAM. It was the source code for *Flappy Bird*. I did this using standard, unmodded Super Nintendo hardware. While this kind of thing has been done before by feeding prerecorded controller inputs into a console from a computer, no human has ever completed this kind of exploit until now.[353]

Rather than writing a movie file and feeding it through a replay board of the sort with which TASBot is equipped, he used the TASing community's now-thorough knowledge of *Super Mario World*'s SRAM and a standard Super Nintendo controller to do something bizarre, pointless, and entertaining enough to garner nearly 1.8 million views. He notes in the video that this was not the first time he had done something like this by hand, either; in a 2015 video, he performed the credits warp by hand using similar techniques.[354] He has since modified these techniques and combined them with new discoveries to do even stranger things, including the installation of a complete "jailbreak" on an otherwise unmodified *Super Mario World* cartridge.[355]

These manual implementations of tool-assisted techniques are notable because they represent an important phenomenon characteristic of many niche hobbies in the age of the internet, namely the ways in which their culture, and all that entails, can ripple out into other communities, even when those communities know fairly little about the technical nuances of the practice. In his YouTube videos and Twitch streams, SethBling is performing an understated, entertainment-driven evangelization for the hobby of TASing. He is thereby drawing in and exposing non-specialist viewers to the values that the hobby represents: an appreciation for the inherent imperfections of technology, a tinkerer's approach to code, and a valorization of the communal character of work over individual acclaim. His videos, and most of the videos of his collaborators, seem to be effective in their popularization of the hobby: his vast viewership includes many creators who have been inspired by his work on both *Minecraft* and *Super Mario World*, and the comment sections of his videos always seem to feature conversations between people who have never heard of TASing and those ready to explain its tricks. His videos undoubtedly work so well in this role because they privilege entertainment. SethBling champions the values described above, but he does so implicitly, by demonstrating them; his stated focus is the pleasure of play. The same is true of TASBot, of course.

The effects of SethBling's work, and the work of the programmers on whom he relies, can also be discerned in the way that specialists have taken it up. Newman's observations about the relationship between different parts of the game modding community are relevant here:

[W]hile the direct modification and manipulation of the code are practised by a minority, the outputs of this work exist within and even create wider cultures, communities and rich contexts for criticism, review and play. As such, even though the highly technical work of creating modifications is open to only a small subset of gamers, the availability of the products of these groups sustains and provides renewed opportunities for a far more extensive group using, discussing and offering critique of these products.[356]

Newman could very well be talking about the discovery and publication of ACE methods. Here, technical knowledge routinely passes back and forth between RTA speedrunners and TASers, constituting new "cultures, communities, and contexts" as it does. *Super Mario World* is a case in point. While runners had performed manual credits warps and even ACEs in other games,[357] SethBling was the first to perform either in *Super Mario World* and the first to reach a massive audience. This affected the rest of the RTA community, which responded eagerly to his achievements. In 2015, a month after first publishing his manual credits warp, runners started to explain how to perform the warp in the friendly format of the YouTube video, providing both technical explanations and simplified versions "for dummies."[358] These linked back to the even more detailed explanations at TASVideos, of course, providing an easy channel along which motivated viewers could migrate. In 2016, a year after SethBling had published his manual credits warp, AGDQ introduced a new category for *Super Mario World* speedrunning, the "0 Exit Race," in which four runners compete against one another to perform the credits warp by hand.[359] By that point, one of the internet's more popular speedrunning records sites had already created the 0 Exit category for RTAs, and runners like Jeffw356, who had inspired SethBling's original attempts at the manual warp, had begun competing; the record fell from 4:59.400 in 2015 to 1:13.320 in early 2017, and it will likely fall further.[360]

The waves of influence and inspiration that ripple out into specialist and non-specialist communities do not stop with gamers. Journalistic coverage of the exploits of runners like SethBling and the TASBot team routinely appears at videogame outlets like *Kotaku* and *Destructoid*, but it also appears in places like *Boing Boing* and *Ars Technica*, bringing the runners' work to readers who might be interested in technology but not necessarily in games. It occasionally reaches an even bigger audience, too. In 2016, speedrunner MitchFlowerPower was invited onto *The Late Show with Stephen Colbert* to promote that year's SGDQ. The setup was typically comedic: MitchFlowerPower would race to complete *Super Mario Bros. 3* against Colbert, who would be racing to microwave and eat a Hot Pocket. Colbert won, but MitchFlowerPower was not far behind: he executed the astoundingly difficult credits warp in a little over three-and-a-half minutes. These sorts of appearances communicate fairly little about the hobby itself, but they at least expose millions of normal viewers to the basic fact of its existence. They work as invitations.

Consoles and Computers

Different members of the TASing community react to public performances like the TASBot block or MitchFlowerPower's television appearance in different ways. When TASBot performs an ACE in front of a large audience at AGDQ, it might well help to create "wider cultures, communities and rich contexts for criticism, review and play," but that criticism might turn out to be strictly negative. TASBot's performance at AGDQ 2017 was a case in point. After (finally) showing off a normal and complete TAS of *Gradius*, TASBot executed three total controls: in *Super Mario Bros. 3*, it jumped to a screen showing the AGDQ 2017 and TASVideos logos; in *Mega Man*, it created a fake operating system that resembled Windows 95; and in *The Legend of Zelda: A Link to the Past*, it repurposed the Super Nintendo as a video playback machine running at approximately 10 frames per second in a 256 color palette and turned the two NES consoles into machines for playing back the left and right audio channels at 54 kHz each, using the three-console assemblage to run movie files for TASes of *Super Mario 64* and *Portal*. With these three data streams at its disposal, TASBot then loaded "sk'Hype," taking video calls from a series of wandering audience members who were in the know and streaming them on-screen. It was, as usual, technically impressive,[361] but the audience reaction seemed somewhat muted, at least to the viewers at home, and none of the TASBot team members on the couch were as visibly delighted as they had been in previous years.

In the AGDQ 2017 thread at the TASVideos forum, the reaction was similarly mixed.[362] Early critical commenters highlighted the team's failure to adequately explain what a TAS is, what was happening in the movie files being played through the three-console assemblage, and what the three total controls were adding up to as they were performed. Masterjun, among others, pointed out the difficulty of explaining any glitch-heavy run, and Cecil defended his choice to hold off on a technical explanation for the latter in order to maintain an air of mystery. Later, however, criticisms from some of the movie files' creators themselves appeared, and then criticisms from team members like true and Greenwood. Cecil's tone shifted; he noted both that he had failed to properly attribute some of the work that had been shown and that his "poor time management" had "caused massive damage to those who were slighted as well as collateral damage to others around me." Cecil temporarily stepped away from the TASBot project in order to spend more time with his family, and the TASBot application for that summer's SGDQ was rejected by the marathon's organizers. At the time of writing, the organizers of AGDQ have asked TASBot to apply for AGDQ 2018, but have requested that the team avoid focusing on the technical wizardry that has been its hallmark. TASBot's run at

GDQ events may not have ended, but any future performances are likely to be far more modest than before.

In that AGDQ 2017 thread, one criticism kept recurring: the TASBot block had become a showcase for technical wizardry that bore almost no relation to the TASes that are TASVideos' bread and butter. Various commenters suggested that TASBot had reduced the consoles and the games to mere computers: "it seems like each AGDQ TASBlock relies more and more on behind the scenes computing and less focus on the consoles/games"; "I do wonder why traditional Tool assisted speed runs seem to be absent from the last two showings"; "[t]he TASBot block for GDQs have become more and more about how much a console and games can be bent from their original purpose to produce things they never were intended to produce." A site editor named Invariel put the point this way:

> In addition to the association of TASing to TASBot, the movies created for *GDQ have moved further and further away from TASVideos' stated goals ("to complete games with extremely high precision"; "[i]t must beat the game") and into the realm of proving that computers are, in fact, computers, leading to runs that are created for the sole purpose of being demonstrated at GDQ and similar events, but not publishable on TASVideos.org, which makes the presentation even less representative of the site.

Although many of the commenters described being thrilled by the technical prowess of the TASBot block, many others shared Invariel's sentiment: consoles are *self-evidently* computers; *of course* they are prone to glitches and therefore susceptible to hacking; *of course* they can take data and do extraordinary things with it. Why would this need to be shown?

Invariel's point was obvious for the literati of TASVideos, but it is not necessarily obvious for the rest of us. And it's forgotten all the time. The generative, open computer effectively becomes an "appliance" when it is housed in smooth plastic and accessed only through the buttons of the controller. Consumers encounter it as a black box, engaging with it on its very limited terms.[363] Consoles like the Xbox and the PlayStation are just like the iPhone in this regard. At the end of the day, however, these consoles are not in fact incomprehensible and inaccessible black boxes, nor appliances limited to the functions that their designers gave them; rather, they are computational machines that are ultimately as generative, and as vulnerable, as any laptop. Computers are imperfect and partially legible; they work at electronic and temporal scales that far exceed the capacity of traditional phenomenological reflection, but they can be partially understood and manipulated, if not totally controlled. The would-be tools of the digerati, computers are just as imperfect as the world that Silicon Valley so often nihilistically rejects.

And they are *fun*, even as appliances. Perhaps especially as appliances, in fact, since appliances invite tinkering and disassembly. The "Spirit of the Hacking Present," to invoke a figure from *The International Journal of Proof-of-Concept or Get The Fuck Out*, might be beset by pragmatism, utility, authority, progress, and the moral panics that arise when these values are jeopardized, but there is no need to turn to a long lost past or a future that might never arrive when the present is still so intriguing:

> Why wait for the Specter of the Future to make an appearance? I say, neighbors, let's make like 1594 at the University of Padua – back when a university used to have quite a different place in this game of ghosts – and have our own Anatomical Theater, a Theater of Literate Disassembly![364]

TASers know about the fun and intrigue of tinkering better than most, and they communicate the pleasure of their platform, as well as their technical and cultural values, through public exhibitions like TASBot. "Each year, TASBlock is becoming less of a speedrunning event and more of a weird art installation," one commenter wrote; for the regular, non-specialist viewer, the block was eye-catching and mind-bending in the mode of other technological artworks, an invitation that worked by arousing curiosity. And the same is true of the other works published by TASVideos: they are always exhibitions of technical prowess and explorations of the ludic language of the game, but they can also function as works of art, shifting assumptions and provoking reflection. In an era characterized by neoliberal ideology and technologized ontology, they are an immanent means of conducting critique.

Conclusion: Memento Mori

Digital technology gives the impression of perfection. Seemingly discrete and apolitical in its sharp demarcation of boundaries, it is light, clean, and clear. It suggests inviolability. The rules of the analog world can be bent, broken, avoided, or overturned, but digital rules? They're fixed. Code is law.

But of course it's not. The impression of perfection might dissuade consumers from playing with their products, but it hits gamers like an invitation. Trifling, metagaming, superplay, counterplay, countergaming, minor practice – whatever you want to call it: players gravitate toward this mode of playing with videogames precisely *because* of their seeming inviolability. They're already playing, after all; it's just a question of what they play with.

These critical, creative, and common modes of play can militate against the ethos and the logic of modern technology, rejecting its various ideals – impregnability, systematicity, autonomy, fungibility, ubiquity, perfectibility – and its threat of totalization. So can game design. The affordances of digital games lend themselves to various forms of power fantasy, the broadest of which concerns the ultimate knowability and availability of the worlds that they represent, but design doesn't have to valorize mastery or entail exhaustion; it can steer players down critical paths, even when those paths are not designed with such a didactic, "serious" end in mind.

Play and design, then, can both function *ludopolitically*, rejecting both the taken-for-granted premises and propositions according to which the world is or should be rendered calculable, controllable, and available for the purposes of goal-driven pursuits, and the more obviously political outcomes that often follow: the black-boxing of digital technologies, the fetishization of tech products, the securitization or exclusion of uncertainty, the elevation of self over other, the refusal of finitude, the rendering homogeneous of things, and the making of the world a standing reserve. Outcomes like these are not inevitable, of course, and they are not only associated with digital media; they do, however, tend to follow from the ontological premises and propositions that some of the games and gaming practices described here symptomatize. Further, these design and play practices are not only ways of engaging with videogames. If videogames are not niche cultural phenomena but are instead exemplary ways "in which we are constantly playing with (and being played by) technical media" in general,[365] then the ways in which we interact with them are significant for understanding and working through the current techno-cultural moment.

Here, it is important to emphasize once more that the critical, creative, and ultimately political valence of play and design is not found in sermons or seminars but in the act and ethos of play itself. Critique operates most powerfully when it knows its subject intimately, and in the context of modern technology, the regime of computation, or the ontotheology of code, its force derives not from an appeal to an outside but from a twisting and a working through. Play functions in this critical, ludopolitical fashion in the trifling modes observed above: in the technical-ethical revelations of speedrunning, in the complication of diegesis performed by datamining and theorycrafting, and in the relativizing self-reflection of mythopoiesis, to name only those examples described above. Design does the same: it can thematize the nihilism inherent in the desire to turn back time, demand choice, refuse responsibility, or lay bare the world. In both play and design, we find an immanent critique of several of these variations on the theme of control, a form of critique grounded in and aiming for fun.

Control can be problematic. Valorizing it thoughtlessly, pursuing it for its own sake – in an existential context in which we all ultimately run out of options and time, this leads to frustration or rage. But it doesn't *only* lead there, and videogames and play practices that emphasize control don't have to lead there either. In one of the very few installments of the videogame podcast *A Life Well Wasted*, the host, Robert Ashley, asks players why they play. He gives the last word to Justin McElroy, and I want to do the same:

I think that I'm probably most inclined to play videogames when I need a sense of satisfaction. It's a very predictable sort of thing, and I think it's why so many kids are drawn to it in a time of their life when they don't really have power or control. By playing a game and following the rules and learning what you need to know, you can get the satisfaction of doing something, of accomplishing something. I think achievements and trophies are sort of a crass way of presenting it, but that's really what's at the heart of it. You put something into it and you get something else out – when you feel like you don't have a lot of control.

My mom died when I was 25 years old, in May of 2005. She died of cancer. And as cancer often does, it took a while. And sort of long after she had stopped responding, there was this period where we were waiting. None of us wanted her to wait alone. So there were a lot of nights where we would take turns…We would sleep in the adjacent hospital room, and we would take turns, take two to three hour shifts and then wake the next person up so they would sit in there basically waiting for her to die – and I would play PSP. I mean, you gotta do something, right? And when I was playing PSP, I was in this scenario where I couldn't do anything. You know, I'm literally in the most helpless [state] I could possibly feel, and for a few minutes while I was playing – I dunno, something stupid – *Pursuit Force* or something like that – I had some control. I was able to *do* something, and for a few minutes get away from where I was at. I guess after something like that, you – *owe* videogames. Which I suppose is as good a reason to play them as any.[366]

McElroy's answer to Ashley's question connects death to control, both of which can be linked in turn to design and play. The dream of perfect control is the logical extension of the power fantasy, and it finds expression in almost all videogames in part because of the way that games afford control over death and time, both within the game and without. Player characters have multiple lives; player characters are invulnerable; players can save and reload; players can start and stop a game when they like. These are different means of exercising control in a world that ultimately offers none. As the temporal fact that most directly indexes our ultimate lack of control, death might therefore present a ludopolitical limit case – a subject that games can thematize better or worse, or a fact that different playstyles might address or ignore. In this context, one might argue that games and play practices that afford escape – that help players to avoid a confrontation with mortality, theirs or that of others – should be condemned for their inauthenticity, or their refusal to grapple with the most basic fact of existence.[367] The refusal of death would be the ultimate desperate act of clinging to control, while the acceptance of death would be its ethical counterpart. Most choices in game design and play would fall into the former camp, but some would fall into the latter. Maybe they could be praised.[368]

If that claim seemed to make sense – if this book seemed to be arguing for splitting game design and play into the authentic and the inauthentic, the ethical and the otherwise, the Good and the Bad – then McElroy's story should give it the lie. There is nothing to condemn in the use that he made of an otherwise unremarkable PlayStation Portable game, finding in it a brief escape and a momentary reclamation of control. It undoubtedly did not diminish the impact of his mother's death. Nor is there anything to condemn in the control-affording use that so many players and designers make of ludic media. We need control to get by in the world; we need to explain and systematize the world to use it to our own ends. We should, by all means, take pleasure in it by playing with it. But we also need to be aware of the speed with which its pursuit and exertion becomes pathological, particularly in the context of digital media and late capitalism.

Games and play are neither good nor bad. They can be instrumentalized or evaluated for what they "do" – for whether, for instance, they can be connected to the quest for control – but any such instrumentalization or evaluation can only ever be qualified or partial. Establishing a single criterion for assessing the critical capacity of something would be the worst contravention of critique, a closure of an opening. Play is generative and unpredictable, even within strictly defined rules – maybe especially then. Play can work against control, but it can do much more.

Endnotes

1   Legend of Grimrock Official Forum, "Alchemist Herb Growth Rate," November 20, 2014: http://www.grimrock. net/forum/viewtopic.php?f=20&t=7572&p=85338&hilit- =crystal+flower#p85338.

2   The longer definition is this: "To play a game is to attempt to achieve a specific state of affairs [prelusory goal], using only means permitted by rules [lusory means], where the rules prohibit use of more efficient in favor or less efficient means [constitutive rules], and where the rules are accepted just because they make possible such activity [lusory attitude]. I also offer the following simpler and, so to speak, more portable version of the above: playing a game is the voluntary attempt to overcome unnecessary obstacles" (Bernard Suits, *The Grasshopper: Games, Life, and Utopia* (Peterborough, Ontario: Broadview Press, 2014), 43).

3   See Martin Heidegger, "The Age of the World Picture," in *The Question concerning Technology and Other Essays*, ed. and trans. William Lovitt (New York: Harper Perennial, 1977), 115-154.

4   On this general phenomenon, see N. Katherine Hayles, *My Mother Was a Computer: Digital Subjects and Literary Texts* (Chicago: University of Chicago Press, 2005), and David Golumbia, *The Cultural Logic of Computation* (Cambridge: Harvard University Press, 2009).

5   The phrase "conduct of conduct" is Michel Foucault's: "[t]he exercise of power consists in guiding the possibility of conduct and putting in order the possible outcome. Basically power is less a confrontation between two adversaries or the linking of one to the other than a question of government" (Michel Foucault, "The Subject and Power," *Critical Inquiry* 8, no. 4 (1982): 789).

6   Modern and pre-modern can't be quite so easily divided, however, and some would undoubtedly question the characterization of Machiavelli as a pre-modern thinker. (For an excellent reading of Machiavelli's relationship to human nature, change, and political order that paints a more nuanced picture, see John G. Gunnell, *Political Philosophy and Time* (Middletown, Connecticut: Wesleyan University Press, 1968), 245-247.) This division is intended to illustrate a particular phenomenon, namely a change in attitudes toward uncertainty, rather than to definitively categorize a political thinker or to characterize a transition between epochs.

7   Niccolò Machiavelli, *The Prince*, ed. and trans. David Wooton (Indianapolis and Cambridge: Hackett, 1995), 74-75. See also Discourse 31 from Niccolò Machiavelli, *The Discourses*, ed. Bernard Crick and trans. Leslie J. Walker (London: Penguin, 1970), 488-492.

8   Thomas Hobbes, *Leviathan*, ed. J. C. A. Gaskin (Oxford and New York: Oxford University Press, 1996), 7.

9   Hobbes, *Leviathan*, 34-35.

10   This formulation fits within what Daniel Innerarity calls "the classic theory of politics," which "was concerned with order stability, integration, and planning" (*The Future and Its Enemies: In Defense of Political Hope*, trans. Sandra Kingery (Stanford: Stanford University Press, 2012), 91). Articulated in nominalist terms by Hobbes, it finds idealist expression in Kant. Where Hobbes is concerned with creating a set of definitions that will engender a mechanics and a politics, Kant believes that the mechanics is already in place: "[p]erpetual peace is *guaranteed* by no less an authority than the great artist *Nature* herself (*natura daedala rerum*). The mechanical process of nature visible exhibits the purposive plan of producing concord among men, even against their will and indeed by means of their discord" (Immanuel

Kant, "Perpetual Peace," in *Political Writings*, ed. H. S. Reiss (Cambridge: Cambridge University Press, 1991), 108).

11   "Metaphors, and senseless and ambiguous words, are like *ignes fatui*; and reasoning upon them, is wandering amongst innumerable absurdities; and their end, contention, and sedition, or contempt" (Hobbes, *Leviathan*, 32).

12   For an entire school of political theory, there is in fact no sovereign without the act of decision. See Carl Schmitt, *Political Theology: Four Chapters on the Concept of Sovereignty*, trans. George Schwab (Chicago: University of Chicago Press, 2005).

13   As Lawrence Lessig puts it, "the invisible hand of cyberspace is building an architecture that is quite the opposite of its architecture at its birth. This invisible hand, pushed by government and by commerce, is constructing an architecture that will perfect control and make highly efficient regulation possible" (Lawrence Lessig, *Code v2* (New York: Basic Books, 2006), 4).

14   Alexander Galloway focuses on control by protocols constituted by code, arguing that protocols like TCP/IP manage to institute control in the Deleuzean sense rather than Foucauldian or Hobbesian ones. This does not make protocol – "that machine, that massive control apparatus that guides distributed networks, creates cultural objects, and engenders life forms" – any less powerful (Alexander Galloway, *Protocol: How Control Exists after Decentralization* (Cambridge: MIT Press, 2004), 243).

15   See the third chapter of Suits, *The Grasshopper*.

16   It should be noted that the definitions of "games" and of "play" are contested, and that they have been of particular concern to game studies scholars in the last two decades. One of the most influential definitions can be found in Jesper Juul's *Half-Real: Video Games between Real Rules and Fictional Worlds*, where he describes a game as "a rule-based

system with a variable and quantifiable outcome, where different outcomes are assigned different values, the player exerts effort in order to influence the outcome, the player feels emotionally attached to the outcome, and the consequences of the activity are negotiable." This definition follows a critique of Suits' definition on the basis that it is impossible to "voluntarily" adopt the "less efficient means" that Suits argues is a requisite part of the "lusory attitude": with the rules literally encoded, the player does not even have the opportunity to cheat (Jesper Juul, *Half-Real: Video Games between Real Rules and Fictional Worlds* (Cambridge and London: MIT Press, 2005), 34-36). Other game scholars offer similar criticisms. Jeremy Leipert, for instance, suggests that "all options, all paths, must be part of the programming," which means that "there is nothing that can be considered an obstacle": players are not voluntarily playing by the rules – they have no choice but to play by them. Leipert continues: "Because no il-lusory moves are possible, the players assume an attitude opposite the lusory attitude necessary for non-digital games, of trying to break the unbreakable lusory means rather than actively enforcing them" (Jeremy Leipert, "On Tilt: The Inheritances and Inheritors of Digital Games" (PhD diss., Trent University, 2015), 300-301). In this, both Juul and Leipert are correct: when it is impossible to voluntarily adopt an inefficient means of achieving a goal, players do not play in same way.

17   As the leading proponent of the virtues of gamification puts it, games "help put people back in control...[P]rogressing toward goals and getting better at a game instils a sense of power and mastery" (Jane McGonigal, *Reality is Broken: Why Games Make Us Better and How They Can Change the World* (New York: Penguin Press, 2011), 149).

18   Lewis Mumford, *Technics and Civilization* (Chicago and London: The University of Chicago Press, 2010), 14.

19   Mumford goes so far as to say that the monastery was the
      original scene for the exercise of this new form of appar-
      ently non-violent power: "It was...in the monasteries of the
      West that the desire for order and power, other than that
      expressed in the military domination of weaker men, first
      manifested itself after the long uncertainty and bloody con-
      fusion that attended the breakdown of the Roman Empire"
      (*Technics and Civilization*, 13).

20   On this connection, and in the context of Mumford's claims
      about the clock, see, for instance, James Carey, "Technology
      and Ideology: The Case of the Telegraph," in *Communica-
      tion as Culture*, rev. ed. (New York and London: Routledge,
      2009), 155-177; Martin Heidegger, "The Question concern-
      ing Technology," in *The Question concerning Technology
      and Other Essays*, ed. and trans. William Lovitt (New York:
      Harper Perennial, 1977), 3-35; Harold Innis, *Empire and
      Communications* (Toronto: Dundurn Press, 2007); Friedrich
      Kittler, *Gramophone, Film, Typewriter*, trans. Geoffrey Win-
      throp-Young and Michael Wutz (Stanford: Stanford Univer-
      sity Press, 1999); Marshall McLuhan, *Understanding Media:
      The Extensions of Man* (New York: Signet, 1964); and Lang-
      don Winner, *Autonomous Technology: Technics-out-of-Control
      as a Theme in Political Thought* (Cambridge: MIT Press, 1977).

21   Something similar holds for history: "[t]ime was a process
      that carried order away; the future and past were unreal –
      only phantoms and decaying images in the mind which ex-
      isted in fiction and memory. In Hobbes's geometric world,
      reality meant the denial of time" (Gunnell, *Political Philoso-
      phy and Time*, 247).

22   In his autobiography, Hobbes wrote that his mother's fears
      of the Spanish Armada caused her to give birth premature-
      ly: "my mother gave birth to twins: fear and myself."

23   Marcel O'Gorman makes a similar observation, noting that
      the "hero system" of "technoculture...mediates the denial of

death in a number of ways, from the sense of belonging one achieves through mere ownership of an iPad...to the hope of achieving immortality through gene therapy and other medical technologies" ("Angels in Digital Armor: Technoculture and Terror Management," *Postmodern Culture: Journal of Interdisciplinary Thought on Contemporary Cultures* 20, no. 3 (2010): http://www.pomoculture.org/2013/09/03/angels-in-digital-armor-technoculture-and-terror-management/).

24 Aubrey D. N. J. de Grey, "Combating the Tithonus Error: What Works?" *Rejuvenation Research* 11, no. 4 (2008): 713.

25 Jacques Derrida describes the archive as "the most archaic place of absolute commencement" (*Archive Fever: A Freudian Impression*, trans. Eric Prenowitz (Chicago: University of Chicago Press, 1996), 91).

26 Liam Mitchell, "Life on Automatic: Facebook's Archival Subject," *First Monday* 19, no. 2 (2014): http://firstmonday.org/article/view/4825/3823#p5.

27 This is a claim also made by several others. O'Gorman, for instance, suggests that "technoculture" is "a distinct heroic action system in which technological production is viewed as an end in itself, and individual recognition and death-denial are hypermediated by technologies that permit us to feel that we transcend time and space with increasing ease" ("Angels in Digital Armor"). For O'Gorman, technoculture functions in the same way as older "heroic action systems" like religion and morality, which, according to Ernest Becker, evolved as a means of coping with the existential reality of human finitude (*The Denial of Death* (New York: Free Press, 1973)). Vincent Mosco makes a similar claim, suggesting that technology functions mythologically: "[t]he thorny questions arising from all the limitations that make us human were once addressed by myths that featured gods, goddesses, and the variety of beings and rituals that

for many provide satisfactory answers. Today, it is the spiritual machines and their world of cyberspace that hold out the hope of overcoming life's limitations" (*The Digital Sublime: Myth, Power, and Cyberspace* (Cambridge: MIT Press, 2005), 78, quoted in O'Gorman, "Angels in Digital Armor").

28 Lorenzo C. Simpson, *Technology, Time, and the Conversations of Modernity* (New York and London: Routledge, 1995), ix. Fifty years earlier, Simone de Beauvoir offered a similar claim: "Today...we are having a hard time living because we are so bent on outwitting death...[T]he scales of measurement have changed; space and time have expanded about us: today it is a small matter that a million men and a century seem to us only a provisional moment; yet, the individual is not touched by this transformation, his life keeps the same rhythm, his death does not retreat before him; he extends his control of the world by instruments which enable him to devour distances and to multiply the output of his effort in time; but he is always only one. However, instead of accepting his limits, he tries to do away with them. He aspires to act upon everything and by knowing everything" (Simone de Beauvoir, *The Ethics of Ambiguity*, trans. Bernard Frechtman (Secaucus: Citadel Press, 1974), 120).

29 As Heidegger famously put it, "the essence of technology is by no means anything technological" (Heidegger, "The Question concerning Technology," 4).

30 Heidegger, "The Question concerning Technology."

31 One popular expression of the determinist argument can be found in Kevin Kelly's *What Technology Wants* (New York: Viking, 2010). Evgeny Morozov offers a critical review of Kelly's claims supplemented by a genealogy of the concept of technology in "e-Salvation," *The New Republic*, March 3, 2011: https://newrepublic.com/article/84525/morozov-kelly-technology-book-wired.

32 Johan Huizinga, *Homo Ludens: A Study of the Play-Element in*

Culture (Boston: The Beacon Press, 1950).

33 Friedrich Nietzsche: "This, yes, this alone is *revenge* itself: the will's antipathy towards time and time's 'It was'" (*Thus Spoke Zarathustra*, translated by R. J. Hollingdale (London and New York: Penguin Books, 1961), 162).

34 Gamergate is often described as a "controversy," but using that term makes it possible for either side to appropriate it. For its mostly male perpetrators, Gamergate was a movement calling for ethics in games journalism. For its mostly female victims, Gamergate was a sustained and misogynistic campaign of harassment intended to produce suffering, fear, and silence. To give any credit to the perpetrators' perspective in this case would be irresponsibly ignorant at best, complicit at worst. For a brilliant analysis connecting Gamergate to wider affective and political phenomena like those described here, see Innuendo Studios' six-part series "Why Are You So Angry?" (YouTube, July 13, 2015: https://www.youtube.com/watch?v=6y8XgGhXkTQ&list=PLJA_jUddXvY62dhVThbeegLPpvQlR4CjF). For an equally important analysis in print format, see Katherine Cross, "'We Will Force Gaming to Be Free': On Gamergate and the License to Inflict Suffering," *First Person Scholar*, October 8, 2014: http://www.firstpersonscholar.com/we-will-force-gaming-to-be-free/.

35 I disagree with John Sharp, for whom the "artgames" of the 2000s were likely an historical anomaly (John Sharp, *Works of Game: On the Aesthetics of Games and Art* (Cambridge and London: MIT Press, 2015), 115). This argument omits the prevalence of artful, control-contravening games in the 2010s, as well as before, and it tends to play down the critical capacity of a wider range of games than he credits. See also Nadav Lipkin, "Examining Indie's Independence: The Meaning of 'Indie' Games, the Politics of Production, and Mainstream Cooptation," *Loading...7*, no. 11 (2013): 8-24.

36 Ian Bogost describes the convincing capacity of gameplay as "*procedural rhetoric*: the art of persuasion through rule-based representations and interactions rather than the spoken word, writing, images, or moving pictures" (*Persuasive Games: The Expressive Power of Videogames* (Cambridge and London: MIT Press, 2007), ix).

37 Jean Baudrillard, *Seduction*, trans. Brian Singer (New York: St. Martin's Press, 1990), 131.

38 Felan Parker argues that "[r]ules are inherently expansive, in that the imposition of limitations creates a specific range of possibilities and outcomes, and this activity takes place in the process of playing a video game – a kind of 'expansive' gameplay" ("The Significance of Jeep Tag: On Player-Imposed Rules in Video Games," *Loading...*2, no. 3 (2008): http://journals.sfu.ca/loading/index.php/loading/article/view/44/41). On the relationship between rules and player practices, see also Rainforest Scully-Blaker, "A Practiced Practice: Speedrunning through Space with de Certeau and Virilio," *Game Studies* 14, no. 1 (2014): http://gamestudies.org/1401/articles/scullyblaker.

39 McKenzie Wark, *Gamer Theory* (Cambridge: Harvard University Press, 2007), §23.

40 As Baudrillard argues with reference to the "play" of "seduction," "[t]he only thing truly at stake is mastery of the strategy of appearances, against the force of being and reality. There is no need to play being against being, or truth against truth; why become stuck undermining foundations, when a *light* manipulation of appearances will do" (Baudrillard, *Seduction*, 10).

41 David Cecchetto, Marc Couroux, Ted Hiebert, and Eldritch Priest agree: "the contemporary world is fabricated such that it is simply as it appears to be: ready-made, functional, and unconcerned with the vagaries of truth. Thus...the proper response to the tragic 'wonderlandification' of the

world is a comic riposte, a rejoinder whose critical purchase lies, paradoxically, in the ironic escalation of its miraculous madness" (*Ludic Dreaming: How to Listen Away from Contemporary Technoculture* (New York and London: Bloomsbury, 2017), 11).

42   See Trevor Owens, "Sid Meier's Colonization: Is It Offensive Enough?" *Play the Past*, November 23, 2010: http://www.playthepast.org/?p=278.

43   Jessica Hammer and Meguey Baker, "Problematizing Power Fantasy," *The Enemy* 1 no. 2 (2014): http://theenemyreader.org/problematizing-power-fantasy/. Hammer and Baker note, however, that videogames' affordance of systemic control means that they can in fact be liberatory contraventions of the status quo rather than replications of it: they offer a place "where ordinary rules of power and authority do not apply." On the connection between power, immersion, and fit, M.-Niclas Heckner argues that "the player character is typically tailored to fit the exact needs of the gamespace," and that, since "the player's pleasure partly derives from fulfilling tasks that her representation is perfectly suited for…the player must suspend abilities that are not part of the game world and only engage with those of the avatar" in order to achieve this sense of power ("Obey-Play: Passive Play and Productive Submission to the Code," in Matthew Wysocki, ed., *Ctrl-Alt-Play: Essays on Control in Video Gaming* (Jefferson and London: McFarland, 2013), 184).

44   Christopher Franklin, "Violence in Games," *Errant Signal*, March 17, 2012: http://www.errantsignal.com/blog/?p=267. On the subject of designing branching conversation systems, see Alexander Freed, "Branching Conversation Systems and the Working Writer, Part 1: Introduction," *Alexander M. Freed*, September 2, 2014: http://www.alexanderfreed.com/2014/09/02/branching-conversation-systems-and-the-working-writer-part-1-introduction/.

45 "Themes get to exist only insofar as they don't make us feel sad, or frustrated, or angry, or inconvenience in any way the sense that we are a super-exceptional superhero," Franklin notes. This is almost an inescapable feature of big budget game development: "Power fantasies are the core defining aesthetic of almost all big budget game development. This is why most huge games that want to bring up serious topics or serious ideas end up with that oil-and-water approach used by games like *The Last of Us* and *Max Payne 3*, where a simple third-person shooter is dressed up with cut scenes in between murder sprees to make it 'about' something more. Meanwhile, games that can't do that, like *Deus Ex* or *Fallout* [4], just end up paying lip service to serious ideas without meaningfully examining them. It is hard to speak truth to power or discuss the nature of power when your game is itself a celebration of unrestrained and unexamined power" (Christopher Franklin, "*Deus Ex: Mankind Divided*," *Errant Signal*, September 21, 2016: http://www.errantsignal.com/blog/?p=919).

46 *IGN*, "*Bulletstorm* – Weapons + Echoes & Anarchy Mode," January 14, 2010: http://ca.ign.com/videos/2011/01/14/bulletstorm-weapons-echoes-anarchy-mode.

47 G. Christopher Williams, "Murder by the Numbers," *Pop Matters*, March 2, 2011: http://www.popmatters.com/post/137527-bulletstorm-murder-by-the-numbers/.

48 Wark, *Gamer Theory*, §31. Alexander Galloway: "To play the game means to play the code of the game. To win means to know the system. And thus to interpret a game means to interpret its algorithm" (*Gaming: Essays on Algorithmic Culture* (Minneapolis: University of Minnesota Press, 2006), 90-91). Lev Manovich: "As the player proceeds through the game, she gradually discovers the rules that operate in the universe constructed by this game. She learns its hidden logic – in short, its algorithm" (*The Language of New Media* (Cam-

bridge and London: MIT Press, 2001), 222). Sharp: "To play a game is to construct theories about how to act in order to best obtain one's goals, whatever they might be" (*Works of Game*, 96). Seb Franklin: "to play a game in any way is to apprehend its underlying structures" ("'We Need Radical Gameplay, Not Just Radical Graphics': Towards a Contemporary Minor Practice in Computer Gaming," *symploke* 17, nos. 1-2 (2009): 164).

49 Wark, *Gamer Theory*, §31. Patrick Jagoda draws on Miriam Hansen to make a similar argument. Where Hansen claims that the cinema provided an "aesthetic horizon for the experience of industrial mass society" ("The Mass Production of the Senses: Classical Cinema as Vernacular Modernism," *Modernism/Modernity* 6, no. 2 (1999): 70), Jagoda argues that "[v]ideogames...provide a comparable 'aesthetic horizon' for the experience of our postindustrial society" ("Fabulously Procedural: *Braid*, Historical Processing, and the Videogame Sensorium," *American Literature* 85, no. 4 (2013): 772).

50 *The Division* is a particularly good example of an obviously racist, classist power fantasy symptomatizing concerns about the loss of security. The game puts the player in the position of a New York-based sleeper agent activated by the government when a smallpox virus hits Manhattan. Released at a time when issues of police violence and structural racism were under continual discussion thanks to the Black Lives Matter movement, the game effectively endorses that violence and racism by giving the player extra-judicial powers: they are able to execute US citizens (whom the game deems killable) even for small violations of (what the game declares) the law. As James Portnow puts it, "in *The Division*, you are a government agent killing US citizens on US soil by government order without due process of law, and those actions are portrayed as heroic. That's

terrifying. This gameworld is a totalitarian wasteland, and [the game] glorifies it." The citizen-criminals the player is tasked with killing "are disaster survivors. They're ordinary people who have lived through a horrific event, and without due process, without acknowledging their fourth amendment rights, you just gun down any of them who appear to be acting out of line." Many of them are what the game classifies as "rioters," who are easy to identify: they all wear hoodies. "Literally everyone you find on the street when wearing a hoodie is a thug to be gunned down on sight in this game, at a time when the hoodie has become a national symbol of racial violence for us" (Extra Credits, "*The Division* – Problematic Meaning in Mechanics – Extra Credits," YouTube, April 13, 2016: https://www.youtube.com/watch?v=4jKsj345Jjw). Austin Walker highlights a similar set of problems (The Beastcast, "Episode 42," March 11, 2016: http://www.giantbomb.com/podcasts/the-giant-beastcast-episode-42/1600-1532/), while Heather Alexandra explicitly describes *The Division*'s legitimation of extra-judicial executions as a "power fantasy" ("Turning in the Badge," *Giant Bomb*, April 1, 2016: http://www.giantbomb.com/articles/guest-column-turning-in-the-badge/1100-5426/). The narrative and aesthetic elements of *The Division* couple with its mechanics to legitimize and entrench a brutal ideology.

51   Alan Emrich, "MicroProse's Strategic Space Opera Is Rated XXXX," *Computer Gaming World* 110 (September 1993), http://www.cgwmuseum.org/galleries/index.php?-year=1993&pub=2&id=110. Emrich was referring to *Master of Orion*, but the description applied equally well to *Civilization*.

52   Ted Friedman, "*Civilization* and Its Discontents: Simulation, Subjectivity, and Space," in *Discovering Discs: Transforming Space and Genre on CD-ROM*, ed. Greg Smith (New

York: New York University Press, 1999), http://web.mit. edu/21w.784/www/BD%20Supplementals/Materials/Unit-Four/friedman.htm. Friedman goes on: "The way computer games teach structures of thought – the way they reorganize perception – is by getting you to internalize the logic of the program. To win, you can't just do whatever you want. You have to figure out what will work within the rules of the game. You must learn to predict the consequences of each move, and anticipate the computer's response. Eventually, your decisions become intuitive, as smooth and rapid-fire as the computer's own machinations."

53 Brian Schrank, *Avant-Garde Videogames: Playing with Technoculture* (Cambridge and London: MIT Press, 2014), 4. For Schrank, videogames are not only "an advanced product of technoculture"; "they are also a major site on which culture naturalizes the ways in which we think and play with technology. In this way, each game becomes a microcosm of technoculture itself" (*Avant-Garde Videogames*, 4). Gerald Voorhees, writing from a psychoanalytic perspective, agrees: the good player will inhabit that role and learn those methods of optimization so thoroughly that they will "desire what the game desires" (Gerald Voorhees, "Materialist Fantasies: The Voice as *objet petit a* in Digital Games," *Journal of Gaming and Virtual Worlds* 8, no. 3 (2016): 255).

54 Samuel Arbesman, "It's Complicated," *Aeon*, January 6, 2014: https://aeon.co/essays/is-technology-making-the-world-indecipherable.

55 Galloway, *Gaming*, 90-91.

56 Galloway, *Gaming*, 90-91. Eric Zimmerman makes a similar point from the perspective of game design: because we live in "an era of games" and "a world of systems," we need to develop the tools necessary for navigating it: a "ludic literacy" for a "ludic century" ("Manifesto for a Ludic Century," in *The Gameful World: Approaches, Issues, Applications*, eds.

Steffen P. Walz and Sebastian Deterding (Cambridge and London: MIT Press, 2014), 19-22).

57 Mark Hansen, "New Media," in *Critical Terms for Media Studies*, eds. W. J. T. Mitchell and Mark Hansen (Chicago and London: University of Chicago Press, 2010), 178.

58 Hansen, "New Media," 181. Wolfgang Ernst notes a similar temporal disjuncture in digital computing, which makes possible "time-axis manipulation" and hence "events" that would "otherwise have not been perceptible to human senses" (*Digital Memory and the Archive* (Minneapolis and London: University of Minnesota Press, 2013), 191).

59 Kittler's terms for such translation are "processing," "computing," or "manipulating": all media transmit, store, and process (Hartmut Winkler, "Processing: The Third and Neglected Media Function," MediaTransatlantic: Media Theory in North America and German-Speaking Europe, April 8, 2010: http://homepages.uni-paderborn.de/winkler/proc_e.pdf).

60 Hansen, "New Media," 180-181.

61 This seems to be a feature of media theory in general, in fact: in arguing that "media determine our situation" or that "the medium is the message," Friedrich Kittler and Marshall McLuhan are not delimiting the scope of the function of the media in advance (though they are suggesting that the media itself works to establish limits). Nor, however, are they presenting their readers with a clear-cut guide to thinking about media new or old.

62 John Durham Peters makes a similar claim about the epistemological and ontological character of media, going so far as to say that media "enter into nature, not only society": "[t]he ozone layer, the arctic ice, and whale populations all are now what they are not only because of how they are covered by reporters, but because of how their being is altered by media, understood as infrastructures of data

and control" (*The Marvelous Clouds: Toward a Philosophy of Elemental Media* (Chicago and London: University of Chicago Press, 2015), 2). In this epistemological, ontological, and ecological function, they affect everything: they are "civilizational ordering devices" (Peters, *The Marvelous Clouds*, 5).

63 Heidegger, "The Question concerning Technology," 26.

64 As Kittler claims, "it is only with Heidegger's help that we can hope to develop something like an ontology of technical media" (Friedrich Kittler, "Towards an Ontology of Media," *Theory, Culture and Society* 26(2-3), 2009: 23). Kittler's insights into this conjunction are particularly significant for my analysis because of his addition of a third term: technology intervenes in the world through the manipulation of *time*. See Friedrich Kittler and Geoffrey Winthrop-Young, "Real Time Analysis, Time Axis Manipulation," *Cultural Politics* 13, no. 1 (2017): 1-18, and Sybille Krämer, "The Cultural Techniques of Time Axis Manipulation: On Friedrich Kittler's Conception of Media," *Theory, Culture and Society* 23, nos. 7-8 (2006): 93-109.

65 Heidegger, "The Question concerning Technology," 25.

66 The translation "all-encompassing imposition," and the interpretation that follows from this careful translation, I owe to Richard Rojcewicz, *The Gods and Technology: A Reading of Heidegger* (Albany: State University of New York Press, 2006).

67 John Durham Peters puts it more provocatively: "[m]edia are not only about the world; in many ways..., they *are* the world" (Peters, *The Marvelous Clouds*, 21).

68 Media can, in and of themselves, lead to certain changes, even massive ones, but they shouldn't be understood only in these causal terms. Media technologies like videogames should be understood symptomatically as well: they indicate a broader understanding of the world that contemporary human beings hold in common. Particular technolo-

gies, in fact, come into existence only when a society has made mental room for them. The designations "cause" and "symptom" speak to a broader conceptual interdependence. Media do both things: they bring about certain ethico-political formations while also demonstrating the assumptions that we have concerning the very possibility of something like politics. But they do not do these things in a straightforward fashion. The relationship between these two fields of concern is recursive at the least, and undoubtedly more complicated than that. In Heidegger's terminology, it's not the case that ontic phenomena merely indicate the existence of an ontological ground-giving, or of a particular mode of revealing. Heidegger's determinism isn't of such a simple sort, and neither is the relationship between medium and message; philosophical foundations give rise to political phenomena, but political phenomena also shape new philosophical foundations, or retrench existing ones. Media contents and effects, likewise, arise on the basis of particular media biases, but they also work to change the contours of the media forms themselves.

69 The approach that Graeme Kirkpatrick takes in *Computer Games and the Social Imaginary* (Cambridge: Polity, 2013) resembles mine in some respects, but he restricts his focus to the technological construction of the *social* world.

70 Galloway, *Gaming*, 90. The methodological challenge facing the media theorist, then, is similar to the challenge facing the philosopher: both are attempting to describe something in which they are completely enmeshed, or something on which they are completely reliant – metaphysical language in the case of the latter and algorithmic entanglements in the case of the former. Both thinkers have to use the terms of their technical and philosophical systems in order to critique those systems. To say that the media theorist in particular can't see the forest for the trees would be a cliché,

but it would be an accurate one, since it points to the media's ontological or ecological character – to understanding it as the ground that supports us, the air we breathe, or, maybe most appropriately, the light that lets us see. McLuhan had a similarly ecological conception of the media in mind when he noted both the difficulty of understanding the role played by the media in structuring human existence and the vital importance of doing so in his reference to the electric light (McLuhan, *Understanding Media*, 24-25). It was and remains a "small thing" only in that it almost always escapes our notice: we see what it illuminates, but we don't see the light itself unless it spells out some sign. But this doesn't stop the electric light from generating massive societal effects: the capitalist organization of contemporary society, to take only the most glaring example, relies heavily on the extra working hours and the leveling constancy enabled by the electric light. From enlightenment comes exploitation, among other things.

71 McLuhan, *Understanding Media*, 208.
72 Paolo Pedercini, "Videogames and the Spirit of Capitalism," *Molleindustria Blog*, February 14, 2015: http://www.molleindustria.org/blog/videogames-and-the-spirit-of-capitalism/.
73 Frank Lantz uses the term in *A Life Well Wasted* (Robert Ashley, "Episode Six: Big Ideas," *A Life Well Wasted*, June 23, 2010: http://alifewellwasted.com/podcast/). Elsewhere, Lantz argues that games "are not media" because media connote novelty, computation, content, and messaging, and games are not new, do not require computers, are not always consumed, and do not necessarily convey messages ("Games Are Not Media," *Game Design Advance*, August 30, 2009: http://gamedesignadvance.com/?p=1567). While Lantz's claim rests on a too-narrow understanding of media as channels of communication, he suggests something about the phenomenological and political role that games

can play that resonates with my overall argument: games, he says, are "a way of actively discovering things about ourselves, and the world, through a process that is deeply collaborative – a collaboration between creator, player, and the world itself." If "meaning" is "actively discovered" in a "collaboration" between creator, player, and world, then the world is not just an inert container or something taken for granted, but something we shape as it shapes us. This sounds an awful lot like the claims that other thinkers make about media.

74   See Hannah Arendt's *Eichmann in Jerusalem: A Report on the Banality of Evil* (New York: Penguin, 2006) and "Understanding and Politics: The Difficulties of Understanding," in *Essays in Understanding 1930-1954: Formation, Exile, and Totalitarianism*, ed. Jerome Kohn (New York: Schocken Books, 2005). Arendt was careful to avoid giving a simple causal account for totalitarianism, of course: the Holocaust was not at all the inevitable product of the march of history or the progress of ideas. See also Tracy B. Strong, who notes that Arendt shares her understanding of "the crisis of our time" with Nietzsche: she understands the disappearance of bannisters and he understands the death of God as both "catastrophe" and "opportunity" (*Politics without Vision: Thinking without a Bannister in the Twentieth Century* (Chicago: University of Chicago Press, 2012), 334).

75   Schrank argues that we are "adapted" to technoculture in "our training in the efficient use of computer interfaces and networks to enact our desire and extend our control" (*Avant-Garde Videogames*, 21).

76   "[P]revention and precaution" take the place of "planning and preparation," Innerarity argues; "the political system is reduced to managing the present" (Innerarity, *The Future and Its Enemies*, 2-4).

77   See Ulrich Beck, *Risk Society: Towards a New Modernity*,

trans. Mark Ritter (London: Sage, 1992).

78   It is "an anatamo-politics of the human body," as Foucault puts it: "its disciplining, the optimization of its capabilities, the extortion of its forces, the parallel increase of its usefulness and its docility, its integration into systems of efficient and economic controls" (Michel Foucault, *The History of Sexuality, Volume 1: An Introduction*, trans. Robert Hurley (New York: Vintage, 1990), 139). See also Michel Foucault, *Discipline and Punish: The Birth of the Prison*, trans. Alan Sheridan (New York: Vintage, 1979).

79   Brian Massumi illustrates: "You see it everywhere today. The tell-tale sign is the positive feedback loop. For example, you buy things with your credit card, presumably to satisfy needs or desires in your life. Needs, desires: you purchase at your soft points. That visceral act is actually an interaction: you have just participated in a data-mining operation. Your input feeds a marketing analysis apparatus, and that feeds a product development machine. The system eventually gets back to you with new products responding to the input and with new ways to reach you, massage your rhythms, air out your viscera, and induce you to spend. New needs and desires are created, even whole new modes of experience, which your life begins to revolve around. You have become, you have changed, in interaction with the system. You have literally shopped yourself into being. At the same time, the system has adapted itself. It's a kind of double capture of mutual responsiveness, in a reciprocal becoming" ("The Thinking-Feeling of What Happens," *Inflexions* 1, no. 1 (2008): http://inflexions.org/n1_The-Thinking-Feeling-of-What-Happens-by-Brian-Massumi.pdf).

80   For an often-referenced argument suggesting a scale change, see Gilles Deleuze, "Postscript on the Societies of Control," *October* 59 (1992): 3-7.

81   For an account of the existential roots of the need to take

hold of the future, see Hal Niedzviecki, *Trees on Mars: Our Obsession with the Future* (New York: Seven Stories, 2015). These existential roots give rise to late capitalist shoots: "modern speculation knows no bounds and is limitless: it operates as if there were no limits to the annexation and incorporation of the future into the present, as if everything in the future were representable, knowable, and calculable in principle, as if nothing of the future could possibly escape valorization through either thought or money" (Uncertain Commons, *Speculate This!* (Durham and London: Duke University Press, 2013)).

82 The increasing importance of technological biopolitics may, however, have more to do with a change in scale or scope – quantity instead of quality. See Liam Cole Young's comments on administration in *List Cultures: Knowledge and Poetics from Mesopotamia to BuzzFeed* (Amsterdam: Amsterdam University Press, 2017).

83 Innerarity, *The Future and Its Enemies*, 92.

84 Peter Thiel, "The Education of a Libertarian," *Cato Unbound*, April 13, 2009: http://www.cato-unbound.org/2009/04/13/peter-thiel/the-education-of-a-libertarian/.

85 On the question of the "originary technicity" of the human, see André Leroi-Gourhan, *Gesture and Speech*, trans. Anna Bostock Berger (Cambridge: MIT Press, 1993), and Bernard Stiegler, *Technics and Time: The Fault of Epimetheus*, trans. Richard Beardsworth and George Collins (Stanford: Stanford University Press, 1998). On the subject of the connection between *ressentiment* and nostalgia, see Bradley Bryan, "Revenge and Nostalgia: Reconciling Nietzsche and Heidegger on the Question of Coming to Terms with the Past," *Philosophy and Social Criticism* 38, no. 1 (2012): 25-38.

86 Wendy Chun, *Control and Freedom: Power and Paranoia in the Age of Fiber Optics* (Cambridge and London: MIT Press, 2006), 3.

87   Chun, *Control and Freedom*, 6. Tung-Hui Hu notes a similar pairing of faith and fallibility at the beginning of his reading of the cloud: "it is designed to get to its destination with 'five-nines' reliability, so that if one hard drive or piece of wire fails en route, another one takes its place, 99.999 percent of the time," but "[a] multi-billion dollar industry that claims 99.999 percent reliability breaks far more often than you'd think, because it sits on top of a few brittle fibers the width of a few hairs" (Tung-Hui Hu, *A Prehistory of the Cloud* (Cambridge and London: MIT Press, 2015), ix).

88   The technologies that enable network media work personally and psychologically as well as politically. They are created to satisfy or cope with desires. For Sherry Turkle, we are simultaneously lonely and afraid of the consequences of intimacy, and we turn to network media, personal robots, and other technologies as a means of reconciling these conflicting forces. In *Alone Together*, Sherry Turkle returns repeatedly to children and the elderly, noting the ways that we provide them with technological surrogates for real people: therapeutic robots are given to nursing homes; Furbies and phones are given to children. As Turkle notes, children and the elderly are important sites for thinking through technology because of their vulnerability: the children of busy parents do not necessarily understand their parents' distance, though they probably know more than we suspect; the elderly who find themselves in nursing homes lack the independence they once had, and know that they are on their way to death. Both groups are uniquely vulnerable – both need care – and so the ways in which that care is provided speaks to our more general approach to vulnerability. For Turkle, the temporary solutions that a therapeutic robot provides leave the underlying problem untouched: "The idea of a robot companion serves as both symptom and dream. Like all psychological symptoms, it

240

obscures a problem by "solving" it without addressing it. The robot will provide companionship and mask our fears of too-risky intimacies. As dream, robots reveal our wish for relationships we can control" (Sherry Turkle, *Alone Together: Why We Expect More from Technology and Less from Each Other* (New York: Basic Books, 2011), 283). If the underlying problems for elderly people include the loss of friends and family and fears about death, then Turkle argues that the answer isn't a fuzzy robot – it's companionship on the one hand and solitude on the other.

89   "Freedom," Chun writes, paraphrasing Hannah Arendt and Jean-Luc Nancy, "is a spacing that constitutes existence": it "spaces in its withdrawal, and that there is something is the gift of this withdrawal; this withdrawal divides and joins, enabling existence, relation, and singularity. Freedom is not the lack of relation but the very possibility of relation, and thus of an existent as such...Freedom cannot be separated from fraternity or equality, for fraternity exists because we all share this nothing, and equality exists because we all measure ourselves against it" (Chun, *Control and Freedom*, 292).

90   Hannah Arendt: "The miracle that saves the world, the realm of human affairs, from its normal, 'natural' ruin is ultimately the fact of natality, in which the faculty of action is ontologically rooted. It is, in other words, the birth of new men and the new beginning, the action they are capable of by virtue of being born" (*The Human Condition*, 2nd ed. (Chicago and London: University of Chicago Press, 1998), 247). For an extended commentary on natality in Arendt and Foucault, see Jeanette Parker, "Natality and the Rise of the Social in Hannah Arendt's Political Thought" (MA thesis, University of Victoria, 2012).

91   Chun, *Control and Freedom*, 3.

92   Edward Tenner, *Why Things Bite Back: Technology and the Re-*

venge of Unintended Consequences (New York: Vintage, 1997).

93 This is true of older rhetoric as well. As David F. Noble argues, "the technological enterprise has been and remains suffused with religious belief" (*The Religion of Technology: The Divinity of Man and the Spirit of Invention* (New York: Penguin, 1999), quoted in O'Gorman, "Angels in Digital Armor").

94 A giant machine and a planetary organism at once, Kelly says, "I don't know what else to call it than The One" ("The Next 5000 Days of the Web," *TED*, December 2007: https://www.ted.com/talks/kevin_kelly_on_the_next_5_000_days_of_the_web?language=en#t-1138198).

95 Ray Kurzweil, *The Singularity Is Near* (Viking, 2006). Singulatarianism is closely related to transhumanism, which, as Robert M. Geraci notes, is a spiritual movement. Geraci goes further, arguing that the design of videogames "promote[s] transhumanist thinking" beyond transhumanist circles, thereby "reshap[ing] our reality" (Robert M. Geraci, "Video Games and the Transhumanist Inclination," *Zygon: Journal of Religion and Science* 47, no. 4 (2012): 735).

96 Donna Haraway, "The Cyborg Manifesto," *Simians, Cyborgs, and Women: The Reinvention of Nature* (New York: Routledge, 1991).

97 Kelly, "The Next 5000 Days of the Web."

98 Divinity is often implicitly ascribed to digital technology. For critical commentary, see Jean Baudrillard, *Screened Out*, trans. Chris Turner (London: Verso, 2002), Wendy Chun, "On 'Sourcery,' or Code as Fetish," *Configurations* 16, no. 3 (2008): 299-324, Ed Finn, *What Algorithms Want: Imagination in the Age of Computing* (Cambridge and London: MIT Press, 2017), Seb Franklin, "Cloud Control, or The Network as Medium," *Cultural Politics* 8 vol. 3 (2012): 443-464, , and Alan Liu and Geert Lovink, "'I Work Here, But I Am Cool': Interview with Alan Liu," *Net Critique*, February 23, 2006:

http://networkcultures.org/geert/interview-with-alan-liu/.

99 Rob Coley and Dean Lockwood, *Cloud Time: The Inception of the Future* (Winchester and Washington: Zero Books, 2012), 1.

100 Coley and Lockwood, *Cloud Time*, 17.

101 Coley and Lockwood, *Cloud Time*, 4.

102 Marina E. Vance et. al., "Nanotechnology in the Real World: Redeveloping the Nanomaterial Consumer Products Inventory," *Beilstein Journal of Nanotechnology* 6 (2015): 1769-1780.

103 Colin Milburn, *Mondo Nano: Fun and Games in the World of Digital Matter* (Durham and London: Duke University Press, 2015).

104 In 1959, in the speculative address that founded the nanotech field, Feynman made a joke about how nanocars might "be useful for the mites to drive around in, [though] I suppose our Christian interests don't go that far" (quoted in Milburn, *Mondo Nano*, 8).

105 For John Robert Marlow, "[t]he coming Age of Nanotechnology might best be described as the Age of Digital Matter, for it will be a time in which it becomes possible to manipulate the physical world in much the same way that a computer now manipulates the digital ones and zeroes on its hard drive." For K. Eric Drexler, nanotechnology is ultimately "about bringing digital control to the atomic level and doing so on a large scale at low cost...This methodology, led by molecular simulation, will be at the heart of the engineering process that will lead us forward into the new world of technology." For J. Storrs Hall, "one way to sum up nanotechnology is that it will make matter into software." See Milburn, *Mondo Nano*, 39.

106 Julian Dibbell traces the nanotech dream to the advent of the computer and notes its central role in what he calls "ludocapitalism": "[l]ubricating the global flow of capital... computers... have been consummate enablers of the post-

modern economic condition. But more than that, the computer has been an icon of that condition – a concrete engine of abstract production and, as such, a tantalizing promise of economies finally set free of matter and its many inefficiencies" (*Play Money: Or, How I Quit My Day Job and Made Millions Trading Virtual Loot* (New York: Basic Books, 2006), 22-23).

107 Milburn, *Mondo Nano*, 61.

108 Hayles, *My Mother Was a Computer: Digital Subjects and Literary Texts*.

109 For more on ontotheology and its relationship to technology, see Iain Thomson's *Heidegger on Ontotheology: Technology and the Politics of Education* (Cambridge, NY: Cambridge University Press, 2005). On the connection to cybernetics, Fred Turner points out that Norbert Wiener, the quintessential twentieth century field's father, argued that "disorganization and randomness, whether in the realm of information or in the realm of politics, was something 'which without too violent a figure of speech we may consider evil'" (*From Counterculture to Cyberculture: Stewart Brand, the Whole Earth Network, and the Rise of Digital Utopianism* (Chicago: University of Chicago Press, 2006), 24). For Wiener, and for so many others, *is* strongly implies *ought*.

110 The mournful subject is capable of acknowledging that a loss has taken place, and is thus able to process it without repression. The melancholic, conversely, disavows the loss. The resulting repression can lead to any number of pathologies, and it is the symptomatic expression of the repression in these pathological forms that allows the underlying melancholia to be identified. This analysis can be applied to individual and group subjects alike: border walls, in the application of this analysis to politics, symptomatize the collective disavowal of the state's loss of sovereignty. The ideal of the bounded nation-state is a fiction, of course, but

it is a fiction that would seem to be under particular threat given the increasing sweep of globalization and the refugee crisis of the late 2010s.

111 Jon Henley, "Walls: An Illusion of Security from Berlin to the West Bank," *The Guardian* (November 19, 2013): http://www.theguardian.com/uk-news/2013/nov/19/walls-barrier-belfast-west-b-ank.

112 Wendy Brown, *Walled States, Waning Sovereignty* (New York: Zone Books, 2010).

113 Sara Ahmed, "Affective Economies," *Social Text* 22, no. 2 (2004): 117-139.

114 For Debord, *détournement* was the only tool equal to the unjust relationship *par excellence*, "the spectacle": "a social relationship between people that is mediated by images," neither "a deliberate distortion of the visual world [n]or...a product of the technology of the mass dissemination of images" but rather "a *Weltanschauung* that has been actualized, translated into the material realm – a world view transformed into an objective force" (Guy Debord, *The Society of the Spectacle*, trans. Donald Nicholson-Smith (New York: Zone Books, 1995), 12-13.) Debord, a critical Marxist theorist, understood better than most the political significance of the game: he took the world of the twentieth century, which is to say a world in which our collective conception of space has been fundamentally altered by electronic communications technologies, as a play of forces that can and must be manipulated. He expressed this understanding in his *Game of War*, a board game in which communication units play a role almost as important as the king in chess. Commenting on its significance, McKenzie Wark argues that the *Game of War* is "a diagram of the strategic possibilities of spectacular time": it "refutes [the] territorial conception of space and [the] hierarchical relation between strategy and tactics [characteristic of the war of position].

Space is always partially unmarked; tactics can sometimes call a strategy into being" ("The Game of War: Debord as Strategist," *Cabinet* 29 (2008): http://www.cabinetmagazine. org/issues/29/wark.php). (Debord's game, as well as a commentary on a playthrough, is available in English as Guy Debord and Alice Becker-Ho, *A Game of War*, trans. Donald Nicholson-Smith (London: Atlas Press, 2007).)

115 Gamer theory, he argues, "starts with a suspension of the assumptions of The Cave: that there is a more real world beyond it, somewhere, and that someone – some priest or professor – knows where it is. The gamer arrives at the beginnings of a reflective life, a gamer theory, by stepping out of The Cave – and returning to it" (Wark, *Gamer Theory*, §19).

116 Wark, *Gamer Theory*, §21.

117 Wark, *Gamer Theory*, §35.

118 Wark, *Gamer Theory*, §22.

119 Roger Caillois distinguishes between *paidia* and *ludus* in *Man, Play, and Games*, trans. Meyer Barash (New York: Free Press of Glencoe, 1961). It's no coincidence that *paidia*, or a spontaneous form of play, resembles *paideia*, or the education of the citizen. See Sebastian Deterding, "Paideia as Paidia: From Game-Based Learning to a Life Well-Played," Games Learning Society 8.0, June 15, 2012: https://www. slideshare.net/dings/paideia-as-paidia-from-gamebased-learning-to-a-life-wellplayed.

120 On critical and ethical game design, see especially Mary Flanagan's *Critical Play: Radical Game Design* (Cambridge and London: MIT Press, 2013) and Miguel Sicart's *Beyond Choices: The Design of Ethical Gameplay* (Cambridge and London: MIT Press, 2013).

121 Videogames, despite their algorithmic character, despite their *structuration*, can give the lie to the fantasy of structure. When Jacques Derrida delivered "Structure, Sign,

and Play" in 1966, he wasn't thinking of *Spacewar!* – but he could have been: "The concept of centered structure…is contradictorily coherent. And, as always, coherence in contradiction expresses the force of a desire." Derrida clearly identified the need for a ground that all structures express: "The concept of centered structure is in fact the concept of a freeplay based on a fundamental ground, a freeplay which is constituted upon a fundamental immobility and a reassuring certitude, which is itself beyond the reach of the freeplay. With this certitude anxiety can be mastered, for anxiety is invariably the result of a certain mode of being implicated in the game, of being caught by the game, of being as it were from the very beginning at stake in the game" (Jacques Derrida, "Structure, Sign, and Play in the Discourse of the Human Sciences," in *The Structuralist Controversy: The Languages of Criticism and the Sciences of Man*, eds Richard Macksey and Eugenio Donato (Baltimore and London: The Johns Hopkins University Press, 1970), 248). In a structuralist conception, freeplay would require a fundamental ground free of the destabilizing challenge of play; it would be the mutual work done by freeplay and ground that would free the structuralist of the anxiety of the game. It would be this interplay – the hierarchical division according to which freeplay takes place on the basis of the stability of ground – that would free the individual of anxiety as such, ultimately a nebulous anxiety that crystallizes around the inevitability of death (Martin Heidegger, *Being and Time*, trans. John Macquarrie and Edward Robinson (San Francisco: Harper and Row, 1962)). It is this anxiety, Derrida suggests, that gives rise to the need for security and control in the context of sure structures, the certainty of which we are guaranteed by the presence of a freeplay that is so clearly their opposite. If there is no absolute origin or final end that would provide a foundation or explanation for the structure of language, society, or the psyche, then there is no absolute reassurance as to how these things function, where they are going, or how they will affect us. This is not to say that there *is* no center, but that the center is a *function* that works in tension with the decentring force of freeplay. We are constituted by a play in uncertainty that continually threatens the disruption of all of our categories and concerns. This suggests the need for a radically different comportment to the world than that provided by the claim to origins, foundations, and stability, since freeplay does not need to be taken as a threat: "As a turning towards the presence, lost or impossible, of the absent origin, this structuralist thematic of broken immediateness is thus the sad, *negative,* nostalgic, guilty, Rousseauist facet of the thinking of freeplay of which the Nietzschean *affirmation* – the joyous affirmation of the freeplay of the world and without truth, without origin, offered to an active interpretation – would be the other side. *This affirmation then determines the non-center otherwise than as a loss of the center.* And it plays the game without security. For there is a *sure* freeplay: that which is limited to the *substitution* of *given and existing, present,* pieces. In absolute chance, affirmation also surrenders itself to *genetic* indetermination, to the *seminal* adventure of the trace" (Derrida, "Structure, Sign, and Play in the Discourse of the Human Sciences," 264). Nietzsche has "showed us the way" to an interpretation of freeplay "which is no longer turned towards the origin, affirms freeplay and tries to pass beyond man and humanism, the name man being the name of that being who, throughout the history of metaphysics or of ontotheology – in other words, through the history of all of his history – has dreamed of full presence, the reassuring foundation, the origin and the end of the game" (Derrida, "Structure, Sign, and Play," 264-265). The answer to the finitude and contingency of the world is *amor fati*: embracing the fact that we do not have control.

122 Ian Bogost is equally uninterested in serious games, albe-it for a different reason: "[g]ames – like photography, like writing, like any medium – shouldn't be shoehorned into one of two kinds of uses, serious or superficial, highbrow or lowbrow, useful or useless," since this sort of division fails to take videogames as a medium with a wide range of pos-sibilities. "After all, we don't distinguish between only two kinds of books, or music, or photography, or film. Rather, we know intuitively that writing, sound, images, and mov-ing pictures can all be put to many different uses" (*How to Do Things with Videogames* (Minneapolis and London: Uni-versity of Minnesota Press, 2011), 5). Understanding this range of uses is part of Bogost's media microecological ap-proach.

123 *The Best Amendment*, for instance, represents the player as a gun-toting white cone, which looks uncomfortably similar to the conical hats of the Ku Klux Klan, tasked with shoot-ing black cones and collecting stars while quotations from the National Rifle Association ("The only thing that stops a bad guy with a gun is a good guy with a gun") appear onscreen.

124 "*Adam Killer* isolates a cause-and-effect loop in first-person shooter games so players can pry it apart in detail...The unspoiled columns of breathing virtual bodies are neatly set up for a hearty slaughter. There is no waiting, no need to move or improve. As the player rains bullets, images of Adam, bullet shells, and blood trails smear in the air. Shoot-ing in mainstream games is limited and reinforced as an intermittent, rather than constant and monolithic, behavior. *Adam Killer* short-circuits the reward cycle into a nauseat-ing overflow. The slaughter fantasy is supersaturated and held in place until it becomes an abject spectacle" (Schrank, *Avant-Garde Videogames*, 44).

125 Brody Condon, interview by Matteo Bittanti, "Interview: Brody Condon's 'Adam Killer' (1999)," *Gamescenes*, May 31, 2010: http://www.gamescenes.org/2010/05/interview-brody-condons-adam-killer-1999.html.

126 Miguel Sicart, *Beyond Choices*, 2.

127 Jacques Ranciere, "Introducing Disagreement," *Angelaki: Journal of the Theoretical Humanities* 9, no. 3 (2004): 3-9.

128 Ranciere refers to this impoverished politics as "the police." Carl Schmitt draws a similar distinction in *The Concept of the Political*, trans. George Schwab (Chicago and London: University of Chicago Press, 1996).

129 Emmanuel Levinas, *Totality and Infinity: An Essay on Exteriority*, trans. Alphonso Lingis (Pittsburgh: Duquesne University Press, 1969). See also Judith Butler, *Giving an Account of Oneself* (New York: Fordham University Press, 2005).

130 Max Weber, "The Profession and Vocation of Politics," in Peter Lassman and Ronald Speirs, eds, *Political Writings* (Cambridge: Cambridge University Press, 1994).

131 Sicart, *Beyond Choices*, 98, 29.

132 In conversation with Miguel Sicart, Manveer Heir suggests that "[o]ne way to handle [the ability to make ethical choices] is to defer the consequence until way later, so the player who wants to change their mind would have to play a lot of content to get back to where they are and decide if that's worth it. I'm not against removing the ability to redo those sorts of decisions without starting a new game, but that would need to be more explicitly clear to the player since this goes against years of training they've received from [other] video games" (Sicart, *Beyond Choices*, 103). While I agree, I also think the potential frustration that the well-trained player might feel would be well worth the novelty of the experience. For more on irreversible decisions in videogames, see Daniel White and Michael Grossfeld, "Irrevocability in Games" (BSc thesis, Worcester Polytechnic

Institute, 2012), as well as *Lisa: The Painful*.

133 Greg Kasavin, "I Don't Want to Know: Delivering Exposition in Games," *GDC Vault*, October 5-8, 2010: http://www.gdcvault.com/play/1013847/I-Don-t-Want-to.

134 Bogost, *Persuasive Games*, ix.

135 Bogost, writing later on the relationship between games and things (in the most general ontological sense), suggests that this attitude is indeed baked into our basic attitude toward the world: the burden of feeling like we are expected to understand the world and ourselves, he writes, "demands that we account for everything in advance, and that we approach the world as a unified and coherent form that we have already mastered. But when we face the world, it doesn't make sense in that way. It's not there for us – not only for us, at least, even the parts that we fashioned expressly for our own ends" (Ian Bogost, *Play Anything: The Pleasure of Limits, the Uses of Boredom and the Secret of Games* (New York: Basic Books, 2016), 56).

136 Schrank, *Avant-Garde Videogames*, 79.

137 Innuendo Studios, "Story Beats: *Bastion*," YouTube, April 15, 2016: https://www.youtube.com/watch?v=IyhrKPLDCyY.

138 Innuendo Studios, "Story Beats: *Bastion*."

139 Innuendo Studios, "Story Beats: *Bastion*." See also Innuendo Studios, "Story Beats: *Dear Esther*," YouTube, March 8, 2016: https://www.youtube.com/watch?v=NOw-Zq1CzcQ, "Story Beats: *Limbo*," YouTube, March 16, 2016: https://www.youtube.com/watch?v=WQ6H8GJBT1k, and "Story Beats: *Ben There, Dan That*," YouTube, March 28, 2016: https://www.youtube.com/watch?v=NtuyTy0EjvM.

140 Raph Koster, "A Letter to Leigh," *Raph Koster's Website*, April 9, 2013: http://www.raphkoster.com/2013/04/09/a-letter-to-leigh/.

141 The title cues the player into the game's theme, and the de-

scription includes an explicit articulation of Quinn's goals: "to illustrate as clearly as possible what depression is like" and to help "other sufferers...come to know that they aren't alone."

142 Quoted in Leigh Alexander, "There Is Nothing to 'Do' in O'Reilly's *Mountain* – and That's a Good Thing," *Gamasutra*, July 8, 2014: http://www.gamasutra.com/view/news/220443/There_is_nothing_to_do_in_OReillys_Mountain__and_thats_a_good_thing.php. O'Reilly's next game, *Everything*, continued this theme: the player can opt to control the game, but they can also sit back and let the game play itself.

143 On Steam, one user wrote the following representative review: "From the reviews on the store page, I thought that it would have some kind of events that happen to liven things up. You could grab random objects, arrange them, see the seasons change, maybe there would be some birds flying around. It gave the impression that even though there wasn't a point to the game, the experience alone would be fun, and you'd stick to it just to see what would happen. But I never saw that. I played for 20 minutes. I spun the camera, i played the keytar, I zoomed in and out, I found every feature on my mountain. It rained, i spun the mountain to make the clouds go away. I saw the little thoughts my mountain had. But nothing happened. I pressed every button, manipulated every control I could think of, and made as many patterns with my mouse as I could imagine, and nothing happened."

144 As Ian Bogost writes in a criticism of "walking simulator" games like *Dear Esther* and *Gone Home*, "[t]he gag of a game with no gameplay might seem political at first, but it quickly devolves into conceptualism" ("Video Games Are Better without Stories," *The Atlantic*, April 25, 2017: https://www.theatlantic.com/technology/archive/2017/04/vid-

eo-games-stories/524148/).

145 Brendan Keogh, *Killing Is Harmless: A Critical Reading of* Spec Ops: The Line (Marden, Australia: Stolen Projects, 2012), 7.

146 On propaganda, see Robert Jackson, BioShock*: Decision, Forced Choice and Propaganda* (Winchester, UK and Washington, DC: Zero Books, 2014). On dystopia, see Rowan Tulloch, "Ludic Dystopias: Power, Politics and Play," *Proceedings of the Sixth Australasian Conference on Interactive Entertainment*, ACM, 2009: 13-23; Lars Schmeink, "Dystopia, Alternate History and the Posthuman in *Bioshock*," *Current Objectives of Postgraduate American Studies* 10 (2009): http://copas.uni-regensburg.de/article/view/113; and Jessica Aldred and Brian Greenspan, "A Man Chooses, A Slave Obeys: *BioShock* and the Dystopian Logic of Convergence," *Games and Culture* 6, no. 5 (2011): 479-496. On objectivism, see Joseph Packer, "The Battle for Galt's Gulch: *Bioshock* as Critique of Objectivism," *Journal of Gaming and Virtual Worlds* 2, no. 3 (2010): 209-224. On education, see Roger Travis, "*Bioshock* in the Cave: Ethical Education in Plato and in Video Games," in Karen Schrier and David Gibson, eds, *Ethics and Game Design: Teaching Values through Play* (Hershey and New York: Information Science Reference, 2010), 86-101. On capitalism, see Thijs van den Berg, "Playing at Resistance to Capitalism: *BioShock* as the Reification of Neoliberal Ideas," *Reconstruction: Studies in Contemporary Culture* 12, no. 2 (2012): http://reconstruction.eserver.org/Issues/122/vandenBerg.shtml. On medical history, see Suzannah Biernoff, "Medical Archives and Digital Culture: From WWI to *BioShock*," *Medical History* 55 (2011): 325-330.

147 In addition to those authors cited below, see Adam Ruch, "Interpretations of Freedom and Control in *BioShock*," *Journal of Gaming and Virtual Worlds* 2, no. 1 (2010): 84-91; Rowan Tulloch, "A Man Chooses, A Slave Obeys: Agency, Interactivity and Freedom in Video Gaming," *Journal of*

Gaming and Virtual Worlds 2, no. 1 (2010): http://www.in-tellectbooks.co.uk/journals/view-Article,id=9436/; Matthew Wysocki and Betsy Brey, "'All That's Left Is the Choosing': *BioShock Infinite* and the Constants and Variables of Control," in Matthew W. Kapell, ed., *The Play versus Story Divide in Game Studies: Critical Essays* (Jefferson: McFarland, 2015), 145-157.

148 Matthew Wysocki and Matthew Schandler, "Would You Kindly? *BioShock* and the Question of Control," in Matthew Wysocki, ed., *Ctrl-Alt-Play: Essays on Control in Video Gaming* (Jefferson and London: McFarland and Company, 2013), 202.

149 As Wysocki and Schandler put it, "if we are willing to accept that we must perform certain actions because 'the game requires it' what does that say about our free will? What does it mean that we find it acceptable to 'kill' other characters because the game tells us they are 'evil'?" (Wysocki and Schandler, "Would You Kindly," 205).

150 Objectivism represents the diametric opposite of the political and ethical stance that I am advocating here: as a philosophy characterized by the fantasy of objective and knowable truth and a belief in the evil of altruism, it hates the vulnerable, unknowable other. *BioShock*'s particular critique of objectivism focuses on science, dealing as the game does with the technological fantasy of the controllability of the body and the environment. Gwyneth Peaty notes that *BioShock* uses its mechanics to play out "contemporary anxieties regarding biomedicine, technology, and the body" ("'Hatched from the Veins in Your Arms': Movement, Ontology, and First-Person Gameplay in *BioShock*," in Gerald Voorhees, Josh Call and Katie Whitlock, eds, *Guns, Grunts, and Grenades: First-Person Shooter Games* (Whitlock: Continuum, 2012), 154). Fantastic as the whole setting of Rapture and the figures of Ryan and Fontaine are, this critique

might seem like it is targeting a straw man; this is not the case, however, since the patent absurdity of objectivism has not prevented it from influencing the real world, particularly through its adoption in the tech sector. (On the lasting influence of objectivism on politics, economics, and technology, see Adam Curtis, "Love and Power," *All Watched over by Machines of Loving Grace*, May 23, 2011, BBC.) Rapture is dystopian, but since its objectivist seeds have been planted elsewhere, a critique of Rapture can also function as a critique of the places that they have taken root.

151 As David Owen points out, "the feeling of having input in the game story – narrative agency – is an illusion akin to suspension of disbelief in theatre...On some level the theatregoer knows they are actors on a stage. Likewise, the game player knows every option available within the game narrative has been predetermined" ("The Illusion of Agency and the Affect of Control within Video Games," in Matthew Wysocki, ed., *Ctrl-Alt-Play: Essays on Control in Video Gaming* (Jefferson and London: McFarland and Company, 2013), 72). Owen is building on several commentaries about the illusory nature of agency in videogames. See, for instance, Alec Charles, "Playing with One's Self: Notions of Subjectivity and Agency in Digital Games," *Eludamos: Journal for Computer Game Culture* 3, no. 2 (2009): 281-294, and Dominic Arsenault and Bernard Perron, "In the Frame of the Magic Circle: The Circle(s) of Gameplay," in Bernard Perron and Mark J. P Wolf, eds, *The Video Game Theory Reader 2* (London and New York: Routledge, 2009), 109-131. Owen, along with Joseph Hogle ("Deus Ex Ludos: Representation, Agency, and Ethics in *Deus Ex: Invisible War*," *Well Played* 1, no. 3 (2012): 49-69), has the good sense to note that players are already aware of the ostensible "problem" of agency that Charles identifies.

152 Clint Hocking, "Ludonarrative Dissonance in *BioShock*,"

Click Nothing: Design from a Long Time Ago, October 7, 2007: http://clicknothing.typepad.com/click_nothing/2007/10/ludonarrative-d.html. Jonathan Blow imagines that the conflict arose because different people were responsible for story and gameplay: "It feels wrong, right? Because on the one hand, the author of the story says, 'These Little Sisters are very important and you should care about them.' And on the other hand, the author of the game design says, 'Well, you can pretty much do what you want. It doesn't matter either way'" ("Conflicts in Game Design," Montreal International Game Summit, November 19, 2008: http://braid-game.com/news/2008/11/a-new-lecture-about-story-and-game-design/). Hocking's term gave rise to a wave of adoption and criticism as designers, players, and critics gave voice to the ways in which mechanics and narrative relate. Dan Olson, blogging at the end of the wave, argues convincingly for its usefulness (see Folding Ideas, "Ludonarrative Dissonance," YouTube, July 19, 2017: https://www.youtube.com/watch?v=04zaTjuV60A).

153 Designer Ken Levine confirms that this was his intention: "I think that it was really the ultimate insult to the player, that [Ryan] chooses to die but you can't choose to do anything. You have no will at all. The rest of the game after that is to establish your will in the world. Will is a very important thing in video games. What will do you have?" (Ken Levine, interview by Chris Remo, "Ken Levine on *BioShock*: The Spoiler Interview," *ShackNews*, August 30, 2007: http://www.shacknews.com/article/48728/ken-levine-on-bioshock-the).

154 Keogh, *Killing Is Harmless*, 7.

155 Keogh, *Killing Is Harmless*. For a longer academic description his method, see Brendan Keogh, "A Play of Bodies: A Phenomenology of Videogame Experience" (PhD diss., RMIT University, 2015).

156 Keogh, *Killing Is Harmless*, 7.

157 Thematically, Keogh and other critics have praised *Spec Ops* for its critique of militarism and the military-entertainment complex, interventionism, American exceptionalism, racism, and masculinity, as well as for its unflinching portrayal of post-traumatic stress disorder. Aesthetically and mechanically, they have noted the realism of the game's depiction of violence, the hyperrealism of its portrayal of the main character's descent into madness, the range of meaningful choices that its mechanics afford, and its effective use of literary and artistic references ranging from Joseph Conrad, Pablo Picasso, and Ernest Hemingway to Francis Ford Coppola and Sam Mendes. This has led critics, designers, and scholars to describe the game's achievements in superlative terms: it is "the harshest indictment of modern military shooter games that I've ever seen" (Extra Credits, "Extra Credits: *Spec Ops: The Line* (Part 1)," YouTube, September 6, 2012: https://www.youtube.com/watch?v=k-jaBsuXWJJ8); it produced "genuine feelings of weariness, guilt, and actual physical sickness" (Zero Punctuation, "*Spec Ops: The Line* (Zero Punctuation)," YouTube, October 24, 2012: http://www.escapistmagazine.com/videos/view/zero-punctuation/6021-Spec-Ops-The-Line); it "is provocative, powerful, and entirely unafraid to sock you square in the jaw" (*EGM Now*, "EGM Review: *Spec Ops: The Line*," June 27, 2012: http://www.egmnow.com/articles/reviews/egm-review-spec-ops-the-line/).

158 Jordan Garland, "Aftermath: Crossing the Line with Walt Williams," *Gaming Bolt*, July 16, 2012: http://gamingbolt.com/aftermath-crossing-the-line-with-walt-williams.

159 Tom Bissell describes the setup and its apparent failings in "Thirteen Ways of Looking at a Shooter," *Grantland*, July 12, 2012: http://grantland.com/features/line-explores-reasons-why-play-shooter-games/.

160 Konrad went rogue because he refused an order to withdraw the 33rd from the city before all of the refugees had been evacuated. When some of Konrad's men disagreed with his refusal and mutinied, he had them executed and strung up as a warning. Worried by the 33rd's actions, many of the refugees rebelled in turn. They were assisted by the CIA, intent on killing off the 33rd and covering up the disaster in order to avoid a political destabilization of the Middle East. This implausible setup is mirrored in its gameplay, but this implausibility has the effect of providing the player with critical distance. Walker, Adams, and Lugo seem just as bulletproof as the player characters in other shooter games. This implausibility is made problematic by the fact that the gameplay is unconvincing: *Spec Ops* pairs dated and frequently tedious cover mechanics with ridiculous shooter conventions like exploding barrels. All of this has the effect of making the player notice the gameplay, calling attention to the "gameness" of the game. Additionally, the game really could not be more conventional. Its white, male, military protagonist is named "Walker," which is as generic (and descriptive) a name as possible, and he is voiced by Nolan North, easily the most recognizable voice in the industry (Keogh, *Killing Is Harmless*, 17-18). The juxtaposition of this disappointingly and noticeably generic gameplay with the serious but absurd narrative works ironically, generating in the player a sense of uncanniness or discomfort as the state of flow that shooters normally engender is broken (Mihály Csíkszentmihályi, *Flow: The Psychology of Optimal Experience* (New York: Harper Perennial, 1991)). Shooters need their players to be immersed in the gameplay, more or less thoughtlessly acting and reacting; the story and aesthetic of the average triple-A shooter should not detract from the twitchy core of the gameplay. Competitive players of games like *Counter-Strike: Global Offensive* will go so

far as to turn down video settings, preload maps, and force the CPU to prioritize the game in order to optimize their frames-per-second rate. "A shooter works by effectively training its players to ignore things like great characterization and thoughtful scenario-making," as Tom Bissell notes (Bissell, "Thirteen Ways of Looking at a Shooter"), but *Spec Ops* does the exact opposite. In generating such "weird, dissociative play" (Extra Credits, "Extra Credits: *Spec Ops: The Line* (Part 2)," YouTube, September 12, 2012: https://www. youtube.com/watch?v=cJZIhcCA2lk), the game provides the player with the distance necessary for critique.

161 This is an unsettling shift, as Keogh observes: "Simply changing the human NPCs I am shooting to an ethnicity that more closely reflects my own is a startlingly powerful way to force me to acknowledge the humanity of the targets I am shooting. You don't have to be a consciously racist person to more easily *other* people whose language and cultures you don't understand" (Keogh, *Killing Is Harmless*, 38).

162 Steven Holmes, "'You Are Not in Control': *Spec Ops: The Line* and the Banality of War," in Steffen Hantke and Agnieszka Soltysik Monnet, eds, *War Gothic in Literature and Culture* (Routledge, 2016), 157.

163 Walt Williams notes that the white phosphorus attack is "even more of a game" than *Spec Ops* itself, "a game within a game": Walker looks down at the targeting camera's depiction of white dots moving around – digitized, sanitized, and distanced, at least in the moment, from the consequences – and fires again and again (Richard Clark and Drew Dixon, "Podcast #18: *Spec Ops: The Line*'s Lead Writer, Walt Williams," *Gamechurch*: http://gamechurch.com/podcast-18-spec-ops-lines-lead-writer-walt-williams/).

164 Keogh, *Killing Is Harmless*, 91.

165 See, for example, Samuel Roberts, "Now Playing: *Spec Ops'*

Most Troubling Scene," *PC Gamer*, December 3, 2014: http://www.pcgamer.com/now-playing-spec-ops-most-troubling-scene/.

166   Keogh, *Killing Is Harmless*, 79.

167   Keogh writes, "Whereas Bioshock's protagonist mistakenly thought he had a choice, Walker mistakenly thought he did not. As long as Walker stayed in Dubai, it was true that he didn't have a choice. But could've he just left Dubai? As long as I played The Line or Bioshock, I didn't have a choice, but could've I just stopped playing the game? Unlike Rapture, Dubai is not at the bottom of the ocean. It is a system and a society that Walker can walk away from. 'There's always a choice,' Lugo once said. Perhaps not. But, at the very least, we have a responsibility. I may not have always had a choice in my actions in *The Line*, but I was still responsible for being present in those choice-less situations. Or, put another way, what I chose to do doesn't matter so much as what I did" (*Killing Is Harmless*, 136).

168   This is true of the false choices with which it repeatedly presents the player throughout the game as well. In these, *Spec Ops* demonstrates to the player the insignificance of killing this person or that person, since everyone with whom the responsibility-denying, delusional Walker comes into contact ends up dead.

169   To say that Konrad figures Walker's conscience isn't quite right. In Freudian terms, Konrad is the incarnation of Walker's superego: he is the "one part of the ego [that] sets itself over against the other, judges it critically, and...takes it as its object" (Sigmund Freud, "Mourning and Melancholia," in *The Standard Edition of the Complete Psychological Works of Sigmund Freud, Volume XIV (1914-1916)*, trans. James Strachey (London: Hogarth Press, 1953), 247). Where Walker's ego is in denial, his superego insists that something is wrong and that he is responsible. Konrad, in other words,

is melancholic. He displays the symptoms: he hallucinates; he exhibits sadism; he (through Konrad) self-castigates; he is suicidal (Freud, "Mourning and Melancholia," 244, 251, 248, and 252). Above all, he denies that which he has lost, or that which he has refused to let go. Konrad, recall, saved Walker's "bleedin' carcass" in Kabul, and Walker and Konrad spoke together about difficult things. We can infer that there is a sense in which Walker *loved* Konrad – not as a man, but as an ideal that Walker is unable to identify or name, and that has disappointed him precisely because it was an ideal. Walker "knows *whom* he has lost but not *what* he has lost in him," in other words (Freud, "Mourning and Melancholia," 245). And because the disappointing object that Konrad figures is unknown, Walker is unable to acknowledge its loss and go through a process of mourning that would result in his eventual shifting of desire to a new object. Instead, Walker internalizes that unknown object as Konrad: the figure of Konrad becomes Walker's superego, enabling Walker to criticize Konrad and the disappointment that he represents by way of his criticism of himself. Konrad's unrelenting criticism of Walker is Walker's criticism of himself. For which disappointment does Konrad stand in, and what does Walker's response to it say about the assessment that *Spec Ops: The Line* makes of the player? Again and again, Walker insists that he "has no choice," but the manifestation of his superego gives that notion the lie. Walker's protestations cover over the knowledge that he could very well turn around and leave the city. As Walker disavows that knowledge, Konrad appears more and more frequently until he eventually materializes, called into being by Walker's guilt. What Walker once aspired to – that which has since become the source of profound disappointment; the ideal that he once loved, and that he projected onto his former commander – was heroism. Konrad says it plainly: "The truth, Walker, is that you're here because you wanted to feel like something you're not. A hero." Understood in slightly different words, Walker once aspired to re-establish order in situations that had spiraled disastrously out of control. Walker "loved" the ideal that military interventionism is supposed to concretize, and he was so disappointed in its failure that he disavowed his responsibility for it. This is what makes the choice that the player makes at the ending so significant. If the superego-Konrad shoots Walker and the player, there is no resolution to Walker's melancholia. If, however, Walker shoots his own reflection, he admits to his delusions, his disavowals, and his fatal investment in heroism, thereby taking responsibility for his actions. In so doing, his superego is not destroyed – it can't be – but it is bypassed.

170 A detailed analysis of *Life Is Strange* would illuminate themes of choice and time alike. See, for example, Innuendo Studios, "Superposition: The Genre of Life Is Strange," YouTube, July 6, 2017: https://www.youtube.com/watch?v=19x-gdLF5agU.

171 Dušan Stamenković and Milan Jaćević, "Time, Space, and Motion in *Braid*: A Cognitive Semantic Approach to a Video Game," *Games and Culture* 10, no. 2 (2015): 197.

172 It would be easy to use the figure of the knight in shining armor as a way of interpreting the Princess as yet another damsel in distress, and thereby to suggest that *Braid* ultimately succumbs to the same sexism that it might otherwise be seen to be critiquing. Anita Sarkeesian, for instance, suggests that *Braid*'s reversal of the trope ("what if...trying to save the damsel... actually makes you the villain?") is laudable, but that "the focus [of games like *The Secret of Monkey Island* and *Braid*] is still squarely on the male characters, and so, at their core, these games are really deconstructing the player's assumptions about the traditional hero archetype"

rather than "truly subverting the trope." Doing so would require "star[ring] the damsel as the main playable character" (feministfrequency, "Damsel in Distress: Part 3 – Tropes vs Women in Video Games," YouTube, August 1, 2013: https://www.youtube.com/watch?v=LjImnqH_KwM). I think that this is a misinterpretation. The Princess's flight from Tim is desperate and active: she is willing to kill him in order to keep him away from her. She tries to drop a chandelier on him, shoot a cannon at him, and drop him into a flaming pit of spikes. She makes recourse to the knight only after acting herself, and in a way that may well have horrified her: how bad must things have become between her and her former partner that she was willing to kill him? Moreover, the text of the epilogue makes it clear that the Princess is a multivalent figure. As Patrick Jagoda argues, the Princess "appears, through the game's connotative plenum, as the love object, the mother, the ultimate platform game trophy, the sovereign, the atom bomb, and 'the end of history'" ("Fabulously Procedural," 758). As multivalent, she cannot simply be a damsel in distress. And when she does appear in this tropic guise, the game makes clear that it is Tim, and therefore the player, who has put her there. While Sarkeesian is certainly right to point out that *Braid* is more concerned with Tim's character than with that of the Princess, it does not reduce her to a damsel in distress, and it does far more than simply "deconstructing the player's assumptions about the traditional hero archetype." Sarkeesian's work is laudable, but her insistence on a single correct way of subverting the trope is problematic. There is more than one way to tell a meaningful story.

173 The best non-academic articulation of *Braid* as a metaphor for the birth of the nuclear age can be found on a European videogame discussion forum: see lewismistreated, "The Story of *Braid*," RLLMUK, August 11, 2008: http://www.

rllmukforum.com/index.php?/topic/190136-the-story-of-braid/.

174 "As *Braid* reminds the player, videogames are historical out-growths of a modernity specific to an informatics, postin-dustrial society"; it, and other videogames, are "entangled in complex late twentieth- and early twenty-first-century histories of media, computing, weapons technology, ethical responsibility, and subject formation that are both broadly geopolitical and uniquely American" (Jagoda, "Fabulously Procedural," 747).

175 Jagoda, citing Paul Saint-Amour ("Bombing and the Symp-tom: Traumatic Earliness and the Nuclear Uncanny," *Dia-critics* 30, no. 4 (2000): 59-82), notes that the inhabitants of Hiroshima were perplexed as to how their city had so far escaped the American bombing runs that had become so common by the end of the war. They expected some sort of attack eventually; they just didn't expect the magnitude of the attack (Jagoda, "Fabulously Procedural," 755).

176 Jagoda, "Fabulously Procedural," 757.

177 Jonathan Blow, interview by Matthew Reynolds, "Braid Ending Explained by Jonathan Blow," *Digital Spy*, Octo-ber 27, 2010: http://www.digitalspy.com/gaming/news/a284605/braid-ending-explained-by-jonathan-blow/. On *Braid*'s incredible attention to detail, with an eye to the re-lationship between the design of the levels and the contents of the Princess's house, see Leda Clark, "The Psychosis of *Braid*," *Very Awkward Girl*, October 21, 2013: https://leedzie.wordpress.com/2013/10/21/the-psychosis-of-braid/.

178 Jagoda, "Fabulously Procedural," 759.

179 Jonathan Blow, interview by Chris Dahlen, "Game Designer Jonathan Blow: What We All Missed about Braid," *AV Club*, August 27, 2008: http://www.avclub.com/article/game-de-signer-jonathan-blow-what-we-all-missed-abo-8626.

180 If Blow has read Roland Barthes ("The Death of the Au-

thor," in *The Rustle of Language*, trans. Richard Howard (Berkeley and Los Angeles: University of California Press, 1989) or Thomas S. Kuhn (*The Structure of Scientific Revolutions*, 3rd ed. (Chicago and London: University of Chicago Press, 1996), he doesn't show any evidence of it.

181 Nietzsche, *Thus Spoke Zarathustra*, 162.

182 Where *Braid*'s critique of scientism is ambivalent, the critique offered by *Inside* is clear. The dystopian indie platformer presents science as a fruitless and violent project of control: the pursuit of security (the guards, sentry robots, dogs, underwater sirens), convenience (the drones who work for the humans), experimentation-for-its-own-sake (the blob seems to be without point), entertainment (the room where the blob is made to dance for a crowd of spectators, some of them clearly children), and scale (the Ballardian facility that is coterminous with the world itself) have nothing to do with the routine practice of science but everything to do with the controlling spirit that would expose the bones of the world and reshape them at a whim.

183 Stamenković and Jaćević, "Time, Space, and Motion in *Braid*," 197-198.

184 Jagoda, "Fabulously Procedural," 766. Astrid Ensslin makes a similar point about the potential of "unnatural narratives," particularly those narratives that employ unusual manipulations of time, for defamiliarization. Videogames that "deliberately violate the ludonarrative conventions of their genre and the medium itself in order to evoke metaludic and metafictional reflections in the player" also have the potential to prompt the player to step back from their immersion in the game, opening up space for "other types of philosophical and critical processes" ("Video Games as Unnatural Narratives," DiGRA 2015: Diversity of Play: Games – Cultures – Identities: https://www.researchgate. net/profile/Astrid_Ensslin/publication/277554116_Vid-

eo_Games_as_Unnatural_Narratives/links/556c5f3508aec-cd7773af8be.pdf, 12).

185 Jagoda, "Fabulously Procedural," 765.

186 Some are straightforward. With Froggit, for instance, the player can "compliment" or "threaten" it instead of fighting or fleeing, and either option will enable the player to spare it on their next turn. Others are more complicated. When the player acts against the Snowdrake rather than fighting it, they have the ability to "heckle," "laugh," or "joke," but choosing any of these fails to do anything but lengthen the fight; in order to successfully spare the Snowdrake, the player needs to first perform a neutral action like "checking" the monster, wait for it tell a joke, laugh in response, and *then* spare it, dodging attacks all the while.

187 Normally, the spare option turns from white to yellow when the player has satisfied the conditions for showing mercy, but the battle with Toriel keeps the spare option white. In order for it to turn yellow, the player needs to choose this seemingly ineffective option 24 times. In the cases where the player does not pick up on the two small clues that imply that Toriel can be spared – a Froggit noting early on that the option will not always be yellow, and Toriel's dialogue changing each time sparing is chosen instead of remaining the same – they will move through the game toward the neutral ending.

188 A few other games have employed a similar tactic – two from the *Metal Gear Solid* series, for instance, have the player restart their console or swap controller ports – but *Undertale* does it with an abrupt, dizzying decisiveness.

189 Both Heckner ("Obey-Play") and Wysocki and Schandler ("Would You Kindly?"), for instance, argue that games often put players in a passive subject position rather than an active one (and that this passivity does not need to be viewed pessimistically), while David Simkins and Con-

stance Steinkuehler argue that roleplaying games can inculcate a "descriptive, critical ethics" that is derived from some of the philosophers I take up below ("Critical Ethical Reasoning and Role-Play," *Games and Culture* 3, no. 3-4 (2008): 334). Moreover, many recent games deliberately put the player in an impotent, frustrated, or even guilty position. In addition to those discussed in the previous chapter, consider games that stimulate feelings of everyday disempowerment like *Cart Life*, *Diaries of a Spaceport Janitor*, and *Papers, Please*. In the latter, the console or computer takes on a life of its own, resulting in a frustrating gameplay experience that pushes the player to make immoral choices (Daniel Johnson, "Animated Frustration or the Ambivalence of Player Agency," *Games and Culture* 10, no. 6 (2015): 593-612). Game designers and critics often agree with these observations. As Mark Brown argues, *Papers Please* shows how people are "driven to do immoral and cruel things by systemic failure, poverty, and desperation. That's a pretty profound message in and of itself, but videogames are uniquely equipped to explore this topic because they aren't limited to just showing and telling: they make you complicit in the system" (Game Maker's Toolkit, "Morality in the Mechanics," YouTube, February 23, 2016: https://www.youtube.com/watch?v=6RHH7M4siPM). Portnow argues that while "almost all games impart [a feeling of control] simply by their nature as part of an interactive medium," designers can deliberately break with this tendency to make players feel disempowered (Extra Credits, "Extra Credits: Why Games Do Cthulhu Wrong: The Problem with Horror Games," YouTube, May 28, 2014: https://www.youtube.com/watch?v=7DyRxlvM9VM). Koster ("A Letter to Leigh") makes a similar claim, suggesting that designers can foster a critical conversation between games and players about the affordances of the medium despite the limitations imposed by these affordances.

190 Wark, *Gamer Theory*, §23, §38.

191 Wark puts it this way: as the analog becomes subsumed by the digital, and as the distinction between the two becomes increasingly binary, we see "a transformation not merely in forms of communication or entertainment, not even in forms of power or of topos, but a change in being itself. The digital appears, finally, to install topology in the world – except in the process it has installed the world within topology" (*Gamer Theory*, §81). Wark's concern is the political valence of digital ontology.

192 To reiterate, Heidegger argues in "The Question concerning Technology" that the essence of technology is a way of revealing the world: the world is always understood in the terms of some ontological pre-understanding. The essence of modern technology reveals the things of the world as *Bestand*, or "standing reserve"; the generalization of this revelation to all things (including the human) is *Ge-stell*, usually translated as "enframing."

193 Nietzsche's work is rarely cited in game studies, however, and his doctrine of the eternal return of the same, which I describe and employ below, is cited even less frequently. When scholars do use it, they sometimes offer misinterpretations. For Tobias Winnerling, for instance, the eternal return denotes that which occurs "again and again in due time" in a finite system governed by hidden but discernible forces wherein "agents...competitively try to achieve self-conquest." This reading applies to videogames, he argues, insofar as they are sets of algorithmic processes that can be executed again and again, "this time taking a new turn and thus (hopefully) surpassing your old player-self" ("The Eternal Recurrence of All Bits: How Historicizing Video Game Series Transform Factual History into Affective History," *Eludamos: Journal for Computer Game Culture*

8, no. 1 (2014): 154-155). Winnerling gets videogames right but Nietzsche wrong: the philosopher is not an advocate of liberal self-improvement, the eternal return is not a model, and the world is not something that can be laid bare. Insofar as videogames work in the ways in which Winnerling describes, and they do, they are in fact clear examples of the avoidance of the challenge of the eternal return.

194 Friedrich Nietzsche, *On the Genealogy of Morals*, trans. Walter Kaufman and R. J. Hollingdale (New York: Vintage Books, 1967), 58.

195 Nietzsche, *On the Genealogy of Morals*, 57.

196 As Coley and Lockwood put it, "Technology has been extremely effective at systematically ordering and opening up the world as resource. This is also a rendering of the world as calculable. The power of digitality in particular lies in its giving over of phenomena to numerical, statistical value, permitting the measure and modulation of any variation in their properties" (Coley and Lockwood, *Cloud Time*, 9).

197 Wark, *Gamer Theory*, §23.

198 Sicart, for instance, suggests that designers can encourage play to "matter personally" by "reducing safety" through restricting players' ability to save and reload (*Beyond Choices*, 102-103).

199 Christopher Franklin, *"Bastion," Errant Signal*, October 10, 2011: http://www.errantsignal.com/blog/?p=184.

200 Supergiant's other release, *Transistor*, does similarly striking and aesthetically significant work with its soundtrack. Thomas Hale argues that the way that the player character interacts with the soundtrack is an instance of ludonarrative resonance: "Darren Korb's soundtrack adds to [the melancholy *fin de siècle* feel of the game], and so can the player: hold down a button, and [player character] Red hums along to the soundtrack. This humming can be heard faintly during combat phases, as a cyberspace-like grid de-

scends on the environment, allowing Red to stop time and plan her attacks; she can also briefly become the ethereal and deadly SuperUser. The implication is that during these moments of clarity, removed temporarily from threats, she is freer to express herself. Not only does this lend the mute Red a voice, it also emphasises her character's connection to the city and her struggle. By making this optional, players must actively choose to join in with the soundtrack; this agency serves to deepen their immersion with the character and the game world" (Thomas Hale, "Press X to Hug: Aesthetic Reinforcement in Videogames," *Media Gluttony*, May 15, 2015: https://mediagluttony.wordpress.com/2015/05/15/press-x-to-hug-aesthetic-reinforcement-in-videogames/#more-121).

201 As L. B. Jeffries points out, however, the narration does not so much direct the player's actions as accompany and enrich them: "*Bastion*'s narrative takes the backseat. It's completely possible to understand everything going on and plow through the game without hearing a word of the story...In many ways, it reverses the formula of systems narrative by having the design slowly come to represent the content. I perform an action, the narrator elaborates. For the first few hours of play I tuned the narrator out. I didn't recognize the weird lingo and nothing seemed to be going on except smashing things. By the end, I was more engaged with the story than I was the design" ("*Bastion* and *Fallout: New Vegas*," *Gamers with Jobs*, January 1, 2012: http://www.gamerswithjobs.com/node/111023).

202 For Heidegger, the eternal return, or eternal recurrence, is not only the heart of Nietzsche's philosophy – it is connected to the most fundamental question that philosophy can pose, namely the question of Being: "[w]ith his doctrine of eternal return Nietzsche in his way thinks nothing else than the thought that pervades the whole of Western philosophy,

a thought that remains concealed but is its genuine driving force. Nietzsche thinks the thought in such a way that in his metaphysics he reverts to the beginnings of Western philosophy" (Martin Heidegger, *Nietzsche Volume I: The Will to Power as Art*, trans. David Farrell Krell (New York: Harper Collins, 1991), 19).

203 Quoted in Martin Heidegger, *Nietzsche Volume II: The Eternal Recurrence of the Same*, trans. David Farrell Krell (New York: Harper Collins, 1991), 11.

204 In *Ecce Homo*, Nietzsche describes the eternal recurrence as the "highest formula of affirmation that is at all attainable" (Friedrich Nietzsche, *Ecce Homo*, trans. Walter Kaufmann (New York: Vintage Books, 1989), 295).

205 Friedrich Nietzsche, *The Gay Science*, trans. Walter Kaufmann (New York: Vintage Books, 1974), §341.

206 Friedrich Nietzsche, *The Will to Power*, trans. Walter Kaufmann and R. J. Hollingdale (New York: Vintage Books, 1968), §585.

207 Nietzsche, *Thus Spoke Zarathustra*, 179.

208 Nietzsche, *Thus Spoke Zarathustra*, 179-180.

209 Nietzsche, *Thus Spoke Zarathustra*, 180.

210 Heidegger, *Nietzsche Volume II*, 179.

211 Nietzsche, *Thus Spoke Zarathustra*, 180.

212 For Heidegger, the bite of the shepherd that follows this awakening evinces an ecstatic conception of temporality of the sort described in the second division of his *Being and Time*. Zarathustra's thought of eternal recurrence arises from an understanding of time as ecstatic – as spread out over the coterminous and equiprimordial constellations of Dasein's simultaneous thrownness, withness, and futurity – but this understanding cannot be attained before the thought of eternal recurrence has itself been affirmed. As Heidegger puts it, "[t]he moment cannot be thought before the bite has occurred, because the bite answers the question

271

as to what the gateway itself – the moment – is: the gateway of the moment is that decision in which prior history, the history of nihilism, is brought to confrontation and forthwith overcome." It is a self-overcoming Dasein who makes this "decision": "The thought of the eternal return of the same *is* only *as* this conquering thought. The overcoming must grant us passage across a gap that seems to be quite narrow. The gap opens between two things that in one way are alike, so that they appear to be the same. On the one side stands the following: "Everything is nought, indifferent, so that nothing is worthwhile – *it is all alike*." And on the other side: "Everything recurs, it depends on each moment, everything matters – *it is all alike*" (Heidegger, *Nietzsche Volume II*, 182). On one side is nihilism, and on the other affirmation. The passage from the one side to the other is made by way of the "rainbow bridge" of the "it is all alike." The Dasein who rejects the thought of eternal recurrence with horror remains despondently lodged in nihilism, and does not change. The Dasein who *affirms* the thought of eternal recurrence with gaiety finds itself transformed.

213 For Heidegger, "nihilism cannot be overcome from the outside. We do not overcome it by tearing away at it or shoving it aside – which is what we do when we replace the Christian God with yet another ideal, such as Reason, Progress, political and economic 'socialism,' or mere Democracy" (*Nietzsche Volume II*, 179).

214 David Farrell Krell, "Introduction to the Paperback Edition: Heidegger Nietzsche Nazism," in Martin Heidegger, *Nietzsche Volume I: The Will to Power as Art and Nietzsche Volume II: The Eternal Recurrence of the Same*, trans. David Farrell Krell (New York: Harper Collins, 1991), xviii. Here, Krell is pointing to the twofold character of finitude: just as the human being dies, the historical epoch to which he belonged eventually comes to an end – and the timing of each

ending is uncertain.

215 Nietzsche, *Thus Spoke Zarathustra*, 234.

216 Nietzsche, *Thus Spoke Zarathustra* , 233.

217 Nietzsche, *Thus Spoke Zarathustra* , 179-180.

218 "I want to learn more and more to see as beautiful what is necessary in things; then I shall be one of those who make things beautiful. *Amor fati*: let that be my love henceforth! I do not want to wage war against what is ugly. I do not want to accuse; I do not even want to accuse those who accuse. *Looking away* shall be my only negation. And all in all and on the whole: some day I wish to be only a Yes-sayer" (Nietzsche, *The Gay Science*, §276).

219 *Ishvara pranidhana*, or surrender to God, is the final observance given in the *Yoga Sutras of Patanjali* and the central lesson of the *Bhagavad Gita* (where it takes the form of a demand to renounce attachment to the fruits of one's actions). Although it relies on a divine conception of the nature and purpose of the world, it demands an ethical stance from its practitioners that bears a striking resemblance to Nietzsche's love of fate. Refigured as the surrender to that which has been given rather than the surrender to God, Nietzsche might recognize himself in Hinduism.

220 On the connection between nostalgia and nihilism, see Bryan, "Revenge and Nostalgia." See also Jean Baudrillard, *Simulations*, trans. Paul Foss, Paul Patton, and Philip Beitchman (New York: Semiotext(e), 1983), 12: "When the real is no longer what it used to be, nostalgia assumes its full meaning." For Baudrillard, "the real is no longer what it used to be" because it has been preceded by simulacra: it is a metaphorical-but-absolute loss of reality. In *Bastion*, the opposite is true: "the real is no longer what it used to be" not because the world that the Caels knew has been replaced by a model, but because it has literally been destroyed. In this context, the nostalgia that takes hold is in-

tense in its longing, and therefore vicious in its nihilistic tendencies.

221 Nietzsche, *On the Genealogy of Morals*, 76.

222 Hobbes, *Leviathan*.

223 Foucault, *The History of Sexuality, Volume 1*.

224 Commenting on the potential of games to generate "meaning-effects," Jonne Arjoranta argues that *Bastion*'s narrator is often used to highlight meaningful and meaningless actions alike ("Narrative Tools for Games: Focalization, Granularity, and the Mode of Narration in Games," *Games and Culture* online, no. 22 (2015): http://gac.sagepub.com/content/early/2015/07/28/1555412015596271.full).

225 Nietzsche, *The Will to Power*, §585.

226 There is, in fact, some evidence that Rucks' awareness of the futility of Restoration is not only hypothetical. It might be the case that Rucks and the Kid are the same person. There are a number of aesthetic similarities between the two: they both sport shock-white hair, and they both wear red bandanas. Additionally, in the game's first Who Knows Where, in which the narrator describes the Kid's history, he says of the Kid's arrival in the Bastion, "Well he finally arrived at Caelondia's vaunted safe haven. He, and no one else" – this despite the fact that Rucks was there to greet him. Later, during the Ura siege, the narrator says "I couldn't stop 'em alone. I ain't a kid no more." Later still, he says that the Kid "reminds me of myself when I was his age. I ever tell you about those days?" Rucks could be the Kid from another timeline – stuck repeating the same hopeless dream of putting things aright.

227 See *On the Genealogy of Morals*, especially Book Three.

228 This ambition expresses what Arthur Kroker calls "the will to technology" – that which has replaced the will to power in an age in which God has been replaced by Technology as such:

"Nietzsche said that the ultimate frustration of the dynamic will is that 'it cannot turn time backwards,' that the will to will is ultimately frustrated by the passing of 'time's it was.' As digital reality, this successor to the exiting of the Christian God, projects itself forward in the accelerated language of light-time and light-space, as the will to universal space defeats, indeed humiliates, the reality of particular time, might there not also be heard in the command language of digital futurism a perceptible hint of ressentiment? Could it be that digital futurism...has about it the familiar scent of revenge-taking?" (Arthur Kroker, *The Will to Technology and the Culture of Nihilism: Heidegger, Nietzsche, and Marx* (Toronto: University of Toronto Press, 2004), 80-81.) Variously expressed as Kevin Kelly's "technium," Ray Kurzweil's "Singularity," or Google's Internet-as-incipient-AI, this vision of Technology is the dream of mechanical mastery dating back to the early days of the Enlightenment. But it boasts its own distinctively digital features, too. In Kroker's more recent work, he argues against writers who would make digitality into a force for certainty, that digital ontology should be understood in terms of relentless drift (see *Body Drift: Butler, Hayles, Haraway* (Minneapolis: University of Minnesota Press, 2012) and *Exits to the Posthuman Future* (Cambridge, UK: Polity, 2014)). This is a vision of technology that rescues it from the boredom of deification, restoring its inherent contingencies and allowing for a new kind of political response.

229 A fairly standard feature for games like this one, New Game + lets the player try playing through the game again, but with a few things changed. Among the many reasons that a player might want to play the game a second time is the desire to know what would happen if the other option were chosen. As popular game reviewer Ben Croshaw puts it, "if you are going to have two endings based on the last decision

we make in the game, for fuck's sake put a save point before it" (Zero Punctuation, "*Bastion* and *From Dust*," YouTube, August 10, 2011: http://www.escapistmagazine.com/videos/view/zero-punctuation/3839-Bastion-and-From-Dust). His frustration – pointing, as it does, to the desire to maintain control over the temporal flow of the gameworld – is instructive.

230 Some of Rucks' lines during these moments include the following: "Just foolin'"; "Kid *almost* falls again"; "The Ura think they got 'im. They're wrong"; "Come on, keep your chin up."

231 Chun, *Control and Freedom*.

232 Turkle, *Alone Together*.

233 On the relationship between protocol and (political) action, see Galloway, *Protocol*.

234 Frederic Jameson, *Postmodernism, or, the Cultural Logic of Late Capitalism* (Durham: Duke University Press, 1991), 38.

235 *Bastion* is therefore a remarkable incidence of ludonarrative resonance, or what Kasavin calls exposition, and of the ethics of deconstruction (Jacques Derrida, *On Cosmopolitanism and Forgiveness*, trans. Mark Dooley and Michael Hughes (London and New York: Routledge, 2001)). Supergiant's third game, *Pyre*, addresses similar themes.

236 Nietzsche, *The Will to Power*, 20-21.

237 Nietzsche, *The Will to Power*, 19-20.

238 It is no surprise that we find escape so difficult: the ascetic ideal that Nietzsche identifies as the root cause of nihilism goes back 2000 years. When we try to cast it off, "[a]bruptly we plunge into the opposite valuations, with all the energy that such an extreme overvaluation of man has generated in man" (*The Will to Power*, 20-21). This should not suggest to us that we have accomplished something, like successfully moving beyond God: "[e]xtreme positions are not succeeded by moderate ones but by extreme positions of the oppo-

site kind. Thus the belief in the absolute immorality of nature…is the psychologically necessary affect once the belief in God and an essentially moral order becomes untenable" (*The Will to Power*, 35).

239 Supergiant Games' second offering, *Transistor*, also features a character who communicates almost exclusively through song. A female protagonist whose voice has been stolen and who is spoken for by the phallogocentric symbol of the titular transistor (Samantha Blackmon, "She Has No Voice So I Must Scream: On Voice and Agency in Video Games," *Not Your Mama's Gamer*, April 15, 2013: http://www.nymgamer.com/?p=2523), Red is nevertheless a powerful feminist figure (Victoria Liao, "Voiceless but Not Powerless: Defying Narrative Convention in Supergiant Games' *Transistor*," *The Spectatorial*, April 23, 2015: https://thespectatorial.wordpress.com/2015/04/23/voiceless-but-not-powerless-defying-narrative-convention-in-supergiant-games-transistor/) – not only empowered, but wise enough to know what to do with that power, in the same manner as Zia.

240 Zulf sings a song too, but his is nostalgic: he sings of "coming home" to "mother."

241 Nietzsche, *On the Genealogy of Morals*, §12.

242 Anita Sarkeesian badly oversimplifies when she characterizes Zia as a damsel in distress, saying that "the only female character in [*Bastion*] doesn't have any depth (to put it mildly); basically, her whole characterization was 'The Female'" ("Interview: Anita Sarkeesian, Games, and Tropes vs. Women," *Destructoid*, February 7, 2012: http://www.destructoid.com/interview-anita-sarkeesian-games-and-tropes-vs-women-230337.phtml.

243 Nietzsche, *The Gay Science*, §276.

244 Galloway, *Gaming*.

245 Huizinga's magic circle is semi-permeable – or, as Stephanie Boluk and Patrick LeMieux would have it, "messy" (Steph-

anie Boluk and Patrick LeMieux, "Metagame," in Henry Lowood and Raiford Guins, eds, *Debugging Game History: A Critical Lexicon* (Cambridge and London: MIT Press, 2016), 318).

246 For Richard Garfield, this means that "[t]here is of course no game without a metagame...A game without a metagame is like an idealized object in physics. It may be a useful construct but it doesn't really exist" ("Metagames," *GDC 2000 Proceedings Archive*, March 8-12, 2000: https://web. archive.org/web/20081221121908/http://www.gamasutra. com/features/gdcarchive/2000/garfield.doc, quoted in Boluk and LeMieux, "Metagame," 318).

247 Gerald Voorhees argues that the game/player distinction is untenable, particularly with regard to their "meaning": "the meaning and significance of games is controlled by neither players nor games but rather lies in the gameplay enacted where player and game interface" ("Criticism and Control: Gameplay in the Space of Possibility," in *Ctrl-Alt-Play: Essays on Control in Video Gaming*, ed. Matthew Wysocki (Jefferson and London: McFarland, 2013), 10).

248 Stephanie Boluk and Patrick Lemieux, *Metagaming: Playing, Competing, Spectating, Cheating, Trading, Making, and Breaking Videogames* (Minneapolis and London: University of Minnesota Press, 2017), 3.

249 Boluk and Lemieux, *Metagaming*, 4.

250 Robert Ashley, "Episode Five: Help," *A Life Well Wasted*, November 25, 2009: http://alifewellwasted.com/2009/11/25/ episode-five-help/.

251 Ashley, "Episode Five," *A Life Well Wasted*.

252 The first *Desert Bus* for Hope telethon ran in 2007, which was the same year that Twitch Interactive's predecessor, Justin.tv, launched.

253 Suits, *The Grasshopper*, 43.

254 Suits, *The Grasshopper*, 51. For a related interpretation of the

relationships of people to social rules and the social system more generally, see Robert K. Merton, *Social Theory and Social Structure* (New York: Free Press, 1968).

255 Huizinga, *Homo Ludens*, 10.

256 Huizinga, *Homo Ludens*, 11.

257 Baudrillard, less concerned with the distinction between cheats and spoilsports, rejects the notion that rules can be "transgressed" – "the cheater cannot transgress the rules since the game, not being a series of interdictions [of the sort established by the Law], does not have lines one can cross" – but still argues for the remarkable significance of the cheater (and the spoilsport): "[i]f games had a finality, the only true player would be the cheater" (Baudrillard, *Seduction*, 140).

258 Huizinga, *Homo Ludens*, 11.

259 Huizinga, *Homo Ludens*, 12.

260 "Any law-abiding community or community of States will have characteristics linking it in one way or another to a play-community. International law between States is maintained by the mutual recognition of certain principles which, in effect, operate like play-rules despite the fact that they may be founded in metaphysics...[T]he integrity of the system rests on a general willingness to keep to the rules. The moment that one or the other party withdraws from this tacit agreement the whole systems of international law must, if only temporarily, collapse unless the remaining parties are strong enough to outlaw the 'spoilsport'" (Huizinga, *Homo Ludens*, 208).

261 Sections of *The Grasshopper* take the form of extended parables. In the story of Ivan and Abdul, in which two retired generals attempt to discover and play a game without rules, Suits offers an allegorical criticism of the rationalism of the Enlightenment. In seeking out a game without rules, the two generals converge on the only possible outcome be-

cause of a "logic" that is "absolutely compelling": "a fight to the finish"; an attempt to gain "final mastery of the situation." They note that the only relevant criterion for victory is "whether we can sustain our position" in the future ("a past victory is worthless unless it can be extended into future domination"), which necessitates the eradication of any and all possible enemies (or players), and they further observe that the promise of that ultimate outcome is the only thing preventing them from committing suicide (Suits, *The Grasshopper*, 64-73). Suits characterizes these two rational figures as players and gameplay itself as a rational process while also contrasting them with the other sorts of players he mentions previously; in so doing, he offers a commentary on the murderous-suicidal ends of rationalism and the non-necessity of a gameplay that would aspire to purity.

262 Huizinga, *Homo Ludens*, 211.

263 Alan Meades conducts a survey of these oppositional but widespread practices in *Understanding Counterplay in Video Games* (New York and London: Routledge, 2015).

264 Meades, *Understanding Counterplay in Video Games*, 12.

265 On the simultaneous destructiveness and creativity of videogame glitch hunters, see Alan Meades, "Why We Glitch: Process, Meaning and Pleasure in the Discovery, Documentation, Sharing and Use of Videogame Exploits," *Well Played* 2, no. 2 (2013): 79-98.

266 Lewis Hyde, *Trickster Makes This World: Mischief, Myth, and Art* (New York: Farrar, Straus and Giroux, 2010), 7.

267 "They are imagined not only to have stolen certain essential goods from heaven and given them to the race but to have gone on and helped shape this world so as to make it a hospitable place for human life...In the Greek tradition, Hermes doesn't simply acquire fire, he invents and spreads a method, a *techne*, for making fire, and when he steals cat-

tle from the gods he is simultaneously presenting the human race with the domestic beasts whose meat that fire will cook. A whole complex of cultural institutions around killing and eating cattle are derived from the liar and thief, Hermes" (Hyde, *Trickster Makes This World*, 8-9).

268 Hyde, *Trickster Makes This World*, 9.

269 Wark, *Gamer Theory*, §40.

270 Similarly, Coley and Lockwood argue that contemporary forms of technological control might be "exercised through ontology itself" – they might create truths "to which there is no alternative" – but this doesn't mean that resistance becomes impossible. Rather, "cheating," as they put it, "still takes place through rule-bound structures, but in this case it is the rules of the games themselves that are subject to change…[W]e are implicated in the discovery of their transition, the emphasis of our creative efforts shift, and we create the truth through our very reactions. Truth, as such, becomes a flexible control method that no longer makes its plea to the transcendental but is collapsed instead into immanence" (Coley and Lockwood, *Cloud Time*, 6).

271 Wark, *Gamer Theory*, §8.

272 Wark, *Gamer Theory*, §21.

273 Wark, *Gamer Theory*, §21. Later, Wark compares the trifler to the artist: "The artist is now the insider who finds a new style of trifling within the game. The artist as outsider is dead, for there is no outside from which to signal back across the border. The limit to the game has to be found from within" (Wark, *Gamer Theory*, §98).

274 Boluk and Lemieux, *Metagaming*, 3-4.

275 For instance, on machinima, see Henry Lowood, "High-Performance Play: The Making of Machinima," *Journal of Media Practice* 7, no. 1 (2006): 25-42, as well as Gabriel Menotti, "Videorec as Gameplay: Recording Playthroughs and Video Game Engagement," *GAME: The Italian Journal of Game*

Studies, 3 (2013): http://www.gamejournal.it/3_menotti/; on let's plays, see René Glas, "Vicarious Play: Engaging the Viewer in Let's Play Videos," *Empedocles: European Journal for the Philosophy of Communication* 5, no. 1-2 (2015): 81-86; on walkthroughs, see Daniel Ashton and James Newman, "Relations of Control: Walkthroughs and the Structuring of Player Agency," *The Fibreculture Journal* 16 (2010): http://sixteen.fibreculturejournal.org/relations-of-control-walk-throughs-and-the-structuring-of-player-agency/, as well as Mia Consalvo, "Zelda 64 and Video Game Fans: A Walk-through of Games, Intertextuality, and Narrative," *Television and New Media* 4, no. 3 (2003): 321-334; on theory-crafting, see Christopher A. Paul, "Optimizing Play: How Theorycraft Changes Gameplay and Design," *Game Studies* 11, no. 2 (2011): http://gamestudies.org/1102/articles/paul, as well as Trina Choontanom and Bonnie Nardi, "Theory-crafting: The Art and Science of Using Numbers to Inter-pret the World," in *Games, Learning, and Society: Learning and Meaning in the Digital Age*, ed. Constance Steinkuhler et al (Cambridge: Cambridge University Press, 2012); on mod-ding, see Olli Sotamaa, "When the Game Is Not Enough: Motivations and Practices among Computer Game Mod-ding Culture," *Games and Culture* 5, no. 3 (2010): 239-255, Nick Dyer-Witheford, "Playing on the Digital Commons: Collectivities, Capital and Contestation in Videogame Cul-ture," *Media, Culture and Society* 29, no. 6 (2009): 934-953, and Will Jordan, "From Rule-Breaking to ROM-Hacking: Theorizing the Computer Game-as-Commodity," *Proceed-ings of DiGRA 2007*, 708-713: http://www.digra.org/wp-con-tent/uploads/digital-library/07311.20061.pdf; and on grief-ing, see Sal Humphreys and Melissa de Zwart, "Griefing, Massacres, Discrimination, and Art: The Limits of Overlap-ping Rule Sets in Online Games," *UC Irvine Law Review* 2, no. 2 (2012): 507-536, as well as Burcu S. Bakioglu, "Spectacular Interventions of Second Life: Goon Culture, Griefing, and Disruption in Virtual Spaces," *Journal of Virtual Worlds Research* 1, no. 3 (2008): 3-21.

276 Patrick LeMieux, "Real Time Attacks: Microtemporal Histories of Speedrunning *Super Mario Bros.*" (paper presented at Extending Play 3, New Brunswick, New Jersey, September 30-October 1, 2016). See also Patrick LeMieux, "From NES-4021 to moSMB3.wmv: Speedrunning the Serial Interface," *Eludamos: Journal for Computer Game Culture* 8, no. 1 (2014): 7-31.

277 *Super Mario Bros.* speedrunning techniques are geared at eliminating "frame rules," the groups of 21 frames that govern when Mario will be able to transition from one level to another.

278 Darbian, "[Tutorial] Super Mario Bros. any %," YouTube, February 1, 2016: https://www.youtube.com/watch?v=PInZ2-qfKEU&t=2652s.

279 Darbian, "[Tutorial] Super Mario Bros. any %," YouTube.

280 Gunnery Sergeant Hartman, "flagpole glitch," YouTube, October 22, 2016: https://www.youtube.com/watch?v=uc-BAwdS3YB4. These instructions were originally discovered and disseminated by Sockfolder, a glitchhunter intimately familiar with the tool-assisted version of the *Super Mario Bros.* any % run.

281 Darbian, "(4:56.878) Super Mario Bros. any% speedrun *World Record*," YouTube, October 6, 2016: https://www.youtube.com/watch?v=j8CHsUFsi1A.

282 James Newman, *Playing with Videogames* (London and New York: Routledge, 2008), 121.

283 Newman, *Playing with Videogames*, 129.

284 "We might be better advised to think of speedrun strategies and techniques, plans and exploits as being the products of group discussion and the speedrunner as a performer enacting the script" (Newman, *Playing with Videogames*, 130).

285 In one of Gardikis's record-setting runs, for instance, he thanks his brother, his friends, and everyone in the speedrunning community who supported him (Newman, *Playing with Videogames*, 131).

286 LeMieux, "From NES-4021 to moSMB3.wmv," *Eludamos*, 22.

287 Newman, *Playing with Videogames*, 126.

288 Franklin, "Towards a Contemporary Minor Practice in Computer Gaming," 176.

289 The Game Theorists, "Game Theory: Why I Gave the Pope *Undertale*," YouTube, July 5, 2016: https://www.youtube.com/watch?v=s8St9oOnkGU.

290 Casual players have a 2.8% chance of encountering any evidence of Gaster, according to Matthew Robert Patrick (The Game Theorists, "Game Theory: Who Is W. D. Gaster? (*Undertale*)," YouTube, Feb. 4, 2017: https://www.youtube.com/watch?v=8wzxbR5vfjE).

291 Tidazi, "Tidazi's 'f/Fun' Theory": https://docs.google.com/document/d/1xvxyX2dxkzDiy2TxRjPq4ryBDrvFG2H-k2q_F-6yLuNg/edit#.

292 Tidazi, "Tidazi's 'f/Fun' Theory. The Distinction between 'fun' and 'Fun,'" Reddit: https://www.reddit.com/r/Undertale/comments/3pwrbf/tidazis_ffun_theory_the_distinction_between_fun/cwa4dh8/.

293 Karibil_Watar, "I Believe I've Solved Gaster," Reddit: https://www.reddit.com/r/Underminers/comments/3wqqez/i_believe_ive_solved_gaster/.

294 This is, again, in sharp contrast to franchises like *Star Wars*. See Henry Jenkins, "Quentin Tarantino's *Star Wars*? Grassroots Creativity Meets the Media Industry," in *The Social Media Reader*, ed. Michael Mandiberg (New York and London: New York University Press, 2012), 203-235.

295 Derek Yu quoted in Noclip, "Rediscovering Mystery – Noclip Documentary (feat. Jonathan Blow / Derek Yu / Jim Crawford)," YouTube, February 27, 2017: https://www.you-

tube.com/watch?v=z2g_0QQRjYY.

296 Noclip, "Rediscovering Mystery," YouTube.

297 David Carr, "Amazon Bets on Content Deal for Twitch," *The New York Times*, August 31, 2014: http://www.nytimes. com/2014/09/01/business/media/amazons-bet-on-content-in-a-hub-for-gamers.html?_r=0.

298 Twitch was originally just one of several content categories on Justin.tv, itself launched in 2007, but it was spun off into its own service in 2011.

299 Bill Wasik, *And Then There's This: How Stories Live and Die in Viral Culture* (New York: Viking Press, 2009), 4.

300 See Elizabeth S. Goodstein, *Experience without Qualities: Boredom and Modernity* (Stanford: Stanford University Press, 2005).

301 The complete logs are available at https://archive.org/details/tpp_logs.

302 Sam Barsanti, "Praise Helix: The Strange Mythology of a Crowdsourced *Pokémon* Game," *The A. V. Club*, March 10, 2014: http://www.avclub.com/article/praise-helix-strange -hilarious-mythology-crowdsour-202017, quoted in Jenny Saucerman and Jeremy Dietmeier, "Twitch Plays Pokemon: A Study in Big G Games," Proceedings of DiGRA 2014, http://library.med.utah.edu/e-channel/wp-content/uploads/2016/04/digra2014_submission_127.pdf.

303 Andrew Cunningham, "The Bizarre, Mind-Numbing, Mesmerizing Beauty of 'Twitch Plays Pokémon,'" *Ars Technica*, February 18, 2014: https://arstechnica.com/gaming/2014/02/ the-bizarre-mind-numbing-mesmerizing-beauty-of-twitch-plays-pokemon/.

304 Shin Hieftje, "The Mythos behind Twitch Plays Pokémon," *Game Informer*, March 12, 2014: http://www.gameinformer. com/b/features/archive/2014/03/12/exploring-the-created-mythos-of-twitch-plays-pokemon.aspx.

305 For instance, see Jordan Devore, "Twitch Plays Pokemon

Is the Best Thing since Salty Bet," *Destructoid*, February 14, 2014: https://www.destructoid.com/twitch-plays-pokemon-is-the-best-thing-since-salty-bet-270580.phtml; Jeff Grubb, "Livestreamer Rigs up Borg-Like Collective of 6,000 Gamers to Play Pokemon," *Venture Beat*, February 14, 2014: http://venturebeat.com/2014/02/14/watch-6000-people-try-to-collectively-play-pokemon-for-game-boy/; and Patricia Hernandez, "The Miraculous Progress of 'Twitch Plays Pokémon,'" *Kotaku*, February 17, 2014: http://kotaku.com/the-miraculous-progress-of-twitch-plays-pokemon-1524605696.

306 Twitch, "TPP Victory! The Thundershock Heard around the World," March 1, 2014: https://blog.twitch.tv/tpp-victory-the-thundershock-heard-around-the-world-3128a5b1cdf5#.j3wdt47lc.

307 "As the conditions of mass leisure emerged," Goodstein writes, "an initially elitist discourse of subjective disaffection gradually took hold in popular culture, so that by the early twentieth century the experience of ennui had become truly universal" (Goodstein, *Experience without Qualities*, 98-99).

308 "Doubt, self-doubt, and deeply felt unfreedom seem to have become constitutive elements of modern identity," Goodstein writes (*Experience without Qualities*, 103).

309 Goodstein, *Experience without Qualities*, 3.

310 For more on the connection between interest and boredom in the context of internet browsing, see Liam Mitchell, "A Phenomenological Study of Social Media: Boredom and Interest on Facebook, Reddit, and 4chan" (PhD diss., University of Victoria, 2012).

311 Derrida, *Archive Fever*.

312 SpeedMarathonArchive, "AGDQ 2015 Various Games Speed Run by TASbot #AGDQ2015," YouTube, January 4, 2015: https://www.youtube.com/watch?v=MjmxmPwmfOk.

313 A complete explanation by the authors of the exploit can be found in Allan Cecil, Ilari Liusvaara, and Jordan Potter, "Pokémon Plays Twitch," *International Journal of Proof-of-Concept or Get The Fuck Out* 11 (January 2016): https://www.alchemistowl.org/pocorgtfo/pocorgtfo10.pdf, 6-23. Hilariously, this pdf also encodes the means for displaying itself as an LSNES movie. A more accessible explanation can be found in Kyle Orland, "Pokémon Plays Twitch: How a Robot Got IRC Running on an Unmodified SNES," *Ars Technica*, January 5, 2015: https://arstechnica.com/gaming/2015/01/pokemon-plays-twitch-how-a-robot-got-irc-running-on-an-unmodified-snes/.

314 TASVideos, "Welcome to TASVideos," last edited February 19, 2017: http://tasvideos.org/WelcomeToTASVideos.html.

315 Steven Messner, "How Tool-Assisted Speedrunning Reveals the Inner-Life of Video Games," *Rock Paper Shotgun*, January 27, 2016: https://www.rockpapershotgun.com/2016/01/27/how-tool-assisted-speedrunning-works/.

316 Newman, *Playing with Videogames*, 143.

317 Newman, *Playing with Videogames*, 133.

318 Doomworld, "About," https://www.doomworld.com/tas/about.html.

319 LeMieux, "From NES-4021 to moSMB3.wmv," *Eludamos*, 11.

320 LeMieux, "From NES-4021 to moSMB3.wmv," 13-14.

321 TASVideos, "SMB3TAS History," last edited October 27, 2010: http://tasvideos.org/SMB3TASHistory.html.

322 LeMieux, "From NES-4021 to moSMB3.wmv," *Eludamos*, 15.

323 Originally hosted at http://bisqwit.iki.fi/jutut/nesvideos.html, the old NESVideos site is still available as an archive: Joel Yliluoma, *Bisqwit's NES Bittorrent Video Downloads*: http://bisqwit.iki.fi/jutut/backup-nesvideos.html.

324 The SGDQ NESbot performance can be seen at UltraJMan, "Summer Games Done Quick – Wizards and Warriors 3 NESbot Demonstration and Burger King Battle," YouTube,

August 27, 2011: https://www.youtube.com/watch?v=KQX-VgMKJEDY&feature=youtu.be. The idea for playing tool-assisted speedruns on real hardware dates back to a tasvideos.org thread from 2006 (TASVideos Discussion Board, "Running Speed Runs on Real Hardware," August 28, 2006: http://tasvideos.org/forum/viewtopic.php?t=4288), though the first attempts to play a movie file on real hardware didn't take place until 2009, and Greenwood's first replay device wasn't completed until 2010 (TASVideos Discussion Board, "Console Verification Thread," July 16, 2010: http://tasvideos.org/forum/viewtopic.php?p=239984). See Allan Cecil's write-up of the history of TASBot for more information: TASVideos, "TAS Bot," last edited May 29, 2017: http://tasvideos.org/TASBot.html.

325 Viewer numbers were drawn from the Twitch API: see http://irc.alligatr.co.uk/agdq14/.

326 TASVideosChannel, "AGDQ 2014 – TASBot Playing SMW Total Control and Various Other TASes," YouTube, January 6, 2014: https://www.youtube.com/watch?v=Uep1H_NvZS0.

327 true used to sell his replay devices at truecontrol.org, but the website has been replaced with a simple splash screen reading: "nothing is happening here. / some things should be forgotten. / some things are best left unsaid."

328 Kyle Orland, "How an Emulator-Fueled Robot Reprogrammed *Super Mario World* on the Fly," *Ars Technica*, January 14, 2014: https://arstechnica.com/gaming/2014/01/how-an-emulator-fueled-robot-reprogrammed-super-mario-world-on-the-fly/.

329 raocow, "Vip4- malfunctions," YouTube, January 7, 2009: https://www.youtube.com/watch?v=xOOT2XIm5o0&t=7m20s.

330 See the comments section of Adam Fabio, "Teaching Mario to Play Pong and Snake through Innumerable Ex-

ploits," *Hackaday*, January 10, 2014: http://hackaday. com/2014/01/10/teaching-mario-to-play-pong-and-snake-through-innumerable-exploits/. Masterjun offers a slightly more technical explanation: when Mario stunned the flying item box, he spawned "a sprite with the ID 0xFA. This ID is not an actual sprite and it is never used in SMW but since it spawned, the game has to run a code for that sprite. The game indexes the code location wrong and the code jumps to $0322. This is a place in the OAM table (OAM is a chunk of memory that stores the data about the sprite tiles to draw onto screen). That means that we can change values of the code being executed by changing the position of sprites" (TASVideos, "Submission #3957: Masterjun's SNES Super Mario World 'Glitched' in 01:39.74," April 26, 2013: http://tasvideos.org/3957S.html).

331 This understanding of cheating turns on my interpretation of Suits, and not all players would agree with it. As Mia Consalvo argues in *Cheating: Gaining Advantage in Videogames* (Cambridge and London: MIT Press, 2007), players define and "negotiate" cheating in different ways, at different times, and in different places depending on the "paratextual" cultural sources on which they draw.

332 TASVideos, "Submission #3767: bortreb's GBC Pokémon Yellow 'Executes Arbitrary Code' in 12:51.87," November 22, 2012: http://tasvideos.org/3767S.html.

333 Orland, "How an Emulator-Fueled Robot Reprogrammed *Super Mario World* on the Fly," *Ars Technica*.

334 TASVideosChannel, "TAS Block at AGDQ 2016 – TASBot," YouTube, January 13, 2016: https://www.youtube.com/watch?v=pj7RE2DcRgc.

335 For an explanation of how TASers trick the game's optical character recognition into receiving such bizarre inputs, see TASVideos, "Brain Age Train Your Brain in Minutes a Day," last edited January 11, 2016: http://tasvideos.org/GameRe-

sources/DS/BrainAgeTrainYourBrainInMinutesADay.html.

336 TASVideos Discussion Board, "AGDQ 2017 Planning and Feedback Thread," November 12, 2016: http://tasvideos. org/forum/viewtopic.php?p=443580#443580.

337 I'm indebted to Allan Cecil for his explanation of this problem. Cecil actually attempted to bypass the problem by replacing the ceramic oscillator on the sound processor of the SNES with a crystal oscillator, but this didn't work either (see dwangoAC's November 26, 2016 post in the AGDQ 2017 planning thread for pictures and a detailed explanation of the process, and his December 14, 2016 post for the reasons that the team abandoned *Donkey Kong Country 2*). Problems of non-determinism are, perhaps by definition, very difficult to analyze and resolve.

338 SpeedMarathonArchive, "AGDQ 2015 Various Games Speed Run by TASbot #AGDQ2015," YouTube.

339 Orland, "Pokémon Plays Twitch," *Ars Technica*.

340 LeMieux, "From NES-4021 to moSMB3.wmv," *Eludamos*, 8.

341 Kyle Orland, "How a Game-Playing Robot Coded 'Super Mario Maker' onto an SNES – Live on Stage," *Ars Technica*, January 11, 2016: https://arstechnica.com/gaming/2016/01/ how-a-game-playing-robot-coded-super-mario-maker-onto-an-snes-live-on-stage/.

342 TASVideos, "Welcome to TASVideos."

343 TASVideos, "Tasing Guide / TAS Art," last edited July 7, 2017: http://tasvideos.org/TasingGuide/TASArt.html. This two-part understanding of the purpose of the hobby goes back to its early days. When TASVideos was still NESVideos, it featured a section titled "What is the purpose of these videos?" in which founder Joel Yliluoma suggested the following: "Short answer 1: They are entertainment. / Short answer 2: They are art" (Yliluoma, *Bisqwit's NES Bittorrent Video Downloads*).

344 TASing might not count as "data art," but some of its out-

comes resonate with the practice. See Mitchell Whitelaw, "Art against Information: Case Studies in Data Practice," *Fibreculture* 11 (2008): http://eleven.fibreculturejournal.org/fcj-067-art-against-information-case-studies-in-data-practice/, and Rosa Menkman, *The Glitch Moment(um)* (Amsterdam: Network Notebooks, 2011).

345 Fabio, "Teaching Mario to Play Pong and Snake through Innumerable Exploits," *Hackaday.*

346 E. Gabriella Coleman, *Coding Freedom: The Ethics and Aesthetics of Hacking* (Princeton and Oxford: Princeton University Press, 2013), 3.

347 Wark's understanding of hacking buys into the value and necessity of control, provided that control is exercised for the right ends. The modern day bourgeoisie, he suggests, is "a class of vectoralists, so named because they control the vectors along which information is abstracted, just as capitalists control the material means with which goods are produced" (29); they seek "always to control information and turn it to [their] own ends, depriving the hacker of control of her or his creation, and thereby denying the world as a whole the right to manage its own development" (McKenzie Wark, *A Hacker Manifesto* (Cambridge and London: Harvard University Press, 2004), §29 and 12). The hacker, then, would wrest control back from the vectoralists, repurposing it for productive ends. Although Wark's notion of "production" is broader than most, it carries with it a problematic assumption about the fundamental character of work. "[T]he liberation of production," as Baudrillard notes of both orthodox Marxism and its more creative twentieth century interpreters, is misrecognized as "the liberation of man"; "use value" is only "the effect of the system of exchange value," but it is (mis)taken as absolute, foundational (Jean Baudrillard, *The Mirror of Production*, trans. Mark Poster (St. Louis: Telos Press, 1975), 21-22). In this

productivist context, the non-work of "play" masquerades as a liberation or an outside; it is a "repressive desublimation" that still "presupposes the full development of productive forces," and thereby leaves the sign of production – the founding symbol of political economy – undisturbed (Baudrillard, *The Mirror of Production*, 39-40). Elsewhere, Baudrillard writes that the "passion for illusion which once characterized [play]" is routinely converted into its opposite: "even as transgression, spontaneity, or aesthetic disinterestedness, play remains only a sublimated form of the old, directive pedagogy that gives it a meaning, assigns it an end, and thereby purges it of its power of seduction" (Baudrillard, *Seduction*, 158. (Bart Simon sums up the problem: "When games become serious, they lose much of their triviality and arguably they are made to fall more easily into the dominant mode of production. In this sense, they become banal. No longer acting as 'ludic gadgets,' games are made to be about something; games are made to definitively refer. They are tamed and made positive" ("What If Baudrillard Was a Gamer?" *Games and Culture* 2, no. 4 (2007): 357).) A radical interpretation of play, hacking, and trifling would therefore reject the work/play dichotomy, along with its inherent and impossible escapism (as Wark's *Gamer Theory* indeed does).

348 Heidegger expresses his understanding of this essential element of the human condition as *Mitsein*, being-with-others; it is, along with thrownness (the having been) and projection (being-toward-death), equiprimordial for *Dasein*, an existential feature of being-in-the-world: "the world is always the one that I share with Others" (*Being and Time*, §26). Noting that there are "numerous mixed forms" of being-with-others, each tending toward what he refers to as either "domination" or "liberation," Heidegger excuses himself from spelling out the political implications of these

forms: "to describe these and classify them would take us beyond the limits of this investigation" (*Being and Time*, §26). In *The Human Condition*, Arendt shares Heidegger's understanding of the existential character of being-with-others in its equiprimordial relationship to thrownness and projection; she, however, emphasizes not the way that *Dasein* is projected onto its inevitable end but out from its birth. Her work on natality is precisely an attempt to "describe" the different forms of being-with-others in order to understand their latent politics.

349 On the ways in which play and authorship are complicated in speedrunning and tool-assisted speedrunning, see Fanny Barnabé, "Le Speedrun: Pratique Compétitive, Ludique ou Créative? Trajectoire d'un Détournement de Jeu Vidéo Institué en Nouveau Game," *Culture Numérique* 2014: http://culture.numerique.free.fr/publications/ludo14/Barnabe_Ludovia_2014.pdf. See also Rainforest Scully-Blaker, "Re-curating the Accident: Speedrunning as Community and Practice" (MA thesis, Concordia University, 2016).

350 On this phenomenon among Minecraft players, see Nicholas Watson, "Procedural Elaboration: How Players Decode Minecraft," *Loading...*10, no. 16 (2017): 75-86.

351 Newman, *Playing with Videogames*, 128.

352 SethBling, "SNES Code Injection -- Flappy Bird in SMW," YouTube, March 28, 2016: https://www.youtube.com/watch?v=hB6eY73sLV0.

353 SethBling, "SNES Code Injection -- Flappy Bird in SMW," YouTube.

354 SethBling, "Super Mario World -- Credits Warp in 5:56.6 (First Time Ever on Console)," YouTube, January 21, 2015: https://www.youtube.com/watch?v=14wqBA5Q1yc&.

355 SethBling, "Jailbreaking Super Mario World to Install a Hex Editor & Mod Loader," YouTube, May 29, 2017: https://www.youtube.com/watch?v=Ixu8tn__91E. The "jailbreak"

meant loading data into the internal storage of the cartridge to "trick the game [into running] custom code," in this case a hex editor that enabled the further manual manipulation of the game.

356 Newman, *Playing with Videogames*, 152.

357 For more early ACE in *Pokémon* games, see Glitch City Laboratories Forum, "Arbitrary Code Execution in Red/Blue Using the '8F' Item," April 25, 2013: http://forums.glitchcity.info/index.php?topic=6638.0.

358 See, for instance, dotsarecool's explanations (dotsarecool, "Super Mario Credits Warp Explained," YouTube, February 20, 2015: https://www.youtube.com/watch?v=vAHXK-2wut_I& and dotsarecool, "Super Mario Credits Warp for Dummies," YouTube, February 7, 2015: https://www.youtube.com/watch?v=rOrTN50QGR8&).

359 GamesDoneQuick, "Super Mario World 0 Exit Race by Various Runners in 5:46 – Awesome Games Done Quick 2016 – Part 86," YouTube, January 31, 2016: https://www.youtube.com/watch?v=rbtXnd_1lJM. SethBling participated, but lost to CarlSagan thanks to a hard lock caused by imperfect execution.

360 Each of these examples illustrates the ways that the techniques discovered by the TAS community can become adopted by the RTA community. Speedrunners of both stripes understand this relationship well. The Speed Demos Archive explains: "TAS can be useful [because] sometimes new techniques or gameplay glitches come out during the vigorous testing of a game's engine that occurs when a TAS video of that game is being made. These discoveries can be useful even when making "normal" speed runs that will be accepted to SDA (speed runs not made using emulators). There are many runs on this site that have been made using techniques that first appeared in TAS videos. Some highly successful speed runners even say that watching TAS is

essential to understanding the game you are attempting to speed run" (Speed Demos Archive, "TAS," http://speed-demosarchive.com/TAS.html).

361 Potter, sitting on the couch, "put [it] into perspective": "if you were to actually convert this to legitimate button press-es, we're pushing approximately a quarter million button presses through these consoles collectively *per second.*" For further explanation, see Kyle Orland, "How a Robot Got *Super Mario 64* and *Portal* "Running" on an SNES," *Ars Technica*, January 15, 2017: https://arstechnica.com/gam-ing/2017/01/how-a-robot-got-super-mario-64-and-portal-running-on-an-snes/.

362 TASVideos Discussion Board, "AGDQ 2017 Planning and Feedback Thread," August 7, 2015: http://tasvideos.org/forum/viewtopic.php?t=17018&highlight=. All quoted com-ments below are drawn from this thread.

363 Jonathan Zittrain, *The Future of the Internet – and How to Stop It* (New Haven and London: Yale University Press, 2008).

364 Pastor Manul Laphroaig, "Three Ghosts and a Little, Brown Dog," *International Journal of Proof-of-Concept or Get The Fuck Out* 11 (January 2016): https://www.alchemistowl.org/po-corgtfo/pocorgtfo10.pdf, 5.

365 Boluk and LeMieux conclude *Metagaming* by noting the im-portance of thinking about videogames in terms of "alle-gories of control," but emphasize this more general corre-spondence between videogames and digital media as such: "[v]ideogames are not only black-boxed technologies or consumable commodities or escapist fantasies or even alle-gories of control. Instead, they stand in for media generally because they highlight our assumptions about the larger technical circuits that operate in excess of (and often at the expense of) human consciousness. From text messaging to ATM machines to ultrafast algorithmic trading to predic-tive search algorithms, the goal of [*Metagaming*] is not only

to consider the way we play videogames, but to become conscious of the ways in which we are constantly playing with (and being played by) technical media" (188).

366 Robert Ashley, "B-Side: Why Game?" *A Life Well Wasted*, May 28, 2009: http://alifewellwasted.com/2009/05/28/b-side-why-game/.

367 This would be an all-too-common misreading of Heidegger's intentions in *Being and Time*.

368 Taking just the question of game design, one might point to any number of games that confront mortality rather than ignoring it: *Passage, The Graveyard, Continue?9876543210*, and *That Dragon, Cancer* stand out for their relatively straightforward narrative depiction of death, while the likes of *High Delivery* depicts it indirectly through mechanics (see Raph Koster, "But Is It Art?" *Raph Koster's Website*, February 16, 2007: http://www.raphkoster.com/2007/02/16/but-is-it-art-2/). For a discussion of artgames that thematize aging and dying rather than death itself, including *Home, I Am a Brave Knight, To the Moon*, and *Alz*, see Cosima Rughiniş, Elisabeta Toma, and Răzvan Rughiniş: they note that most mainstream games do not feature older characters, and most artgames portray aging as a depressing, inevitable, and purposeless process, thereby instrumentalizing their older characters "in order to support an argument about the finitude of life" ("Time to Reminisce and Die: Representing Old Age in Art Games," *Proceedings of DiGRA 2011 Conference: Think Design Play* (2011): https://www.researchgate.net/profile/Cosima_Rughinis/publication/280319689_Time_to_Reminisce_and_Die_Representing_Old_Age_in_Art_Games/links/55b29a6b08ae9289a0858d7a.pdf). Finally, for a discussion of the capacity of games that seem to have nothing to do with death to nonetheless evoke it, see Brendan Keogh, "When Game Over Means Game Over: Using Permanent Death to Craft Living Stories in *Minecraft*,"

Proceedings of The 9th Australasian Conference on Interactive Entertainment: Matters of Life and Death, article no. 20 (2013): http://dl.acm.org/citation.cfm?id=2513572&preflayout=tabs, and Jenn Frank's poignant meditation on *Super Hexagon*, "Allow Natural Death," *Unwinnable*, November 19, 2012: http://www.unwinnable.com/2012/11/29/allow-natural-death/.

Bibliography

Ahmed, Sara. "Affective Economies." *Social Text* 22, no. 2 (2004): 117-139.

Aldred, Jessica and Brian Greenspan. "A Man Chooses, A Slave Obeys: *BioShock* and the Dystopian Logic of Convergence." *Games and Culture* 6, no. 5 (2011): 479-496.

Alexander, Leigh. "There Is Nothing to 'Do' in O'Reilly's Mountain – and That's a Good Thing." *Gamasutra*, July 8, 2014: http://www.gamasutra.com/view/news/220443/There_is_nothing_to_do_in_OReillys_Mountain__and_thats_a_good_thing.php.

Alexandra, Heather. "Turning in the Badge." *Giant Bomb*, April 1, 2016: http://www.giantbomb.com/articles/guest-column-turning-in-the-badge/1100-5426/.

Arbesman, Samuel. "It's Complicated." *Aeon*, January 6, 2014: https://aeon.co/essays/is-technology-making-the-world-indecipherable.

Arendt, Hannah. *Eichmann in Jerusalem: A Report on the Banality of Evil*. New York: Penguin, 2006.

Arendt, Hannah. *The Human Condition*. 2nd ed. Chicago and London: University of Chicago Press, 1998.

Arendt, Hannah. "Understanding and Politics: The Difficulties of Understanding." In *Essays in Understanding 1930-1954: Formation, Exile, and Totalitarianism*, edited by Jerome Kohn, 307-327. New York: Schocken Books, 2005.

Arjoranta, Jonne. "Narrative Tools for Games: Focalization, Granularity, and the Mode of Narration in Games." *Games and Culture* online, no. 22 (2015): http://gac.sagepub.com/content/early/2015/07/28/1555412015596271.full.

Arsenault, Dominic and Bernard Perron. "In the Frame of the Magic Circle: The Circle(s) of Gameplay." In *The Video Game Theory Reader 2*, edited by Bernard Perron and Mark J. P Wolf,

109-131. London and New York: Routledge, 2009.

Ashley, Robert. "B-Side: Why Game?" *A Life Well Wasted*, May 28, 2009: http://alifewellwasted.com/2009/05/28/b-side-why-game/.

Ashley, Robert. "Episode Five: Help." *A Life Well Wasted*, November 25, 2009: http://alifewellwasted.com/2009/11/25/episode-five-help/.

Ashley, Robert. "Episode Six: Big Ideas." *A Life Well Wasted*, June 23, 2010: http://alifewellwasted.com/podcast/.

Ashton, Daniel and James Newman. "Relations of Control: Walkthroughs and the Structuring of Player Agency." *The Fibreculture Journal* 16 (2010): http://sixteen.fibreculturejournal.org/relations-of-control-walkthroughs-and-the-structuring-of-player-agency/.

Bakioglu, Burcu S. "Spectacular Interventions of Second Life: Goon Culture, Griefing, and Disruption in Virtual Spaces," *Journal of Virtual Worlds Research* 1, no. 3 (2008): 3-21.

Barnabé, Fanny. "Le Speedrun: Pratique Compétitive, Ludique ou Créative? Trajectoire d'un Détournement de Jeu Vidéo Institué en Nouveau Game." *Culture Numérique* 2014: http://culture.numerique.free.fr/publications/ludo14/Barnabe_Ludovia_2014.pdf.

Barsanti, Sam. "Praise Helix: The Strange Mythology of a Crowdsourced *Pokémon* Game." *The A. V. Club*, March 10, 2014: http://www.avclub.com/article/praise-helix-strange-hilarious-mythology-crowdsour-202017.

Barthes, Roland. "The Death of the Author." In *The Rustle of Language*, translated by Richard Howard, 49-55. Berkeley and Los Angeles: University of California Press, 1989.

Baudrillard, Jean. *The Mirror of Production*. Translated by Mark Poster. St. Louis: Telos Press, 1975.

Baudrillard, Jean. *Screened Out*. Translated by Chris Turner. London: Verso, 2002.

Baudrillard, Jean. *Seduction*. Translated by Brian Singer. New

York: St. Martin's Press, 1990.

Baudrillard, Jean. *Simulations*. Translated by Paul Foss, Paul Patton, and Philip Beitchman. New York: Semiotext(e), 1983.

The Beastcast. "Episode 42." March 11, 2016: http://www.giantbomb.com/podcasts/the-giant-beastcast-episode-42/1600-1532/.

Beck, Ulrich. *Risk Society: Towards a New Modernity*. Translated by Mark Ritter. London: Sage, 1992.

Becker, Ernest. *The Denial of Death*. New York: Free Press, 1973.

Biernoff, Suzannah. "Medical Archives and Digital Culture: From WWI to *BioShock*." *Medical History* 55 (2011): 325-330.

Bissell, Tom. "Thirteen Ways of Looking at a Shooter." *Grantland*, July 12, 2012: http://grantland.com/features/line-explores-reasons-why-play-shooter-games/.

Blackmon, Samantha "She Has No Voice So I Must Scream: On Voice and Agency in Video Games." *Not Your Mama's Gamer*, April 15, 2013: http://www.nymgamer.com/?p=2523.

Blow, Jonathan. "Conflicts in Game Design." Montreal International Game Summit, November 19, 2008: http://braid-game.com/news/2008/11/a-new-lecture-about-story-and-game-design/.

Blow, Jonathan, interview by Chris Dahlen. "Game Designer Jonathan Blow: What We All Missed about Braid." *AV Club*, August 27, 2008: http://www.avclub.com/article/game-designer-jonathan-blow-what-we-all-missed-abo-8626.

Blow, Jonathan, interview by Matthew Reynolds. "Braid Ending Explained by Jonathan Blow." *Digital Spy*, October 27, 2010: http://www.digitalspy.com/gaming/news/a284605/braid-ending-explained-by-jonathan-blow/.

Bogost, Ian. *How to Do Things with Videogames*. Minneapolis and London: University of Minnesota Press, 2011.

Bogost, Ian. *Persuasive Games: The Expressive Power of Videogames*. Cambridge and London: MIT Press, 2007.

Bogost, Ian. *Play Anything: The Pleasure of Limits, the Uses of Bore-*

dom and the Secret of Games. New York: Basic Books, 2016.

Bogost, Ian. "Video Games Are Better without Stories." *The Atlantic*, April 25, 2017: https://www.theatlantic.com/technology/archive/2017/04/video-games-stories/524148/.

Boluk, Stephanie and Patrick LeMieux. "Metagame." In *Debugging Game History: A Critical Lexicon*, edited by Henry Lowood and Raiford Guins, 313-324. Cambridge and London: MIT Press, 2016.

Boluk, Stephanie and Patrick Lemieux. *Metagaming: Playing, Competing, Spectating, Cheating, Trading, Making, and Breaking Videogames*. Minneapolis and London: University of Minnesota Press, 2017.

Brown, Wendy. *Walled States, Waning Sovereignty*. New York: Zone Books, 2010.

Bryan, Bradley. "Revenge and Nostalgia: Reconciling Nietzsche and Heidegger on the Question of Coming to Terms with the Past." *Philosophy and Social Criticism* 38, no. 1 (2012): 25-38.

Butler, Judith. *Giving an Account of Oneself*. New York: Fordham University Press, 2005.

Caillois, Roger. *Man, Play, and Games*. Translated by Meyer Barash. New York: Free Press of Glencoe, 1961.

Carey, James. "Technology and Ideology: The Case of the Telegraph." In *Communication as Culture*, rev. ed., 155-177. New York and London: Routledge, 2009.

Carr, David. "Amazon Bets on Content Deal for Twitch." *The New York Times*, August 31, 2014: http://www.nytimes.com/2014/09/01/business/media/amazons-bet-on-content-in-a-hub-for-gamers.html?_r=0.

Cecchetto, David, Marc Couroux, Ted Hiebert, and Eldritch Priest. *Ludic Dreaming: How to Listen Away from Contemporary Technoculture*. New York and London: Bloomsbury, 2017.

Cecil, Allan, Ilari Liusvaara, and Jordan Potter. "Pokémon Plays Twitch." *International Journal of Proof-of-Concept or Get The Fuck Out* 11 (January 2016): https://www.alchemistowl.org/

pocorgtfo/pocorgtfo10.pdf, 6-23.

Charles, Alec. "Playing with One's Self: Notions of Subjectivity and Agency in Digital Games." *Eludamos: Journal for Computer Game Culture* 3, no. 2 (2009): 281-294.

Choontanom, Trina and Bonnie Nardi. "Theorycrafting: The Art and Science of Using Numbers to Interpret the World." In *Games, Learning, and Society: Learning and Meaning in the Digital Age*, edited by Constance Steinkuhler, Kurt Squire, and Sasha Barab, 185-209. Cambridge: Cambridge University Press, 2012.

Chun, Wendy. *Control and Freedom: Power and Paranoia in the Age of Fiber Optics*. Cambridge and London: MIT Press, 2006.

Chun, Wendy. "On 'Sourcery,' or Code as Fetish." *Configurations* 16, no. 3 (2008): 299-324.

Clark, Leda. "The Psychosis of *Braid*." *Very Awkward Girl*, October 21, 2013: https://leedzie.wordpress.com/2013/10/21/the-psychosis-of-braid/.

Clark, Richard and Drew Dixon. "Podcast #18: *Spec Ops: The Line*'s Lead Writer, Walt Williams." *Gamechurch*: http://gamechurch.com/podcast-18-spec-ops-lines-lead-writer-walt-williams/.

Coleman, E. Gabriella. *Coding Freedom: The Ethics and Aesthetics of Hacking*. Princeton and Oxford: Princeton University Press, 2013.

Coley, Rob and Dean Lockwood. *Cloud Time: The Inception of the Future*. Winchester and Washington: Zero Books, 2012.

Condon, Brody, interview by Matteo Bittanti. "Interview: Brody Condon's 'Adam Killer' (1999)." *Gamescenes*, May 31, 2010: http://www.gamescenes.org/2010/05/interview-brody-condons-adam-killer-1999.html.

Consalvo, Mia. *Cheating: Gaining Advantage in Videogames*. Cambridge and London: MIT Press, 2007.

Consalvo, Mia. "Zelda 64 and Video Game Fans: A Walkthrough of Games, Intertextuality, and Narrative." *Television and New*

Media 4, no. 3 (2003): 321-334.

Cross, Katherine. "'We Will Force Gaming to Be Free': On Gamergate and the License to Inflict Suffering." *First Person Scholar*, October 8, 2014: http://www.firstpersonscholar.com/we-will-force-gaming-to-be-free/.

Csíkszentmihályi, Mihály. *Flow: The Psychology of Optimal Experience*. New York: Harper Perennial, 1991.

Cunningham, Andrew. "The Bizarre, Mind-Numbing, Mesmerizing Beauty of 'Twitch Plays Pokémon.'" *Ars Technica*, February 18, 2014: https://arstechnica.com/gaming/2014/02/the-bizarre-mind-numbing-mesmerizing-beauty-of-twitch-plays-pokemon/.

Curtis, Adam. "Love and Power." *All Watched over by Machines of Loving Grace*, May 23, 2011, BBC.

Darbian. "[Tutorial] Super Mario Bros. any %." YouTube, February 1, 2016: https://www.youtube.com/watch?v=PInZ2-qfKEU&t=2652s.

Darbian. "(4:56.878) Super Mario Bros. any% speedrun *World Record*." YouTube, October 6, 2016: https://www.youtube.com/watch?v=j8CHsUFsi1A.

De Beauvoir, Simone. *The Ethics of Ambiguity*. Translated by Bernard Frechtman. Secaucus: Citadel Press, 1974.

De Grey, Aubrey D. N. J. "Combating the Tithonus Error: What Works?" *Rejuvenation Resesarch* 11, no. 4 (2008): 713-715.

Debord, Guy. *The Society of the Spectacle*. Translated by Donald Nicholson-Smith. New York: Zone Books, 1995.

Debord, Guy and Alice Becker-Ho. *A Game of War*. Translated by Donald Nicholson-Smith. London: Atlas Press, 2007.

Deleuze, Gilles. "Postscript on the Societies of Control." *October* 59 (1992): 3-7.

Derrida, Jacques. *Archive Fever: A Freudian Impression*. Translated by Eric Prenowitz. Chicago: University of Chicago Press, 1996.

Derrida, Jacques. *On Cosmopolitanism and Forgiveness*. Translated by Mark Dooley and Michael Hughes. London and New York: Routledge, 2001.

Derrida, Jacques. "Structure, Sign, and Play in the Discourse of the Human Sciences." In *The Structuralist Controversy: The Languages of Criticism and the Sciences of Man*, edited by Richard Macksey and Eugenio Donato, 247-272. Baltimore and London: The Johns Hopkins University Press, 1970.

Deterding, Sebastian. "Paideia as Paidia: From Game-Based Learning to a Life Well-Played." Games Learning Society 8.0, June 15, 2012: https://www.slideshare.net/dings/paideia-as-paidia-from-gamebased-learning-to-a-life-wellplayed.

Devore, Jordan. "Twitch Plays Pokemon Is the Best Thing since Salty Bet." *Destructoid*, February 14, 2014: https://www.destructoid.com/twitch-plays-pokemon-is-the-best-thing-since-salty-bet-270580.phtml.

Dibbell, Julian. *Play Money: Or, How I Quit My Day Job and Made Millions Trading Virtual Loot*. New York: Basic Books, 2006.

Doomworld. "About." https://www.doomworld.com/tas/about.html.

dotsarecool. "Super Mario Credits Warp Explained." YouTube, February 20, 2015: https://www.youtube.com/watch?v=-vAHXK2wut_I&.

dotsarecool. "Super Mario Credits Warp for Dummies." YouTube, February 7, 2015: https://www.youtube.com/watch?v=rOrT-N50QGR8&).

Dyer-Witheford, Nick. "Playing on the Digital Commons: Collectivities, Capital and Contestation in Videogame Culture." *Media, Culture and Society* 29, no. 6 (2009): 934-953.

EGM Now. "EGM Review: *Spec Ops: The Line*." June 27, 2012: http://www.egmnow.com/articles/reviews/egm-review-spec-ops-the-line/.

Emrich, Alan. "MicroProse's Strategic Space Opera Is Rated XXXX." *Computer Gaming World* 110 (September 1993): http://www.cgwmuseum.org/galleries/index.php?year=1993&-

pub=2&id=110.

Ensslin, Astrid. "Video Games as Unnatural Narratives." DiG-RA 2015: Diversity of Play: Games – Cultures – Identities: https://www.researchgate.net/profile/Astrid_Ensslin/publication/277554116_Video_Games_as_Unnatural_Narratives/links/556c5f3508aeccd7773af8be.pdf.

Ernst, Wolfgang. *Digital Memory and the Archive* (Minneapolis and London: University of Minnesota Press, 2013).

Extra Credits. "Extra Credits: *Spec Ops: The Line* (Part 1)." YouTube, September 6, 2012: https://www.youtube.com/watch?v=kjaBsuXWJJ8.

Extra Credits. "Extra Credits: Why Games Do Cthulhu Wrong: The Problem with Horror Games." YouTube, May 28, 2014: https://www.youtube.com/watch?v=7DyRxlvM9VM.

Extra Credits. "*The Division* – Problematic Meaning in Mechanics – Extra Credits." YouTube, April 13, 2016: https://www.youtube.com/watch?v=4jKsj345Jjw.

Extra Credits. "Extra Credits: *Spec Ops: The Line* (Part 2)." YouTube, September 12, 2012: https://www.youtube.com/watch?v=cJZIhcCA2lk.

Fabio, Adam. "Teaching Mario to Play Pong and Snake through Innumerable Exploits." *Hackaday*, January 10, 2014: http://hackaday.com/2014/01/10/teaching-mario-to-play-pong-and-snake-through-innumerable-exploits/.

feministfrequency. "Damsel in Distress: Part 3 – Tropes vs Women in Video Games." YouTube, August 1, 2013: https://www.youtube.com/watch?v=LjImnqH_KwM.

Finn, Ed. *What Algorithms Want: Imagination in the Age of Computing*. Cambridge and London: MIT Press, 2017.

Flanagan, Mary. *Critical Play: Radical Game Design*. Cambridge and London: MIT Press, 2013.

Folding Ideas. "Ludonarrative Dissonance." YouTube, July 19, 2017: https://www.youtube.com/watch?v=04zaTjuV60A.

Foucault, Michel. *Discipline and Punish: The Birth of the Prison.*

Translated by Alan Sheridan. New York: Vintage, 1979.

Foucault, Michel. *The History of Sexuality, Volume 1: An Introduction*. Translated by Robert Hurley. New York: Vintage, 1990.

Foucault, Michel. "The Subject and Power." *Critical Inquiry* 8, no. 4 (1982): 777-795.

Frank, Jenn. "Allow Natural Death." *Unwinnable*, November 19, 2012: http://www.unwinnable.com/2012/11/29/allow-natural-death/.

Franklin, Christopher. "*Bastion*." *Errant Signal*, October 10, 2011: http://www.errantsignal.com/blog/?p=184.

Franklin, Christopher. "*Deus Ex: Mankind Divided*." *Errant Signal*, September 21, 2016: http://www.errantsignal.com/blog/?p=919.

Franklin, Christopher. "Violence in Games." *Errant Signal*, March 17, 2012: http://www.errantsignal.com/blog/?p=267.

Franklin, Seb. "Cloud Control, or The Network as Medium." *Cultural Politics* 8 no. 3 (2012): 443-464.

Franklin, Seb. "'We Need Radical Gameplay, Not Just Radical Graphics': Towards a Contemporary Minor Practice in Computer Gaming." *symploke* 17, nos. 1-2 (2009): 163-180.

Freed, Alexander. "Branching Conversation Systems and the Working Writer, Part 1: Introduction." *Alexander M. Freed*, September 2, 2014: http://www.alexanderfreed.com/2014/09/02/branching-conversation-systems-and-the-working-writer-part-1-introduction/.

Freud, Sigmund. "Mourning and Melancholia." In *The Standard Edition of the Complete Psychological Works of Sigmund Freud, Volume XIV (1914-1916)*, translated by James Strachey, 243-258. London: Hogarth Press, 1953.

Friedman, Ted. "*Civilization* and Its Discontents: Simulation, Subjectivity, and Space." In *Discovering Discs: Transforming Space and Genre on CD-ROM*, edited by Greg Smith, http://web.mit.edu/21w.784/www/BD%20Supplementals/Materials/UnitFour/friedman.htm. New York: New York University

Press, 1999.

Galloway, Alexander. *Gaming: Essays on Algorithmic Culture*. Minneapolis: University of Minnesota Press, 2006.

Galloway, Alexander. *Protocol: How Control Exists after Decentralization*. Cambridge: MIT Press, 2004.

Game Maker's Toolkit. "Morality in the Mechanics." YouTube, February 23, 2016: https://www.youtube.com/watch?v=6RHH7M4siPM.

The Game Theorists. "Game Theory: Who Is W. D. Gaster? (*Undertale*)." YouTube, Februrary 4, 2017: https://www.youtube.com/watch?v=8wzxbR5vfjE.

The Game Theorists. "Game Theory: Why I Gave the Pope *Undertale*." YouTube, July 5, 2016: https://www.youtube.com/watch?v=s8St9oOnkGU.

GamesDoneQuick. "Super Mario World 0 Exit Race by Various Runners in 5:46 – Awesome Games Done Quick 2016 – Part 86." YouTube, January 31, 2016: https://www.youtube.com/watch?v=rbtXnd_1lJM.

Garfield, Richard. "Metagames." *GDC 2000 Proceedings Archive*, March 8-12, 2000: http://web.archive.org/web/20081221121908/http://www.gamasutra.com/features/gdcarchive/2000/garfield.doc.

Garland, Jordan. "Aftermath: Crossing the Line with Walt Williams." *Gaming Bolt*, July 16, 2012: http://gamingbolt.com/aftermath-crossing-the-line-with-walt-williams.

Geraci, Robert M. "Video Games and the Transhumanist Inclination." *Zygon: Journal of Religion and Science* 47, no. 4 (2012): 735-756.

Glas, René. "Vicarious Play: Engaging the Viewer in Let's Play Videos," *Empedocles: European Journal for the Philosophy of Communication* 5, no. 1-2 (2015): 81-86.

Glitch City Laboratories Forum. "Arbitrary Code Execution in Red/Blue Using the '8F' Item." April 25, 2013: http://forums.

glitchcity.info/index.php?topic=6638.0.

Golumbia, David. *The Cultural Logic of Computation*. Cambridge: Harvard University Press, 2009.

Goodstein, Elizabeth S. *Experience without Qualities: Boredom and Modernity*. Stanford: Stanford University Press, 2005.

Grubb, Jeff. "Livestreamer Rigs up Borg-Like Collective of 6,000 Gamers to Play Pokemon." *Venture Beat*, February 14, 2014: http://venturebeat.com/2014/02/14/watch-6000-people-try-to-collectively-play-pokemon-for-game-boy/.

Gunnell, John G. *Political Philosophy and Time*. Middletown, Connecticut: Wesleyan University Press, 1968.

Gunnery Sergeant Hartman. "flagpole glitch." YouTube, October 22, 2016: https://www.youtube.com/watch?v=ucBAwdS3YB4.

Hale, Thomas. "Press X to Hug: Aesthetic Reinforcement in Videogames." *Media Gluttony*, May 15, 2015: https://mediagluttony.wordpress.com/2015/05/15/press-x-to-hug-aesthetic-reinforcement-in-videogames/#more-121.

Hammer, Jessica and Meguey Baker. "Problematizing Power Fantasy." *The Enemy* 1 no. 2 (2014): http://theenemyreader.org/problematizing-power-fantasy/.

Hansen, Mark. "New Media." In *Critical Terms for Media Studies*, edited by W. J. T. Mitchell and Mark Hansen, 172-195. Chicago and London: University of Chicago Press, 2010.

Hansen, Miriam. "The Mass Production of the Senses: Classical Cinema as Vernacular Modernism." *Modernism/Modernity* 6, no. 2 (1999): 59-77.

Haraway, Donna. "The Cyborg Manifesto." In *Simians, Cyborgs, and Women: The Reinvention of Nature*, 149-182. New York: Routledge, 1991.

Hayles, N. Katherine. *My Mother Was a Computer: Digital Subjects and Literary Texts*. Chicago: University of Chicago Press, 2005.

Heckner, M.-Niclas. "Obey-Play: Passive Play and Productive Submission to the Code." In *Ctrl-Alt-Play: Essays on Control in Video Gaming*, edited by Matthew Wysocki, 183-195. Jefferson and London: McFarland, 2013.

Heidegger, Martin. "The Age of the World Picture." In *The Question concerning Technology and Other Essays*, edited and translated by William Lovitt, 115-154. New York: Harper Perennial, 1977.

Heidegger, Martin. *Being and Time*. Translated by John Macquarrie and Edward Robinson. San Francisco: Harper and Row, 1962.

Heidegger, Martin. *Nietzsche Volume I: The Will to Power as Art*. Translated by David Farrell Krell. New York: Harper Collins, 1991.

Heidegger, Martin. *Nietzsche Volume II: The Eternal Recurrence of the Same*. Translated by David Farrell Krell. New York: Harper Collins, 1991.

Heidegger, Martin. "The Question concerning Technology." In *The Question concerning Technology and Other Essays*, edited and translated by William Lovitt, 3-35. New York: Harper Perennial, 1977.

Henley, Jon. "Walls: An Illusion of Security from Berlin to the West Bank." *The Guardian*, November 19, 2013: http://www.theguardian.com/uk-news/2013/nov/19/walls-barrier-belfast-west-b-ank.

Hernandez, Patricía. "The Miraculous Progress of 'Twitch Plays Pokémon.'" *Kotaku*, February 17, 2014: http://kotaku.com/the-miraculous-progress-of-twitch-plays-pokemon-1524605696.

Hieftje, Shin. "The Mythos behind Twitch Plays Pokémon." *Game Informer*, March 12, 2014: http://www.gameinformer.com/b/features/archive/2014/03/12/exploring-the-created-mythos-of-twitch-plays-pokemon.aspx.

Hobbes, Thomas. *Leviathan*. Edited by J. C. A. Gaskin. Oxford and New York: Oxford University Press, 1996.

Hocking, Clint. "Ludonarrative Dissonance in *BioShock*." *Click Nothing: Design from a Long Time Ago*, October 7, 2007: http://clicknothing.typepad.com/click_nothing/2007/10/ludonarrative-d.html.

Hogle, Joseph. "Deus Ex Ludos: Representation, Agency, and Ethics in *Deus Ex: Invisible War*." *Well Played* 1, no. 3 (2012): 49-69.

Holmes, Steven. "'You Are Not in Control': *Spec Ops: The Line* and the Banality of War." In *War Gothic in Literature and Culture*, edited by Steffen Hantke and Agnieszka Soltysik Monnet, 157-175. Routledge, 2016.

Hu, Tung-Hui. *A Prehistory of the Cloud*. Cambridge and London: MIT Press, 2015.

Huizinga, Johan. *Homo Ludens: A Study of the Play-Element in Culture*. Boston: The Beacon Press, 1950.

Humphreys, Sal and Melissa de Zwart. "Griefing, Massacres, Discrimination, and Art: The Limits of Overlapping Rule Sets in Online Games." *UC Irvine Law Review* 2, no. 2 (2012): 507-536.

Hyde, Lewis. *Trickster Makes This World: Mischief, Myth, and Art*. New York: Farrar, Straus and Giroux, 2010.

IGN. "*Bulletstorm* – Weapons + Echoes & Anarchy Mode." January 14, 2010: http://ca.ign.com/videos/2011/01/14/bulletstorm-weapons-echoes-anarchy-mode.

Innerarity, Daniel. *The Future and Its Enemies: In Defense of Political Hope*. Translated by Sandra Kingery. Stanford: Stanford University Press, 2012.

Innis, Harold. *Empire and Communications*. Toronto: Dundurn Press, 2007.

Innuendo Studios. "Story Beats: *Bastion*." YouTube, April 15, 2016: https://www.youtube.com/watch?v=IyhrKPLDCyY.

Innuendo Studios. "Story Beats: *Ben There, Dan That*." YouTube, March 28, 2016: https://www.youtube.com/watch?v=Ntuy-Ty0EjvM.

Innuendo Studios. "Story Beats: *Dear Esther*." YouTube, March 8, 2016: https://www.youtube.com/watch?v=NOw-Zq1CzcQ.

Innuendo Studios. "Story Beats: *Limbo*." YouTube, March 16,

2016: https://www.youtube.com/watch?v=WQ6H8GJBT1k.

Innuendo Studios. "Superposition: The Genre of Life Is Strange." YouTube, July 6, 2017: https://www.youtube.com/watch?v=19xgdLF5agU.

Innuendo Studios. "Why Are You So Angry?" YouTube, July 13, 2015: https://www.youtube.com/watch?v=6y8XgGhXk-TQ&list=PLJA_jUddXvY62dhVThbeegLPpvQlR4CjF.

Jackson, Robert. BioShock: *Decision, Forced Choice and Propaganda*. Winchester, UK and Washington, DC: Zero Books, 2014.

Jagoda, Patrick. "Fabulously Procedural: *Braid*, Historical Processing, and the Videogame Sensorium." *American Literature* 85, no. 4 (2013): 745-779.

Jameson, Frederic. *Postmodernism, or, the Cultural Logic of Late Capitalism*. Durham: Duke University Press, 1991.

Jeffries, L. B. "*Bastion* and *Fallout: New Vegas*." *Gamers with Jobs*, January 1, 2012: http://www.gamerswithjobs.com/node/111023.

Jenkins, Henry. "Quentin Tarantino's *Star Wars*? Grassroots Creativity Meets the Media Industry." In *The Social Media Reader*, edited by Michael Mandiberg, 203-235. New York and London: New York University Press, 2012.

Johnson, Daniel. "Animated Frustration or the Ambivalence of Player Agency." *Games and Culture* 10, no. 6 (2015): 593-612.

Jordan, Will. "From Rule-Breaking to ROM-Hacking: Theorizing the Computer Game-as-Commodity." *Proceedings of DiGRA 2007*, 708-713: http://www.digra.org/wp-content/uploads/digital-library/07311.20061.pdf.

Juul, Jesper. *Half-Real: Video Games between Real Rules and Fictional Worlds*. Cambridge and London: MIT Press, 2005.

Kant, Immanuel. "Perpetual Peace." In *Political Writings*, edited by H. S. Reiss, 93-130. Cambridge: Cambridge University Press, 1991.

Karibil_Watar. "I Believe I've Solved Gaster." Reddit: https://www.reddit.com/r/Underminers/comments/3wqqez/i_believe_ive_solved_gaster/.

Kasavin, Greg. "I Don't Want to Know: Delivering Exposition in Games." *GDC Vault*, October 5-8, 2010: http://www.gdcvault.com/play/1013847/I-Don-t-Want-to.

Kelly, Kevin. "The Next 5000 Days of the Web." *TED*, December 2007: https://www.ted.com/talks/kevin_kelly_on_the_next_5_000_days_of_the_web?language=en#t-1138198.

Kelly, Kevin. *What Technology Wants*. New York: Viking, 2010.

Keogh, Brendan. *Killing Is Harmless: A Critical Reading of* Spec Ops: The Line. Marden, Australia: Stolen Projects, 2012.

Keogh, Brendan. "A Play of Bodies: A Phenomenology of Videogame Experience." PhD diss., RMIT University, 2015.

Keogh, Brendan. "When Game Over Means Game Over: Using Permanent Death to Craft Living Stories in Minecraft." *Proceedings of the 9th Australasian Conference on Interactive Entertainment: Matters of Life and Death*, article no. 20 (2013): http://dl.acm.org/citation.cfm?id=2513572&preflayout=tabs.

Kirkpatrick, Graeme. *Computer Games and the Social Imaginary*. Cambridge: Polity, 2013.

Kirschenbaum, Matthew. *Mechanisms: New Media and the Forensic Imagination*. Cambridge: MIT Press, 2008.

Kittler, Friedrich. *Gramophone, Film, Typewriter*. Translated by Geoffrey Winthrop-Young and Michael Wutz. Stanford: Stanford University Press, 1999.

Kittler, Friedrich. "Towards an Ontology of Media." *Theory, Culture and Society* 26, nos. 2-3 (2009): 23-31.

Kittler, Friedrich and Geoffrey Winthrop-Young. "Real Time Analysis, Time Axis Manipulation." *Cultural Politics* 13, no. 1 (2017): 1-18.

Koster, Raph. "A Letter to Leigh," *Raph Koster's Website*, April 9, 2013: http://www.raphkoster.com/2013/04/09/a-letter-to-leigh/.

Koster, Raph. "But Is It Art?" *Raph Koster's Website*, February 16, 2007: http://www.raphkoster.com/2007/02/16/but-is-it-art-2/.

Krämer, Sybille. "The Cultural Techniques of Time Axis Manipulation: On Friedrich Kittler's Conception of Media." *Theory, Culture and Society* 23, nos. 7-8 (2006): 93-109.

Krell, David Farrell. "Introduction to the Paperback Edition: Heidegger Nietzsche Nazism." In Martin Heidegger, *Nietzsche Volume I: The Will to Power as Art and Nietzsche Volume II: The Eternal Recurrence of the Same*, translated by David Farrell Krell, ix-xxvii. New York: Harper Collins, 1991.

Kroker, Arthur. *Body Drift: Butler, Hayles, Haraway*. Minneapolis: University of Minnesota Press, 2012.

Kroker, Arthur. *Exits to the Posthuman Future*. Cambridge: Polity, 2014.

Kroker, Arthur. *The Will to Technology and the Culture of Nihilism: Heidegger, Nietzsche, and Marx*. Toronto: University of Toronto Press, 2004.

Kuhn, Thomas S. *The Structure of Scientific Revolutions*, 3rd ed. Chicago and London: University of Chicago Press, 1996.

Kurzweil, Ray. *The Singularity Is Near*. Viking, 2006.

Lantz, Frank. "Games Are Not Media." *Game Design Advance*, August 30, 2009: http://gamedesignadvance.com/?p=1567.

Legend of Grimrock Official Forum. "Alchemist Herb Growth Rate." November 20, 2014: http://www.grimrock.net/forum/viewtopic.php?f=20&t=7572&p=85338&hilit=crystal+flower#p85338.

Leipert, Jeremy. "On Tilt: The Inheritances and Inheritors of Digital Games." PhD diss., Trent University, 2015.

LeMieux, Patrick. "Real Time Attacks: Microtemporal Histories of Speedrunning *Super Mario Bros.*" Paper presented at Extending Play 3, New Brunswick, New Jersey, September 30-October 1, 2016.

LeMieux, Patrick. "From NES-4021 to moSMB3.wmv: Speedrunning the Serial Interface." *Eludamos: Journal for Computer Game Culture* 8, no. 1 (2014): 7-31.

Leroi-Gourhan, André. *Gesture and Speech*. Translated by Anna

Bostock Berger. Cambridge: MIT Press, 1993.

Lessig, Lawrence. *Code v2*. New York: Basic Books, 2006.

Levinas, Emmanuel. *Totality and Infinity: An Essay on Exteriority*. Translated by Alphonso Lingis. Pittsburgh: Duquesne University Press, 1969.

Levine, Ken, interview by Chris Remo. "Ken Levine on *BioShock*: The Spoiler Interview." *ShackNews*, August 30, 2007: http://www.shacknews.com/article/48728/ken-levine-on-bioshock-the.

Lewismistreated. "The Story of *Braid*." RLLMUK, August 11, 2008: http://www.rllmukforum.com/index.php?/topic/190 136-the-story-of-braid/.

Liao, Victoria. "Voiceless but Not Powerless: Defying Narrative Convention in Supergiant Games' *Transistor*." *The Spectatorial*, April 23, 2015: https://thespectatorial.wordpress.com/2015/04/23/voiceless-but-not-powerless-defying-narrative-convention-in-supergiant-games-transistor/.

Lipkin, Nadav. "Examining Indie's Independence: The Meaning of 'Indie' Games, the Politics of Production, and Mainstream Cooptation." *Loading...*7, no. 11 (2013): 8-24.

Liu, Alan, interview by Geert Lovink. "'I Work Here, But I Am Cool': Interview with Alan Liu." *Net Critique*, February 28, 2006: http://networkcultures.org/geert/interview-with-alan-liu/.

Lowood, Henry. "High-Performance Play: The Making of Machinima." *Journal of Media Practice* 7, no. 1 (2006): 25-42.

McGonigal, Jane. *Reality is Broken: Why Games Make Us Better and How They Can Change the World*. New York: Penguin Press, 2011.

McLuhan, Marshall. *The Gutenberg Galaxy: The Making of Typographic Man*. Toronto: University of Toronto Press, 1962.

McLuhan, Marshall. *Understanding Media: The Extensions of Man*. New York: Signet, 1964.

Machiavelli, Niccolò. *The Discourses*. Edited by Bernard Crick and translated by Leslie J. Walker. London: Penguin, 1970.

Machiavelli, Niccolò. *The Prince*. Edited and translated by David Wooton. Indianapolis and Cambridge: Hackett, 1995.

Manovich, Lev. *The Language of New Media*. Cambridge and London: MIT Press, 2001.

Massumi, Brian. "The Thinking-Feeling of What Happens." *Inflexions* 1, no. 1 (2008): http://inflexions.org/n1_The-Thinking-Feeling-of-What-Happens-by-Brian-Massumi.pdf.

Meades, Alan. *Understanding Counterplay in Video Games*. New York and London: Routledge, 2015.

Meades, Alan. "Why We Glitch: Process, Meaning and Pleasure in the Discovery, Documentation, Sharing and Use of Videogame Exploits." *Well Played* 2, no. 2 (2013): 79-98.

Menkman, Rosa. *The Glitch Moment(um)*. Amsterdam: Network Notebooks, 2011.

Menotti, Gabriel. "Videorec as Gameplay: Recording Playthroughs and Video Game Engagement." *GAME: The Italian Journal of Game Studies*, 3 (2013): http://www.gamejournal.it/3_menotti/.

Merton, Robert K. *Social Theory and Social Structure*. New York: Free Press, 1968.

Messner, Steven. "How Tool-Assisted Speedrunning Reveals the Inner-Life of Video Games." *Rock Paper Shotgun*, January 27, 2016: https://www.rockpapershotgun.com/2016/01/27/how-tool-assisted-speedrunning-works/.

Milburn, Colin. *Mondo Nano: Fun and Games in the World of Digital Matter*. Durham and London: Duke University Press, 2015.

Mitchell, Liam. "Life on Automatic: Facebook's Archival Subject." *First Monday* 19, no. 2 (2014): http://firstmonday.org/article/view/4825/3823#p5.

Mitchell, Liam. "A Phenomenological Study of Social Media: Boredom and Interest on Facebook, Reddit, and 4chan." PhD diss., University of Victoria, 2012.

Morozov, Evgeny. "e-Salvation." *The New Republic*, March 3,

2011: https://newrepublic.com/article/84525/morozov-kelly-technology-book-wired.

Mosco, Vincent. *The Digital Sublime: Myth, Power, and Cyberspace*. Cambridge: MIT Press, 2005.

Mumford, Lewis. *Technics and Civilization*. Chicago and London: The University of Chicago Press, 2010.

Newman, James. *Playing with Videogames*. London and New York: Routledge, 2008.

Niedzviecki, Hal. *Trees on Mars: Our Obsession with the Future*. New York: Seven Stories, 2015.

Nietzsche, Friedrich. *Beyond Good and Evil: Prelude to a Philosophy of the Future*. Translated by Walter Kaufmann. New York: Vintage Books, 1966.

Nietzsche, Friedrich. *Ecce Homo*. Translated by Walter Kaufman. New York: Vintage Books, 1989.

Nietzsche, Friedrich. *The Gay Science*. Translated by Walter Kaufman. New York: Vintage Books, 1984.

Nietzsche, Friedrich. *On the Genealogy of Morals*. Translated by Walter Kaufmann and R. J. Hollingdale. New York: Vintage Books, 1989.

Nietzsche, Friedrich. *Thus Spoke Zarathustra*. Translated by R. J. Hollingdale. London and New York: Penguin Books.

Nietzsche, Friedrich. *Twilight of the Idols, or, How to Philosophize with a Hammer*. Translated by R. J. Hollingdale. Harmondsworth: Penguin, 1968.

Nietzsche, Friedrich. *The Will to Power*. Translated by Walter Kaufmann and R. J. Hollingdale. New York: Random House, 1968.

Noble, David F. *The Religion of Technology: The Divinity of Man and the Spirit of Invention*. New York: Penguin, 1999.

Noclip. "Rediscovering Mystery – Noclip Documentary (feat. Jonathan Blow / Derek Yu / Jim Crawford)." YouTube, February 27, 2017: https://www.youtube.com/watch?v=z2g_0QQRjYY.

O'Gorman, Marcel. "Angels in Digital Armor: Technoculture and Terror Management." *Postmodern Culture: Journal of Interdisciplinary Thought on Contemporary Cultures* 20, no. 3 (2010): http://www.pomoculture.org/2013/09/03/angels-in-digital-armor-technoculture-and-terror-management/.

Orland, Kyle. "How an Emulator-Fueled Robot Reprogrammed *Super Mario World* on the Fly." *Ars Technica*, January 14, 2014: https://arstechnica.com/gaming/2014/01/how-an-emulator-fueled-robot-reprogrammed-super-mario-world-on-the-fly/.

Orland, Kyle. "How a Game-Playing Robot Coded 'Super Mario Maker' onto an SNES – Live on Stage." *Ars Technica*, January 11, 2016: https://arstechnica.com/gaming/2016/01/how-a-game-playing-robot-coded-super-mario-maker-onto-an-snes-live-on-stage/.

Orland, Kyle. "How a Robot Got *Super Mario 64* and *Portal* "Running" on an SNES." *Ars Technica*, January 15, 2017: https://arstechnica.com/gaming/2017/01/how-a-robot-got-super-mario-64-and-portal-running-on-an-snes/.

Orland, Kyle. "Pokémon Plays Twitch: How a Robot Got IRC Running on an Unmodified SNES." *Ars Technica*, January 5, 2015: https://arstechnica.com/gaming/2015/01/pokemon-plays-twitch-how-a-robot-got-irc-running-on-an-unmodified-snes/.

Owen, David. "The Illusion of Agency and the Affect of Control within Video Games." In *Ctrl-Alt-Play: Essays on Control in Video Gaming*, edited by Matthew Wysocki, 72-82. Jefferson and London: McFarland and Company, 2013.

Owens, Trevor. "Sid Meier's Colonization: Is It Offensive Enough?" *Play the Past*, November 23, 2010: http://www.playthepast.org/?p=278.

Packer, Joseph. "The Battle for Galt's Gulch: *Bioshock as Critique of Objectivism*." *Journal of Gaming and Virtual Worlds* 2, no. 3 (2010): 209-224.

Parker, Felan. "The Significance of Jeep Tag: On Player-Imposed

Rules in Video Games." *Loading...*2, no. 3 (2008): http://journals.sfu.ca/loading/index.php/loading/article/view/44/41.

Parker, Jeanette. "Natality and the Rise of the Social in Hannah Arendt's Political Thought." MA thesis, University of Victoria, 2012.

Pastor Manul Laphroaig. "Three Ghosts and a Little, Brown Dog." *International Journal of Proof-of-Concept or Get The Fuck Out* 11 (January 2016): https://www.alchemistowl.org/pocorgtfo/pocorgtfo10.pdf, 4-5.

Paul, Christopher A. "Optimizing Play: How Theorycraft Changes Gameplay and Design." *Game Studies* 11, no. 2 (2011): http://gamestudies.org/1102/articles/paul.

Peaty, Gwyneth. "'Hatched from the Veins in Your Arms': Movement, Ontology, and First-Person Gameplay in *BioShock*." In *Guns, Grunts, and Grenades: First-Person Shooter Games*, edited by Gerald Voorhees, Josh Call and Katie Whitlock, 153-174. Whitlock: Continuum, 2012.

Pedercini, Paolo. "Videogames and the Spirit of Capitalism." *Molleindustria Blog*, February 14, 2015: http://www.molleindustria.org/blog/videogames-and-the-spirit-of-capitalism/.

Peters, John Durham. *The Marvelous Clouds: Toward a Philosophy of Elemental Media*. Chicago and London: University of Chicago Press, 2015.

Ranciere, Jacques. "Introducing Disagreement." *Angelaki: Journal of the Theoretical Humanities* 9, no. 3 (2004): 3-9.

raocow. "Vip4- malfunctions." YouTube, January 7, 2009: https://www.youtube.com/watch?v=xOOT2XIm5o0&t=7m20s.

Roberts, Samuel. "Now Playing: *Spec Ops'* Most Troubling Scene." *PC Gamer*, December 3, 2014: http://www.pcgamer.com/now-playing-spec-ops-most-troubling-scene/.

Rojcewicz, Richard. *The Gods and Technology: A Reading of Heidegger*. Albany: State University of New York Press, 2006.

Ruch, Adam. "Interpretations of Freedom and Control in *BioShock*." *Journal of Gaming and Virtual Worlds* 2, no. 1 (2010):

84-91.

Rughiniș, Cosima, Elisabeta Toma, and Răzvan Rughiniș. "Time to Reminisce and Die: Representing Old Age in Art Games." *Proceedings of DiGRA 2011 Conference: Think Design Play* (2011): https://www.researchgate.net/profile/Cosima_Rughinis/publication/280319689_Time_to_Reminisce_and_Die_Representing_Old_Age_in_Art_Games/links/55b29a6b08ae9289a-0858d7a.pdf.

Saint-Amour, Paul. "Bombing and the Symptom: Traumatic Earliness and the Nuclear Uncanny." *Diacritics* 30, no. 4 (2000): 59-82.

Sarkeesian, Anita. "Interview: Anita Sarkeesian, Games, and Tropes vs. Women." *Destructoid*, February 7, 2012: http://www.destructoid.com/interview-anita-sarkeesian-games-and-tropes-vs-women-230337.phtml.

Saucerman, Jenny and Jeremy Dietmeier. "Twitch Plays Pokemon: A Study in Big G Games." Proceedings of DiGRA 2014: http://library.med.utah.edu/e-channel/wp-content/uploads/2016/04/digra2014_submission_127.pdf.

Schmeink, Lars. "Dystopia, Alternate History and the Posthuman in *Bioshock*." *Current Objectives of Postgraduate American Studies* 10 (2009): http://copas.uni-regensburg.de/article/view/113.

Schmitt, Carl. *The Concept of the Political*. Translated by George Schwab. Chicago and London: University of Chicago Press, 1996.

Schmitt, Carl. *Political Theology: Four Chapters on the Concept of Sovereignty*. Translated by George Schwab. Chicago: University of Chicago Press, 2005.

Schrank, Brian. *Avant-Garde Videogames: Playing with Technoculture*. Cambridge and London: MIT Press, 2014.

Scully-Blaker, Rainforest. "A Practiced Practice: Speedrunning through Space with de Certeau and Virilio." *Game Studies* 14, no. 1 (2014): http://gamestudies.org/1401/articles/scullyblaker.

Scully-Blaker, Rainforest. "Re-curating the Accident: Speedrunning as Community and Practice." MA thesis, Concordia University, 2016.

SethBling. "Jailbreaking Super Mario World to Install a Hex Editor & Mod Loader." YouTube, May 29, 2017: https://www.youtube.com/watch?v=Ixu8tn__91E.

SethBling. "SNES Code Injection -- Flappy Bird in SMW." YouTube, March 28, 2016: https://www.youtube.com/watch?v=h-B6eY73sLV0.

SethBling. "Super Mario World -- Credits Warp in 5:56.6 (First Time Ever on Console)." YouTube, January 21, 2015: https://www.youtube.com/watch?v=14wqBA5Q1yc&.

Sharp, John. *Works of Game: On the Aesthetics of Games and Art*. Cambridge and London: MIT Press, 2015.

Sicart, Miguel. *Beyond Choices: The Design of Ethical Gameplay*. Cambridge and London: MIT Press, 2013.

Simkins, David W. and Constance Steinkuehler. "Critical Ethical Reasoning and Role-Play." *Games and Culture* 3, no. 3-4 (2008): 333-355.

Simon, Bart. "What If Baudrillard Was a Gamer?" *Games and Culture* 2, no. 4 (2007): 355-357.

Simpson, Lorenzo C. *Technology, Time, and the Conversations of Modernity*. New York and London: Routledge, 1995.

Sotamaa, Olli. "When the Game Is Not Enough: Motivations and Practices among Computer Game Modding Culture." *Games and Culture* 5, no. 3 (2010): 239-255.

SpeedMarathonArchive. "AGDQ 2015 Various Games Speed Run by TASbot #AGDQ2015." YouTube, January 4, 2015: https://www.youtube.com/watch?v=MjmxmPwmfOk.

Speed Demos Archive. "TAS." http://speeddemosarchive.com/TAS.html.

Stamenković, Dušan and Milan Jaćević. "Time, Space, and Motion in *Braid*: A Cognitive Semantic Approach to a Video Game." *Games and Culture* 10, no. 2 (2015): 178-203.

Stiegler, Bernard. *Technics and Time: The Fault of Epimetheus.* Translated by Richard Beardsworth and George Collins. Stanford: Stanford University Press, 1998.

Strong, Tracy B. *Politics without Vision: Thinking without a Bannister in the Twentieth Century.* Chicago: University of Chicago Press, 2012.

Suits, Bernard. *The Grasshopper: Games, Life, and Utopia.* Peterborough, Ontario: Broadview Press, 2014.

TASVideos. "Brain Age Train Your Brain in Minutes a Day." Last edited January 11, 2016: http://tasvideos.org/GameResources/DS/BrainAgeTrainYourBrainInMinutesADay.html.

TASVideos. "SMB3TAS History." Last edited October 27, 2010: http://tasvideos.org/SMB3TASHistory.html.

TASVideos. "Submission #3767: bortreb's GBC Pokémon Yellow 'Executes Arbitrary Code' in 12:51.87." November 22, 2012: http://tasvideos.org/3767S.html.

TASVideos. "Submission #3957: Masterjun's SNES Super Mario World 'Glitched' in 01:39.74." April 26, 2013: http://tasvideos.org/3957S.html.

TASVideos. "TAS Bot." Last edited May 29, 2017: http://tasvideos.org/TASBot.html.

TASVideos. "Welcome to TASVideos." Last edited February 19, 2017: http://tasvideos.org/WelcomeToTASVideos.html.

TASVideosChannel. "AGDQ 2014 – TASBot Playing SMW Total Control and Various Other TASes." YouTube, January 6, 2014: https://www.youtube.com/watch?v=Uep1H_NvZS0.

TASVideosChannel. "TAS Block at AGDQ 2016 – TASBot." YouTube, January 13, 2016: https://www.youtube.com/watch?v=pj7RE2DcRgc.

TASVideos Discussion Board. "AGDQ 2017 Planning and Feedback Thread." November 12, 2016: http://tasvideos.org/forum/viewtopic.php?p=443580#443580.

TASVideos Discussion Board. "Console Verification Thread." July 16, 2010: http://tasvideos.org/forum/viewtopic.php?

p=239984.

TASVideos Discussion Board. "Running Speed Runs on Real Hardware." August 28, 2006: http://tasvideos.org/forum/viewtopic.php?t=4288.

Tenner, Edward. *Why Things Bite Back: Technology and the Revenge of Unintended Consequences.* New York: Vintage, 1997.

Thiel, Peter. "The Education of a Libertarian." *Cato Unbound,* April 13, 2009: http://www.cato-unbound.org/2009/04/13/peter-thiel/the-education-of-a-libertarian/.

Thomson, Iain. *Heidegger on Ontotheology: Technology and the Politics of Education.* Cambridge, NY: Cambridge University Press, 2005.

Tidazi. "Tidazi's 'f/Fun' Theory." https://docs.google.com/document/d/1xvxyX2dxkzDiy2TxRjPq4ryBDrvFG2H-k2q_F-6yLuNg/edit#.

Tidazi. "Tidazi's 'f/Fun' Theory. The Distinction between 'fun' and 'Fun.'" Reddit: https://www.reddit.com/r/Undertale/comments/3pwrbf/tidazis_ffun_theory_the_distinction_between_fun/cwa4dh8/.

Travis, Roger. "*Bioshock* in the Cave: Ethical Education in Plato and in Video Games." In *Ethics and Game Design: Teaching Values through Play,* edited by Karen Schrier and David Gibson, 86-101. Hershey and New York: Information Science Reference, 2010.

Tulloch, Rowan. "Ludic Dystopias: Power, Politics and Play." *Proceedings of the Sixth Australasian Conference on Interactive Entertainment,* ACM, 2009: 13-23.

Tulloch, Rowan. "A Man Chooses, A Slave Obeys: Agency, Interactivity and Freedom in Video Gaming." *Journal of Gaming and Virtual Worlds* 2, no. 1 (2010): http://www.intellectbooks.co.uk/journals/view-Article,id=9436/.

Turkle, Sherry. *Alone Together: Why We Expect More from Technology and Less from Each Other.* New York: Basic Books, 2011.

Turner, Fred. *From Counterculture to Cyberculture: Stewart Brand, the Whole Earth Network, and the Rise of Digital Utopianism.* Chicago: University of Chicago Press, 2006.

Twitch. "TPP Victory! The Thundershock Heard around the World." March 1, 2014: https://blog.twitch.tv/tpp-victory-the-thundershock-heard-around-the-world-3128a5b1cdf5#.j3wdt47lc.

UltraJMan. "Summer Games Done Quick – Wizards and Warriors 3 NESbot Demonstration and Burger King Battle." YouTube, August 27, 2011: https://www.youtube.com/watch?v=KQX-VgMKJEDY&feature=youtu.be.

Uncertain Commons. *Speculate This!* Durham and London: Duke University Press, 2013.

Van den Berg, Thijs. "Playing at Resistance to Capitalism: *Bio-Shock* as the Reification of Neoliberal Ideas." *Reconstruction: Studies in Contemporary Culture* 12, no. 2 (2012): http://reconstruction.eserver.org/Issues/122/vandenBerg.shtml.

Vance, Marina E., Todd Kuiken, Eric P. Vejerano, Sean P. McGinnis, Michael F. Hochella Jr., David Rejeski, and Matthew S. Hull. "Nanotechnology in the Real World: Redeveloping the Nanomaterial Consumer Products Inventory." *Beilstein Journal of Nanotechnology* 6 (2015): 1769-1780.

Voorhees, Gerald. "Criticism and Control: Gameplay in the Space of Possibility." In *Ctrl-Alt-Play: Essays on Control in Video Gaming,* edited by Matthew Wysocki, 9-20. Jefferson and London: McFarland, 2013.

Voorhees, Gerald. "Materialist Fantasies: The Voice as *objet petit a* in Digital Games." *Journal of Gaming and Virtual Worlds* 8, no. 3 (2016): 247-264.

Wark, McKenzie. "The Game of War: Debord as Strategist." *Cabinet* 29 (2008): http://www.cabinetmagazine.org/issues/29/wark.php.

Wark, McKenzie. *Gamer Theory.* Cambridge: Harvard University Press, 2007.

Wark, McKenzie. *A Hacker Manifesto.* Cambridge and London:

Harvard University Press, 2004.

Wasik, Bill. *And Then There's This: How Stories Live and Die in Viral Culture*. New York: Viking Press, 2009.

Watson, Nicholas. "Procedural Elaboration: How Players Decode Minecraft." *Loading...*10, no. 16 (2017): 75-86.

Weber, Max. "The Profession and Vocation of Politics." In *Political Writings*, edited by Peter Lassman and Ronald Speirs, 309-369. Cambridge: Cambridge University Press, 1994.

White, Daniel and Michael Grossfeld. "Irrevocability in Games." BSc thesis, Worcester Polytechnic Institute, 2012.

Whitelaw, Mitchell. "Art against Information: Case Studies in Data Practice." *Fibreculture* 11 (2008): http://eleven.fibreculturejournal.org/fcj-067-art-against-information-case-studies-in-data-practice/.

Williams, G. Christopher "Murder by the Numbers." *Pop Matters*, March 2, 2011: http://www.popmatters.com/post/137527-bulletstorm-murder-by-the-numbers/.

Winkler, Hartmut. "Processing: The Third and Neglected Media Function." MediaTransatlantic: Media Theory in North America and German-Speaking Europe, April 8, 2010: http://homepages.uni-paderborn.de/winkler/proc_e.pdf.

Winner, Langdon. *Autonomous Technology: Technics-out-of-Control as a Theme in Political Thought*. Cambridge: MIT Press, 1977.

Winnerling, Tobias. "The Eternal Recurrence of All Bits: How Historicizing Video Game Series Transform Factual History into Affective History." *Eludamos: Journal for Computer Game Culture* 8, no. 1 (2014): 151-170.

Wysocki, Matthew and Betsy Brey. "'All That's Left Is the Choosing': *BioShock Infinite* and the Constants and Variables of Control." In *The Play versus Story Divide in Game Studies: Critical Essays*, edited by Matthew W. Kapell, 145-157. Jefferson: McFarland, 2015.

Wysocki, Matthew and Matthew Schandler. "Would You Kindly? *BioShock* and the Question of Control." In *Ctrl-Alt-Play:*

Essays on Control in Video Gaming, edited by Matthew Wysocki, 196-207. Jefferson and London: McFarland and Company, 2013.

Yliluoma, Joel. *Bisqwit's NES Bittorrent Video Downloads*. http://bisqwit.iki.fi/jutut/backup-nesvideos.html.

Young, Liam Cole. *List Cultures: Knowledge and Poetics from Mesopotamia to BuzzFeed*. Amsterdam: Amsterdam University Press, 2017.

Zero Punctuation. "*Bastion* and *From Dust*." YouTube, August 10, 2011: http://www.escapistmagazine.com/videos/view/zero-punctuation/3839-Bastion-and-From-Dust.

Zero Punctuation. "*Spec Ops: The Line*." YouTube, October 24, 2012: http://www.escapistmagazine.com/videos/view/zero-punctuation/6021-Spec-Ops-The-Line.

Zimmerman, Eric. "Manifesto for a Ludic Century." In *The Gameful World: Approaches, Issues, Applications*, edited by Steffen P. Walz and Sebastian Deterding, 19-22. Cambridge and London: MIT Press, 2014.

Zittrain, Jonathan. *The Future of the Internet – and How to Stop It*. New Haven and London: Yale University Press, 2008.

Ludography

Alz. Dylan Carter. 2014.

Bastion. Supergiant Games. Warner Bros. Interactive Entertainment, 2011.

Battle Chess. Interplay Entertainment and Silicon and Synapse. Interplay Entertainment, 1988.

Ben There, Dan That. Size Five Games, 2008.

The Best Amendment. Molleindustria. Molleindustria, 2013.

BioShock. 2K Boston and 2K Australia. 2K Games, 2007.

Braid. Number None. Number None and Microsoft Game Studios, 2008.

Brain Age. Nintendo Software Planning and Development. Nintendo, 2006.

Bulletstorm. People Can Fly and Epic Games. Electronic Arts, 2011.

Candy Crush. King. King, 2012.

Cart Life. Richard Hofmeier, 2011.

Civilization. MPS Labs. MicroProse, 1991.

Clicker Heroes. Playsaurus. Playsaurus, 2014.

Colonization. MicroProse. MicroProse, 1994.

Color a Dinosaur. FarSight Studios. Virgin Games, 1993.

Continue?9876543210. Jason Oda. Starvingeyes, 2014.

Counter-Strike: Global Offensive. Hidden Path Entertainment and Valve Corporation. Valve Corporation, 2012.

Dear Esther. Thechineseroom. Thechineseroom, 2012.

Depression Quest. The Quinnspiracy. The Quinnspiracy, 2013.

Desert Bus. Imagineering. Absolute Entertainment, 1995.

Deus Ex: Human Revolution. Eidos Montréal. Square Enix, 2011.

Deus Ex: Mankind Divided. Eidos Montréal. Square Enix, 2016.

Diaries of a Spaceport Janitor. Sundae Month. tinyBuild, 2016.

The Division. Massive Entertainment, Ubisoft, 2016.

Donkey Kong Country 2. Rare. Nintendo, 1995.

DOOM. id Software. GT Interactive, 1993.

Duke Nukem 3D. 3D Realms. GT Interactive, 1996.

EarthBound. Ape and HAL Laboratory. Nintendo, 1995.

The Elder Scrolls V: Skyrim. Bethesda Game Studios. Bethesda Softworks, 2011.

Everything. David O'Reilly. Double Fine Productions, 2017.

Eye of the Beholder. Westwood Associates. Strategic Simulations, Inc., 1991.

Fallout 3. Bethesda Game Studios. Bethesda Softworks, 2008.

Fallout 4. Bethesda Game Studios. Bethesda Softworks, 2015.

Flappy Bird. dotGEARS. dotGEARS, 2013.

Freedom Bridge. Necessary Games, 2011.

Galaga. Namco. Namco and Midway, 1981.

Gears of War. Epic Games. Microsoft Studios, 2006.

Gone Home. The Fullbright Company. The Fullbright Company, 2013.

Gradius. Konami. Konami, 1985.

The Graveyard. Tale of Tales. Valve Corporation and Apple, 2008.

Gyromite. Nintendo Research and Development 1. Nintendo, 1985.

Half-Life. Valve Corporation. Sierra Studios, 1998.

High Delivery. Ferry Halim, 2004.

Home. Steven Lavelle. Increpare Games, 2009.

I Am a Brave Knight. Tree Interactive. Tree Interactive, 2014.

Inside. Playdead. Playdead, 2016.

The Last of Us. Naughty Dog. Sony Computer Entertainment, 2013.

Legend of Grimrock 2. Almost Human. Almost Human, 2014.

The Legend of Zelda: A Link to the Past. Nintendo Entertainment Analysis and Development. Nintendo, 1991.

Life Is Strange. Dontnod Entertainment. Square Enix and Feral Interactive, 2015.

Limbo. Playdead. Playdead, 2010.

Lisa: The Painful. Dingaling Productions. Dingaling Productions,

2014.

Lose/Lose. Zack Gauge, 2009.

McDonald's Videogame. Molleindustria. Molleindustria, 2006.

Master of Orion. Simtex. MicroProse, 1993.

Max Payne 3. Rockstar Studios. Rockstar Games, 2012.

Mega Man. Capcom. Capcom, 1987.

Mega Man 2. Capcom. Capcom, 1988.

Minecraft. Mojang. Mojang, 2011.

Missile Command. Atari, Inc. Atari, Inc. and Sega, 1980.

Mountain. David O'Reilly. Double Fine Productions, 2014.

Papers, Please. 3903 LLC. 3903 LLC, 2013.

Passage. Jason Rohrer. Jason Rohrer, 2007.

Phone Story. Molleindustria. Molleindustria, 2011.

Pokémon Red. Game Freak. Nintendo, 1996.

Pokémon Yellow. Game Freak. Nintendo, 1998.

Pong. Atari. Atari, 1972.

Portal. Valve Corporation. Valve Corporation, 2007.

Pyre. Supergiant Games. Supergiant Games, 2014.

Quake. id Software. GT Interactive, 1996.

Quest for Glory: So You Want to Be a Hero. Sierra Entertainment.
Sierra Entertainment, 1989.

The Secret of Monkey Island. Lucasfilm Games. Lucasfilm Games,
1990.

Spacewar! Steve Russell. Steve Russell, 1962.

Spec Ops: The Line. Yager Development. 2K Games, 2013.

Splatoon. Nintendo Entertainment Analysis and Development.
Nintendo, 2015.

Stack Up. Nintendo Research and Development 1. Nintendo,
1985.

The Stanley Parable. Galactic Cafe. Galactic Cafe, 2013.

Starcraft. Blizzard Entertainment. Blizzard Entertainment, 1998.

Super Hexagon. Terry Cavanagh. Terry Cavanagh, 2012.

Super Mario 64. Nintendo Entertainment Analysis and Development. Nintendo, 1996.

Super Mario All-Stars. Nintendo Entertainment Analysis and Development. Nintendo, 1993.

Super Mario Bros. Nintendo Research and Development 4. Nintendo, 1985.

Super Mario Bros. 3. Nintendo Research and Development 4. Nintendo, 1990.

Super Mario Kart 64. Nintendo Entertainment Analysis and Development. Nintendo, 1997.

Super Mario Maker. Nintendo Entertainment Analysis and Development. Nintendo, 2015.

Super Mario World. Nintendo Entertainment Analysis and Development. Nintendo, 1991.

A Tale in the Desert. Pluribus Games and eGenesis. Pluribus Games, 2003.

That Dragon, Cancer. Numinous Games. Numinous Games, 2016.

To Build a Better Mousetrap. Molleindustria. Molleindustria, 2014.

To the Moon. Freebird Games. Freebird Games, 2011.

Transistor. Supergiant Games. Supergiant Games, 2014.

Undertale. Toby Fox. Toby Fox, 2015.

The Witness. Thekla, Inc. Thekla, Inc., 2016.

Yume Nikki. Kikiyama. 2004.

Index

non-determinism, 196, 290n337

normalization, 7, 58

nostalgia, 84, 124, 128, 130, 137, 169

null sprite glitch, 188-189, 288n330

O'Reilly, David, 68-69

objectivism, 70, 72, 254n150

ontology, 1, 15-16, 35-37, 52, 115, 213. *See also* being, world

ontotheology, 43, 50-52, 200, 215, 244n109

Oppenheimer, J. Robert, 90

Orientalism, 183

Orland, Kyle, 187, 190, 199

p4plus2. *See* Potter, Jordan (p4plus)

Page, Larry, 45

paidia, 54, 142, 246n119

Papers, Please, 266n189

Pedercini, Paolo, 39

platformers, 84-85

play, 10-11, 23, 54, 139; as critique, 2, 21, 54, 177, 213, 215, 218; definition of, 142, 219n2, 221n16

Pokémon Plays Twitch, 175-176, 190

Pokémon Red, 166-169, 175

Pokémon Yellow, 189

politics and the political, 2, 26-27, 34, 49, 51, 58-59, 114-115, 140. *See also* ludopolitics

Pong, 187

Portal, 210

Potter, Jordan (p4plus2), 189-193, 206, 287n313, 295n361

power: algorithmic, 32; as conduct, 7, 219n5, 223n19; and immersion, 228n43; as increase of a number, 107, 110; ontological, 2, 47-49; transformations of, 41, 45

power fantasy, 2, 27-29, 62, 214, 217, 228n43; and choice, 64; as learning and mastery of algorithms, 22, 30-33, 113-114; and mainstream games, 229n45; and time, 84

procedural rhetoric, 64, 227n36

protocol, 221n14

Quake, 180

quantification, 6, 18, 36, 39, 107, 110, 157. *See also* digitality and digitization

Quest for Glory: So You Want to Be a Hero, 19

Quinn, Zoe, 66

racism, 183, 230n50

rationalism, 43, 279n261

real, the, 198, 273n220

reality, 124, 127, 146, 198, 201;

Zero Books

CULTURE, SOCIETY & POLITICS

Contemporary culture has eliminated the concept and public figure of the intellectual. A cretinous anti-intellectualism presides, cheer-led by hacks in the pay of multinational corporations who reassure their bored readers that there is no need to rouse themselves from their stupor. Zer0 Books knows that another kind of discourse – intellectual without being academic, popular without being populist – is not only possible: it is already flourishing. Zer0 is convinced that in the unthinking, blandly consensual culture in which we live, critical and engaged theoretical reflection is more important than ever before.
If you have enjoyed this book, why not tell other readers by posting a review on your preferred book site.
Recent bestsellers from Zero Books are:

In the Dust of This Planet
Horror of Philosophy vol. 1
Eugene Thacker
In the first of a series of three books on the Horror of Philosophy, *In the Dust of This Planet* offers the genre of horror as a way of thinking about the unthinkable.
Paperback: 978-1-84694-676-9 ebook: 978-1-78099-010-1

Capitalist Realism
Is there no alternative?
Mark Fisher
An analysis of the ways in which capitalism has presented itself
as the only realistic political-economic system.
Paperback: 978-1-84694-317-1 ebook: 978-1-78099-734-6

Rebel Rebel
Chris O'Leary
David Bowie: every single song. Everything you want to know,
everything you didn't know.
Paperback: 978-1-78099-244-0 ebook: 978-1-78099-713-1

Cartographies of the Absolute
Alberto Toscano, Jeff Kinkle
An aesthetics of the economy for the twenty-first century.
Paperback: 978-1-78099-275-4 ebook: 978-1-78279-973-3

Malign Velocities
Accelerationism and Capitalism
Benjamin Noys
Long listed for the Bread and Roses Prize 2015, *Malign
Velocities* argues against the need for speed, tracking
acceleration as the symptom of the ongoing crises of capitalism.
Paperback: 978-1-78279-300-7 ebook: 978-1-78279-299-4

Meat Market
Female flesh under Capitalism
Laurie Penny
A feminist dissection of women's bodies as the fleshy fulcrum
of capitalist cannibalism, whereby women are both consumers
and consumed.
Paperback: 978-1-84694-521-2 ebook: 978-1-84694-782-7

Poor but Sexy
Culture Clashes in Europe East and West
Agata Pyzik
How the East stayed East and the West stayed West.
Paperback: 978-1-78099-394-2 ebook: 978-1-78099-395-9

Sweetening the Pill
or How we Got Hooked on Hormonal Birth Control
Holly Grigg-Spall
Has contraception liberated or oppressed women? *Sweetening the Pill* breaks the silence on the dark side of hormonal contraception.
Paperback: 978-1-78099-607-3 ebook: 978-1-78099-608-0

Why Are We The Good Guys?
Reclaiming your Mind from the Delusions of Propaganda
David Cromwell
A provocative challenge to the standard ideology that Western power is a benevolent force in the world.
Paperback: 978-1-78099-365-2 ebook: 978-1-78099-366-9

Readers of ebooks can buy or view any of these bestsellers by clicking on the live link in the title. Most titles are published in paperback and as an ebook. Paperbacks are available in traditional bookshops. Both print and ebook formats are available online.

Find more titles and sign up to our readers' newsletter at http://www.johnhuntpublishing.com/culture-and-politics

Follow us on Facebook
at https://www.facebook.com/ZeroBooks

and Twitter at https://twitter.com/Zer0Books